For Elizabeth

You were Tech's finest. mother fits into that category, too. Best wishes, ever.

[signature]
Dec. 16, 1986

FRAGMENTS

Wiley W. Hilburn, Jr.'s North Louisiana

"Actually, that first lick was the only one I landed."
—p. 163

FRAGMENTS

Wiley W. Hilburn, Jr.'s North Louisiana

A Compilation from *The Times* (of Shreveport) Column
With An Introduction by Jim Montgomery

Edited by Billy H. Gilley

DEPARTMENT OF HISTORY
LOUISIANA TECH UNIVERSITY

Ruston, Louisiana
1987

© McGinty Publications, 1987
All rights reserved. No part of this publication may be reproduced in any form or by any means, electronic, mechanical, photocopying, recording, or otherwise, without the prior written permission of the publisher, except by a reviewer who may quote passages in a review.

Printed in the United States of America

Library of Congress Catalog Card Number: 86-62677
ISBN   0-940231-00-X

For Ellen

CONTENTS

Illustrations	xi
Foreword	xiii
Acknowledgments	xv
Introduction	xvii

Part One: Portraits — 1

Tom Sawyer: Alive in Ruston	3
A Hudson, "Ebbtide," and Girls	5
Berry and Baseball, and the Summer of 1948	8
The Milkshake King of Winnfield	12
Unionville and the Store: Hamming Up History	13
Eyeball to Eyeball with Rosalynn	16
"Hey Boots!": Kendall Flournoy Was Back	19
The Curmudgeon Whom We All Admired	22
Dr. Roane: He Knew It Hurt . . . and Cared	25
Educating "The Barbarians"	27
"She Gave You Your First Book, Son"	29
Miss Butler, Miss Pepper, Miss . . .	31
Johnny Perritt, a "Rare Survivor"	33
A Fig Tree Grows in Shreveport	34
The Yankee-Killer Who Came Home	35
Christmas, in the Lap of Vulcan	38
"I Don't Have a Country"	41
The Major Against the Mob	44
A Garden in Webster Parish	47
A Quiet Theologian	50
A Measure of Goodness and Grace	54
A "Little Ride" with Jay Taylor	56

CONTENTS

The Minnesota Fats of Forestry   59
Constancy, Character, Cornish Hens   63
Under a Pink Dogwood   66

Part Two: Governors and Other Such People   69

Waggonner: "I Like Him"   71
Sam Jones, and Earl's Ghost   72
Russell: A Different Long   78
Huckaby: From Plum Patch to Power   85
Bob Kennon, Ozymandias and the Governors of Louisiana   89
We Sang It All Together Just One More Time   92
Treen: No Spitballs. No Scandals   94
Louisiana's Political Schizophrenia   96
When Big John Outshined Them All   102
Loy Weaver: The Best and the Brightest   106
Edwards: History's Main Chance   110
On "Discovering" Jim Brown   113
Huey's Ghost: Where It Led   117
Earl: "Boy, I'm Gonna Give You a Scoop"   120

Part Three: Some Personal Things   127

Mr. Bronson: Rights and Wrongs   129
End of *The World*—Almost   130
Football: For the Losers   132
State Fair: The Four Bears   135
Ange, Barn, Op and Aunt Bee   139
Come, Let Us Reason Together   141
Saturday Afternoons at the Dixie   143
He Fired Me Three Times . . . and I Deserved It   145
Was It Only a Post-Operative Hallucination?   148
Edwin and Dave: I Hardly Knew You   150
"Uh, It Sounds Like the Tappets . . ."   153
One Wrong Turn and I Was Lost   156

CONTENTS

VDTs Are Here, but I'll Go Down with My Typewriter	158
The Bruised (Me) Legend of the First Lick	161
What? An Eraser in His Ear?	164
Oliver. Frog. Fish. Bootsie. *Lance*	167
"Major Credit Card, Please"	170
The "Compliments" He Gets	172
Biting Through Red Hair	173
Another Failure for Hilburn	175
Of BB Guns and Blooper Balls	177

Part Four: Laughing—Inside and Out — 181

Taylor and Turkey Creek	183
A Forearm, a Rural Mailbox, and . . . Arrrrrrah!	184
A Thanksgiving Bet, 1932	186
The Haunting of Clear Lake	188
I Think He's Naked in the Tank	190
"I Did Quit . . . But *They* Blew Smoke in My Face"	193
The Last Practical Joke at Tech	196
An Explosive Gun Safety Lesson	199
"I Don't Mow," He Told Us	200
Country Pride at the Crossroads	203
That Buzzard Wasn't a Chicken	205
C. L., and the Hot Breath of Hell	207
"I Came to Collect My 'A'"	210
What's This? Dirty Movies in Ruston?	212
Atlanta, If You Change Coke Again, Don't Tell Us	215

Part Five: One Man's Family — 219

At Pop's: A Monkey in the Bed	221
Growing Up, Goodbyes, Neighbors	224
Of Parties and Pierced Ears	226
Life in America's Lourdes	228
Time Is Measured by a Senior Ring	231

CONTENTS

"He's at Home in the Garden, Happy, . . ."	233
Magic Decoders and Ginsu Knives	234
They Gave a Revival and Nobody Came	237
The Day Pop Integrated the Parade	239
Bob and the Great Soapbox Derby	241
They Even Took My Razor	243
"He's Graduating?"	245
Frustration: Cars and Collisions	246
Vacation: "Green . . . It's Green"	249
The Night the Gin Burned Down	251
Little League: Twelve "Don'ts" for Dads	255
The Little Girl Is Growing Up	258
Batman, Where Have You Gone?	260
Barbados: A Glad Hour in the Sun	261
"Was That Mule Drinking, Son?"	265
He Was Gone . . . But Not Gently	266
The Cubs Were a Family Affair	269
In Praise (?) of Poor Grades	272
Part Six: A Place in Time	277
Storming Down Interstate-20	279
For Christmas: An Old Barn	281
A Sanctuary for the New Year	282
February, and Forever, in Boeuf Prairie	284
The Free Ferry at Duty	287
Yes, It Is November in North Louisiana	289
Milkworms and Magic and Morgan's Pond	291
A Crazy-Quilt for Thanksgiving	296
"'Way up Saline, a Dog Died"	297
Kate's House: The Last Moonrise	299
Vienna's Syrup Bucket Mystery	302
Let Us Look, Please, Before Winter Comes	305
A Book About Us, a Century Ago	308
Maybe Some Things Are Forever	311
Index	315

ILLUSTRATIONS

Frontispiece ii
A Quiet Theologian 52
"Uncle Earl" 122
The Four Bears 136
Encounter with C.L. 208
The Gin 252
Morgan's Pond 292

FOREWORD

Traditionally, New Orleans and its Creole culture and Cajan *joie de vivre* have characterized the image of Louisiana. Wiley W. Hilburn, Jr., in his *The Times* (of Shreveport) "Fragments" column, evokes a contrasting image of the other (North) Louisiana—a Louisiana peopled by rural and piney woods, Protestant and Scots-Irish Southerners.

In *Fragments: Wiley W. Hilburn, Jr.'s North Louisiana*, Hilburn defines his Louisiana in sketches of people, analyses of populistic politics, and personal experiences. Also recounted are humorous stories and descriptions of the Hilburn family (a mirror of typical North Louisiana small town and rural families). Finally, Hilburn paints a vivid picture of the North Louisiana landscape.

The editor and McGinty Publications especially wanted to publish Hilburn's descriptions of North Louisiana life because they radiate a wealth of warmth and personal feeling.

A number of people have contributed to this work and to each of them I am indebted: special thanks to *The Times* (of Shreveport) and to its parent company Gannett Co., Inc. for permission to publish the "Fragments" selections that comprise this book; Albino Hinojosa, Louisiana, Tech University, for the jacket design and illustrations; Steve Rodakis, Louisiana Tech University, for the photographic study of Mr. Hilburn; Mrs. Nell R. Hutchins, who typed the manuscript; and Dr. William Y. Thompson and Dr. Kenneth Rea, of the Louisiana Tech University Department of History's McGinty Publications Committee for many helpful suggestions.

Louisiana Tech University Billy H. Gilley
Ruston, Louisiana
1986

ACKNOWLEDGMENTS

Louisiana Tech University President F. Jay Taylor often says, "I'm one of your fans. I read you." This kind of encouragement from the boss has been appreciated, but it takes an even stronger presidential hide to cheerfully (most of the time) accept kidding from my column and criticism from the campus newspaper, *The Tech Talk*, which I oversee. It takes a big man. He is a big man.

At *The Times* (of Shreveport), the same kind of support has come from retired Editor Raymond McDaniel, who had the idea for my first *Times-* published book, *Reflections of North Louisiana*, and from Publisher Howard Bronson. I've had the pleasure of working for both Howard and his father, the late William Bronson, also a *Times* publisher.

In fact, the whole *Times* is family. I've worked for the newspaper since 1962 as editorial writer and columnist, continuing without break to produce for *The Times* after coming to Tech in 1968. My editor in this capacity is Editorial Page Editor Jim Montgomery. Typically, his introduction is better than the book.

At the same time, I have worked closely with *The Times* editorial department, including George Bradley and Diana Taylor.

Back at Tech, this book is the result, really, of a long and special relationship between the university's journalism and history departments. I have worked with Dr. William Y. Thompson, history chairman, on many projects.

Dr. Billy H. Gilley has done a superb editing job on this work for the sponsoring McGinty Publications in the Louisiana Tech University Department of History. I am honored that McGinty Publications felt the columns were worthy of publication in book form. And my work, in all areas, has benefited from the support

ACKNOWLEDGMENTS

of Dr. Paul J. Pennington, dean of the College of Arts and Sciences, and Dr. Kenneth Rea, associate dean.

The journalism faculty has seen me through dozens of crises, at Tech and at *The Times*, and I'm grateful to Ron White, Sallie Rose Hollis, Pam Ledford, Pat Moncrief and Mary Campbell. The same gratitude is extended to what is now a generation of our journalism students.

Tech's journalism department, of course, has had the constant support of Mr. and Mrs. Clarence Faulk of Ruston, former publishers and broadcasters. In a great sense, the Faulks raised me, personally and professionally, and those days I spent at the Ruston *Daily Leader* were golden times.

My parents, Mr. and Mrs. W.W. Hilburn, Sr. of Ruston have provided abiding support. My Riser in-laws are family. And my children, Greg, Kevin and Anne Marie Hilburn, have grown up on the editorial pages of *The Times*—seeing their misadventures, and never their considerable achievements, mirrored in three states. They didn't complain much.

This book is dedicated to my wife, Ellen. She has not only edited and sometimes censored every column and editorial that has come to *The Times* editorial department, she has provided the peace of mind and the environment of love and support that made this book possible.

Finally, I am grateful to the people of North Louisiana. They wrote the book, and they are still writing the column.

Wiley W. Hilburn, Jr.
Department of Journalism
Louisiana Tech University
August 20, 1986

INTRODUCTION

What you should know about Wiley Hilburn's column, "Fragments," is that he never really wanted to write it.

Readers of what is arguably the most popular local newspaper column in North Louisiana, East Texas and South Arkansas (not to mention the hundreds of readers who get tattered clippings of "Fragments" by mail from friends and relatives who just can't resist sending them along) may find it hard to believe that Wiley didn't want to write it, but it's true.

Perhaps the best way to explain it is just to tell the story.

After growing up in Ruston, La., graduating from Louisiana Tech University and taking a graduate degree from Louisiana State University in journalism—and working for several newspapers along the way—Wiley wound up in Shreveport as an editorial writer for what was then *The Shreveport Times*, now just *The Times*.

All during those years and for all the years since—from the nights spent with his grandparents, Pop and Peg, as a child in Ruston, to the long days and evenings as a working journalist, part-time brawler at service stations and eternal source of consternation for his childhood sweetheart and long-time wife, Ellen—Wiley has been what you might call a sponge: He soaks up everything. Every detail. Every . . . fragment.

Every little nuance of human feeling, every twitch of an eyebrow and every other oddity that tells a human story, funny or sad, seems to go into a personal memory bank, to be called up years later when it's needed to tell a tale.

Even during his six years as a full-time editorial writer for *The Times*, Wiley used this capacity—albeit sparingly—to bring wel-

INTRODUCTION

come vitality to the normally gray, on-the-other-hand, issue-oriented world of editorial pages.

His touch was such that even when he decided to forsake the world of daily journalism and move to academia—as chairman of Louisiana Tech University's journalism department—the management of *The Times* asked him to continue writing at least some editorials on a part-time basis. He did, much to the delight of editorial page readers, who reveled especially in his editorials about changing seasons in North Louisiana. These became a hallmark for *The Times,* and many of them were collected in a slim volume called *Reflections of North Louisiana,* published by *The Times* in 1978.

All the while, though, Wiley was trying to write . . . well, *other* things and get them published as editorials in the newspaper. That's about where I came in.

Wiley was long-gone to Louisiana Tech by the time I came to the editorial department as a writer in 1974 and editorial page editor in 1976. But as a mentor, confidant and friend, he's a continuing presence. Sometimes by mail, sometimes by telephone (never by computer, which he abhors to this day) and often in person ("Meet me in Minden for lunch") he was and is constantly in touch.

So when he kept sending those *other* things, I kept talking to him about them. They are completely familiar now to readers as "Fragments," but at the time—submitted as *editorials,* remember—they were a little strange and difficult to describe. Only one thing was certain in my mind. They weren't editorials, and shouldn't be published as such.

"Why not?" Wiley demanded by telephone one day.

"Well, because they're just not," I replied with what must have seemed parental exasperation (as in: "Why?" "Because I said so.").

I think I can be a little more articulate about it now. Editorials, while they strive for personality and vivacity, tend by nature to deal with a lamentably impersonal world. Besides that, they're

INTRODUCTION

often a collective opinion reflecting thoughts of the writer, the publisher, the editor and anyone else empowered to influence editorial policy at a newspaper.

Yet here were these *other* things from Wiley, reflecting with humor, humility and verve a highly personal view of some wonderfully personal stories. People, high and low (everyone from Russell Long to a nameless town drunk). Animal stories (Buckwheat, the ubiquitous spaniel who owns the Hilburns). Children (Anne Marie, Greg and Kevin, whose personal crises have been worked out in print by their waste-no-detail father). Fantasies ("I always really wanted to be named *Lance*"). And, as always, there were stories about poor, dear, bright Ellen, who has discovered that a firm hand and laconic wit are really the only ways to deal with this fourth child to whom she's been married for more than a quarter-century.

They were not editorials, but these antic tales told with a penchant for very human insight would make an ideal personal, by-lined column. I knew that. I wanted it. I wanted it for *The Times*. I wanted it for our readers. And I wanted it every week, rain or shine, good mood or bad, come what may. There, as they say, was the rub.

These *other* things had been coming at a markedly eratic pace. One this week. Another one three weeks later. Then a month or two would pass before yet another one arrived.

Finally, when I had about eight or ten of them tucked away in an envelope, unpublished, Wiley called again.

"Why can't you run them—as a column, maybe?" he begged. At last, I thought, he was beginning to catch on.

"Meet me at Strawn's for lunch," I said. Next day, he did.

What I tried to explain was my feeling about a bylined column: "It's regular. It's where readers can count on finding it, same place, same time, every week."

What I couldn't quite say to him—not so he'd understand it, anyway—was that I thought I knew what was in store for these unusual pieces: Outrageous popularity. If we had published one or two, then stopped until Wiley cranked out another one, *The Times'* readers would never have forgiven us. They would have demanded them on a regular basis. If we couldn't promise them that, we'd do better not to start.

"But I don't have time," he whined, listing an endless array of family, professional and civic obligations.

"All right," I said, taking the gamble, "then don't write them and don't send them to me anymore. Not until you're ready to do them on a weekly basis."

He did not take it well. Wiley's brow wasn't just furrowed. It looked like a cotton patch before planting. Pain and rejection were written all over that serious, warm, slightly chubby little face. I felt like Simon Legree. But I'd already learned something from Ellen: Be firm with him. I wanted the column. The only way to get it was to demand it.

We walked out of Strawn's into the yellow afternoon light on Kings Highway, Wiley's shoulders slumping, my cheeks aching from suppressing a grin. He opened his car door, then turned and stood with arms across the door's top, hands flopped down, head bowed and said, "Well." That's all. No answer. He got into the car and drove back to Ruston.

A couple of weeks later the answer arrived: a package of columns, enough to run for several weeks, with a note suggesting that the column be named "Fragments." It was, and it's been there on Sunday opposite the editorial page of *The Times* ever since.

Now you might think that's the end of the story, but it isn't. With Wiley, there's never really an end to any story, just an interruption.

A few years later, there came another crisis ("Meet me in Minden for lunch"). It was like reliving the Strawn's scene all over.

"I just don't have the time for all I'm doing," he said worriedly, as he says many things much of the time. "The work at Tech is increasing all the time, the editorials and the columns take

INTRODUCTION

up more and more time, I've got family demands. I'm just going to have to stop writing the column."

Precisely what I said after this announcement escapes me, but it was something on the order of, "The hell you will!"

He could stop writing editorials, I said. We'd even call President F. Jay Taylor at Tech and tell him to slack off on university work, if necessary. The one option not allowed—and not even considered—was to let him stop writing "Fragments." Again, the reason: Our readers would never forgive us. His death—and death alone—might be the only legitimate reason to stop them, and even then the readers would probably demand posthumous reruns.

That time, I believe he finally understood. Somehow, it got through to him that people *wanted* to read his unusual little stories of life in general—that he was, in fact, something of a fixture in the life of *Times* readers. A key word made the difference.

"They *depend* on you, Wiley," I pleaded. He looked up, stunned, then a grin broke out. That did it, and I felt foolish for not having thought to say it that way a long time ago. Nothing gets Hilburn hooked faster than to know that somebody—anybody—is depending on him.

This time he left not slumping but strutting. The columns never stopped. He also found time to keep writing editorials and keep doing everything he does at Louisiana Tech—which includes the unpaid, untitled position of counselor-at-large and shoulder-to-cry-on for everyone from President Taylor to a freshman student with personal problems.

He still finds time for all of it because, more than anything else, he *cares*. About people. About their problems. About their peccadillos and even about their bean patches.

It was this caring, so gentle yet not cloying, unapologetically sentimental sometimes, dramatically revealing at others, that distinguished those *other* things that began arriving intermittently on my desk in the mid 1970s. It's what still distinguishes

INTRODUCTION

them today, which is to say that it's what makes Wiley W. Hilburn, Jr., the man he is.

The columns are, indeed, "Fragments" of his life and the lives around him. They've now become fragments of our lives, too.

And I'll never again listen to his requests to stop writing them.

—Jim Montgomery
Editorial Page Editor
The Times
Shreveport, Louisiana

FRAGMENTS

Wiley W. Hilburn, Jr.'s North Louisiana

//
PART ONE

PORTRAITS

Tom Sawyer: Alive in Ruston

December 17, 1978

Tom Sawyer isn't dead.

Naw, old Tom is alive in Ruston, disguised in a fuzzy pink jumpsuit and hiding out in Shipley's Cafe under the alias of Sonny Barnard. Sonny, you see, has somehow conned about the whole of this college town into painting his picket fence—or, as it happens, building and selling his invention.

The invention is called a "Dirt Extractor," and it cleans automobile carpets. Nobody will deny that the idea for the machine, for which there are now several dozen orders, was Sonny's. He put the thing together in his mind down at what might be loosely—very loosely—described as "the office."

That office can be seen as one enters Ruston via North Vienna, but look quickly because it's unlikely that this place will ever be set aside as one of Lincoln Parish's architectural landmarks. Actually, Sonny is headquartered in the remains of an old washateria, and it still smells faintly of detergent and grease. What the whole thing looks like, from the inside, is Dr. Frankenstein's laboratory right after Boris Karloff went crazy and busted everything up. The concrete floor is littered with wire, pieces of pipe and bits of metal.

The only furniture in Barnard's lab is an old rocking chair, where Sonny rocks and dreams of inventions—like the dirt extractor—and plays the part of either the mad scientist or Tom Sawyer, depending on what work needs to be done.

If the rocking chair is empty, then Sonny is for sure at Shipley's where he can be identified by a braying blast of a laugh—the decibel count of which has been known to make all the doughnuts in the place go flat.

But, like I said, the idea for the dirt extractor is solely Sonny's, and half of Ruston thinks Barnard is going to get rich off of it. If he does, a good part of the reason will have to be chalked up to no developmental overhead. Enter Tom Sawyer and the picket fence. Or, think of it the way Jack Moran did over coffee at Shipley's the other day. Sonny, he says, has put together a Ruston think tank, and done it without a single consultant's fee.

Consider, Sonny got Moran, who is a furniture maker and artisan, to make the hand tools. Mike Wells, a machinist, constructed the case. Billy Davison made the cabinet. And that only starts it. Ken Young, a troubleshooter for IBM, wired the contraption.

Dr. Buck Brown, a member of Louisiana Tech's electrical engineering faculty, came up with a cut-off switch. Bill Bayne, a mechanic, supplied and installed the hose. John "Red" LaRue, a realtor, has demonstrated the machine for potential buyers (Moran calls him "sales director for the Southeastern United States").

No, even with all that help on the production side, Sonny isn't taking sales for granted. Dr. James Hester, chairman of the business department at Tech, wandered into Sonny's Shipley spider web and is now advising on sales flow and management. Two other Tech Ph.D's have also been victimized and are helping out. As noted, Shipley's is the business office. (Moran, with a gift for rhetoric, calls it Ruston corporate headquarters), thanks to proprietors Tommy and Fern Mercer.

Of course, Sonny takes his time thinking these things out, and once the extractor was about built, he bogged down on deciding on a sign or insignia to show it off. Days passed and Sonny rocked and drank coffee at Shipley's. Finally Harry Farrar, who has a locksmith and sign business next door to Sonny's lab, lost patience at the hold-up and made the appropriate sign. Free, of course. "Here's your damned sign," he told Sonny. "Now let's get on with the invention."

Others have been drawn into Sonny's net. John Hays, publisher of *The Morning Paper*, is doing pictures for the brochure. Eddie Hood, who owns X-Press Printing, has done some of the printing. Free, of course. I've been elected project historian (the position of least status). Jimmy Alexander has been named chaplain. He's praying for all of us.

The truth is that everybody likes Sonny, a big, dark-haired fellow who has himself helped a lot of people. And who wouldn't like Tom Sawyer? As for the invention, tell Tech and T. L. James to move over: Lincoln Parish has a new industry. And who knows, when the thing goes over big, the Peach Festival people might even put Sonny's old washateria on the things-to-see list.

A Hudson, "Ebbtide," and Girls

April 29, 1979

If our '50s gang had a Fonzie, it had to be Bill. It wasn't that we worshiped Bill the way the "Happy Days" crowd does the Fonz.

A HUDSON, "EBBTIDE," AND GIRLS

Bill was liked and very much a part of the group. But envy, more than reverence, characterized our attitude toward him.

For if our Bill didn't look at all like Henry Winkler, he did share one crucial characteristic of the Fonzie persona: The entire female population of Lincoln Parish, it seemed, was crazy about Bill. And that, in turn, drove us crazy with envy. Of course it wasn't only envy either; it was also a consuming curiosity about how Bill succeeded where we failed.

Maybe it was the car he drove; some of us thought so. Bill had a green Hudson that he washed carefully every summer afternoon in his aunt's front yard. More important, that Hudson had an automatic gas cap. You pressed a button, and it popped open. We rationalized that, without the automatic gas cap to show off, Bill's appeal for women would vanish.

In our saner moments we knew better, but it did seem that Bill knew all the right props to succeed at the dating game while we almost literally groped in the dark. He kept a small bottle of wine (Bill could recite the "good years" for wine even then) in a bamboo flask in the backseat of the Hudson. Was it the wine, we wondered, or the bamboo flask? We could get wine, of course (even if we didn't know the "good years"), but nobody could ever locate a bamboo flask exactly like Bill's.

If the car and the wine didn't win the women, then Bill could always sing. It seemed unfair to us that, on top of all his other talents, Bill could sing, too. Strumming effortlessly on his "git-fiddle" (it always occupied the Hudson's backseat with the bamboo flask), Bill could string out "Ebbtide" and "You'll Never Walk Alone" just like Roy Hamilton.

Inevitably a whole crowd of girls would make a circle around him, leaving their dates, getting close to catch his golden voice: "First the tide rushes in . . ." Bill would try to get me to provide the chorus, but I knew better than to do that.

If Hudson, wine and song failed, which was extremely unlikely, then old Bill could resort to poetry. That's right; he wrote poetry, composing it on the concrete sidings of Interstate 20

A HUDSON, "EBBTIDE," AND GIRLS

overpasses where his efforts could be seen by all who happened along, especially females.

An English teacher at Louisiana Tech dismissed Bill's romantic rhymes as "unintellectual," but Bill couldn't have cared less that his overpass writings didn't exactly compare with the best of T. S. Eliot. A coed's face would go all soft when Bill began to recite some of his "unintellectual" stuff.

Bill, of course, was aware that he had a certain attraction for women and affected a casual arrogance about it. "I'm not spending any more summers in Ruston," he told me one August. "Why not?" I asked. "Not enough good-lookin' girls to choose from around here in the summer," he said calmly, and from then on Bill found other places to be a good part of June, July and August.

Sometimes the green-eyed monster would get the best of us and somebody would throw a sharp barb at Bill. But he had a way of utterly deflating our best efforts. Once I got three invitations to the March of Dimes Dance in the Men's Old Gym at Tech and couldn't wait to confront Bill (who for once didn't get asked) with my news. "Caught in the last-minute rush, huh?" he observed without a trace of interest.

Bill wasn't much of an athlete (hard to believe, isn't it?), but he did become the best of the marginal people on the Ruston High School track squad and promptly styled himself "King of the rinky-dinks." Bill not only won a letter with a minimum of running, he was sort of a star, too.

Even where food and dress were concerned, Bill could somehow anticipate things and turn them to his advantage with the girls. When we didn't know any salad dressing but Thousand Island existed, Bill was ordering oil-and-vinegar and grilling steaks for his dates.

And while we all wore nauseous pink shirts and black slacks Bill opted for a battered soft jacket, whitened blue jeans and felt shoes. Bill just knew things the rest of us didn't, anticipated the trends, and the girls loved him for it.

Some twenty years have passed since those days. I don't see Bill much, but the other day I did run into him. His hair is calculatedly shaggy, he drives one of those "z" cars, and his girl is a knockout. Bill is still the Fonz, I guess, and in a way I still admire him: He's sort of scoring for all of us.

Berry, and Baseball, and the Summer of 1948

May 20, 1979

"Blind Tom!"

The singular, sandpaper voice carried over my head into the Little League outfield this recent cool May night at the ballpark, but it summoned me back to the summer of 1948—and my own childhood in Ruston.

The voice, I knew instantly, belonged to Berry Hinton. Now, in the ripening spring of 1979, he sat well behind me, cheering for a grandson and jeering at the umpires. But before, in the summer of '48, Berry was on the baseball field himself.

In 1948, summer was forever in Lincoln Parish, and the place to be every Sunday afternoon was Fraser Field. That's where Berry played baseball and managed the old Ruston Volunteers of the Big Eight League.

Kids had baseball heroes then, and Berry was mine; Berry and his Vols.

Ruston actually had two baseball teams in those days, Berry's Vols and the Rebels. And the Rebels, truth to tell, had a far larger following than the Vols. The Rebels were a young and brawling bunch; fellows who worked on oil rigs and in the construction business.

BERRY, AND BASEBALL, AND THE SUMMER OF 1948

The Rebels could steal bases and run fast and score runs in bursts. Of course, the Vols were established first, and they looked it; I mean they looked older than the Rebels because they were older.

Though the Vols were to somehow defeat the Rebels in the championship playoffs of 1948 on guts and guile and pure love of the game, it was plain even to my young eyes that Hinton's old soldiers had retreated to the last ditch. The lithe, swift Rebels were on the rise.

But the rivalry between the two hometown ball clubs was deep and pretty bitter, and when they played—the Vols limping slightly in their soiled white uniforms and the Rebels dashing in their pressed racehorse gray—well, likely as not 2,000 people would turn up on a hot Sunday afternoon to watch 'em go at it.

Everybody took sides and, as John Foster Dulles used to say before it was all right to lose a war, neutrality was considered immoral. The Vols had Willet, Prudhomme, Hicks, Foster, Berry and his brother Billy, Davis, Lewis, Herrin, Harrison, Thigpen and Pace.

The Rebels countered with Reed, Williamson, Null, Beard, Holstead (the dark-haired, yelling Racer Holstead at third was the fountain of the Rebels' youthful vitality), Hall, Lann, Cassibry and Griner. The Rebels, as noted, got the big cheers. That was because the Rebels were a flashy and talented team but also, I think, because of Berry.

Berry, you see, was a very good baseball player, and he knew it, and sometimes showed that he knew it. A discernible mutter of disapproval rippled through the crowd when Berry slouched to bat in his rumpled red and white uniform.

Before Berry ever took even a practice swing, he would carefully and yet casually knock imaginary dirt out of his cleats with the bat, taking his good time about it, too. Then he would finally stand in, wagging the lumber, pointing it down the barrel like a rifle at the pitcher, and prancing in wide circles after each throw, his cheek bulging all the time with Beechnut.

BERRY, AND BASEBALL, AND THE SUMMER OF 1948

Ruston is a sedate sort of town, and a lot of people didn't take kindly to Berry's ritually repeated performance. But Hinton went right ahead with it, as if he enjoyed the fans' impatience. In fact, if somebody got particularly abusive, Berry would ease over toward the grandstand in a measured, infinitely slow tread and grin malignantly at the offender before cutting loose an arrogant aim of tobacco juice.

Some people just hated all of that, but I loved it, and loved Berry. It was just a game and Hinton was the original and everlasting boy of summer, playing every moment right into the dusty red ground of Fraser Field with a boiling aggression that did—I freely admit—border on cussedness.

And the thing was, Berry could back up that bravado on the field, though like most of the Vols at that stage of his semi-pro career, he was already old enough to be playing slow-pitch softball. He was that good; Fraser Field rang with the crack of his line drives. No long ball hitter, he bulls'-eyed every gap in the defensive perimeter with shots aimed like bullets.

He played every position on the infield and caught when "Round Man" Willet got booted out of a game. Even Berry's multitude of detractors concede he would have made the big leagues but for one fatal flaw—an arm so wounded he nearly had to run the put-out to first base.

No matter. It wasn't that Berry hit .400 for several summers, which he did. It was those other things. Like the time he was being given an intentional walk. Ball one. Ball two. Then suddenly there was Berry lunging across the plate to one-arm a looping, game-winning single to right field. The other team was infuriated. So were Hinton's critics in the stands. As usual, I loved it.

But sometimes Berry would embarrass even me. There was that time he was lodged on third base, the tying run with two out. Berry looked as condemned and hopeless as an inmate of

BERRY, AND BASEBALL, AND THE SUMMER OF 1948

deathrow as he took his lead off third. That was because his brother, Billy, was at bat.

Now Billy was a fine athlete and good on defense, but he owned a singularly quiet bat. Berry, hung up on third with that game-tying run, knew it. And after Billy went down two strikes, Berry simply couldn't stand it. He tried to steal home.

He was doomed, out two miles in a cloud of dust, and there was brother Billy watching it all, helpless, bat in hand. I was embarrassed for Billy. But I thought in my ten-year-old mind, "Oh, that Berry. That Berry."

I might have been a silent admirer of Berry all those summers, but we kids had a habit of sitting on the Vol dugout during the game, drinking RC's jammed up to the neck with fresh-roasted peanuts and observing the players close-up. And once, in a night game, Berry came out of the dugout for a drink of water.

Summoning all my courage, I flung out at him: "Mr. Hinton, I'm for the Vols!" I did not realize it in that second, but it was the start of a life-long friendship. Berry's brown eyes, squinted down to slant-holes from tracking pop-flies in the sun, gathered me in. "You want a drink of water?" he said in that sandpaper voice, offering me the dipper.

I drank, as if from the Holy Grail. Then he invited me to sit in the dugout for the rest of the game. It was unbelievable. I didn't sleep for two nights.

It's the spring of '79 now and I'm forty-one and Berry is watching his grandson play Little League baseball. But Hinton is still one of Lincoln Parish's meanest bowlers, and when he yells "Blind Tom" at the umpire I go and sit beside him.

"Wiley," he tells me in the sandpaper voice, punctuating the words with an arrogant aim of Beechnut, "your boy has a good glove down there at second base." After that, I beamed for two days. Berry Hinton had said that my son Kevin is a good baseball player. And I have drunk from Berry's cup one more time.

The Milkshake King of Winnfield

October 21, 1979

Some people go through life without leaving much of a trace. Others, giving of themselves, steer a phosphorescent passage that glimmers long after they are gone. The late Howard A. "Dick" Porter of Winnfield gave off such a light, and it lingers yet.

Dick Porter wasn't a political power or a captain of great corporations. He operated a soda fountain on Winnfield's Main Street when cokes were a nickel and the sawmill and the rock quarry were "industry" in the town. In fact, Dick Porter ran the Dixie Drugstore for fifty-three years and the day he closed was the day he went to the hospital for the last time. He died March 11, 1978.

I met Mr. Porter right after he had finished waxing the drugstore floor. He poured me the best milkshake from Ruston south to the Gulf in that liver-smelling place. And somehow I felt right at home in that brief time, and he stuck in my mind.

So it was that I wrote a very small thing about this man I had remembered meeting in the Dixie Drugstore coming home one day from Baton Rouge. And when the little item was printed long after that meeting, well, I quickly found out that Mr. Porter was a very big man.

A lot of people called and wrote to say that Dick Porter had touched their lives, but Eck Bozeman told the best story of this enduring North Louisiana man in a letter to "Fragments". Here, in part, is what Mr. Bozeman wrote about Mr. Porter:

"Yes, when Dick Porter died, so did the Dixie Drugstore. And with it went a legend of service to Winnfield in more ways than one. There is no way of knowing how many boys got their start 'jerking soda' for Dick Porter. I was one of those boys.

"I well remember the day Dick opened for business. My father and mother operated a dairy in Winnfield. A day or two before the opening date Dick put in an order for twenty-five gallons of milk for his famous milkshakes. We delivered the milk early that morning which was on a Saturday. When the phone rang we were eating lunch. It was Dick Porter. He needed another twenty-five gallons of milk as soon as we could get it to the store. Before nine o'clock that night they were out of milk. For years Dick Porter was the 'milkshake king' of Winnfield.

"Dick Porter loved to play his violin. At night when there was very little business he would take his violin out of its case and he would play for the benefit of those who were in the store. It was always a treat to hear him play. In his declining years—in fact up until the year before he died—he played for the annual reunion of former Winnfield High School students dating back to 1908.

"Yes, Howard Allen 'Dick' Porter and the Dixie Drugstore were as much a part of Winnfield's Main Street as the Red Onion Cafe was to Ruston in the years past.

"Now that I am nearing the seventy-one-year mark, I look back to when the Dixie Drugstore was every boy's favorite hangout—and Dick Porter's place was the place. That was when the boys wore pompadour hairdos and bell bottom pants."

Unionville and the Store: Hamming Up History

June 29, 1980

UNIONVILLE—Here in the piney woods and red clay heartland of North Central Louisiana, Buck Guynes is selling Ball

UNIONVILLE AND THE STORE: HAMMING UP HISTORY

freeze jars, Pampers, turnip seeds, hawgjowls, Vita-Fresh orange juice, neck bones and wigs—all incongruously mixed up on the shelves—out of the Colvin-Jones General Store.

Most of all, though, Buck is selling history, Smoke-House bacon slabs and Red-Eye Gravy hams. If Buck puts the ham ahead of the history (or more likely combines the two), that's all right. In Unionville, they go together like ham hocks and butterbeans.

The history actually came first. The store was established in 1853 by the Stone Colvin family and that same hill-country dynasty has hung on to it through all the generations. The general store is the genuine historical article, parked haphazardly on U.S. 167 between Ruston and Dubach, not far from where it stood when these uplands were on the frontier.

What Colvin in-law Buck has done is promote the history part since he took over the store as manager in 1977. For though the manager wears Roundhouse overalls, cracked cowboy boots and calls himself a "country boy," he is first of all a promoter—and a very successful one at that.

He admits it. The store, despite its history, was struggling to survive in 1977. Buck wrangled a feature story in Ruston's *Morning Paper* that came down heavily on the store's ties to "an era bygone, an age simpler, more innocent, perhaps better." It was just what Buck had been wanting.

That piece appeared in February of 1978. "March business jumped three thousand dollars and we caught on," Buck told me the other day in his almost indecipherable Southern drawl. Since then Buck has taken the Monroe *Morning World*, the Ruston *Daily Leader*, *The Times* and several area television crews on his nostalgia tour of the store. The nostalgia-history bit worked.

When Buck could break away from interviews, he sold 1,189 bacon slabs and grossed well over $135,000 last year. His business has extended well beyond Unionville's hardy 500 residents. Now "Fragments" has been added to Buck's media scalps—bought for two containers (one sour) of Vita Fresh orange juice. I expect to see Charles Kuralt's "On-the-Road" van

UNIONVILLE AND THE STORE: HAMMING UP HISTORY

parked outside the store the next time I drive up. Until then, Buck says he will settle for one of Tom Erwin's features on KSLA-TV. Watch out, Tom. Buck wants you.

Naturally, Buck isn't out a nickel on all this free historical advertising. He does place a weekly ad in John Hays' *Morning Paper*, the source of his original breakthrough, but he and John are on the barter system: hams for Hays, newspaper space for Buck's folksy ads.

Of course, some of the news on Buck and the store has not been on the feature side—like the time he took on the Louisiana Department of Transportation when the state expropriated the store for $11,002 to make way for a 4.8-mile road project.

The DOT said Guynes could not file suit to recover any damages suffered while the business had to close to move off the right-of-way. This time progress waited on Buck, and history, for a solid two years while the battle raged. Buck won in the end.

"I didn't want to hold up the highway project . . . it was needed," Buck told *Times* bureau chief Tom Morris. "But all the factors involved do not give the state a right to destroy a business and a livelihood."

Buck did move the old store on his own time and terms, but then the question became: Would this mess of unsheeted tin and pine flooring stand up to its sixty-foot migration? There was pot-betting among Unionville residents that the store would fall in on Buck. However, the building survived the move, though even Buck admits "the termites had long ago deserted some of that wood."

Is Buck combative by nature? "You could say that . . . especially when it comes to makin' a living," Buck says. "If something is worth having, it's worth fighting for. I fought for this store."

Guynes, a native of Dry Prong and a former high school French teacher, also conceded that his independent ways "have alienated some people around here." He points out that he has turned an 80 percent credit business to an 80 percent cash business.

Maybe Buck has made some people mad and maybe he is literally hamming up history, but there was a lot of traffic around the Colvin-Jones General Store the two days I visited. Among the customers was Melvin Kay, who settled down on the whittled-up oak bench outside the store, propped his feet on a stack of black locust wood, and expertly rolled himself a Prince Albert.

Mr. Kay felt right at home.

And so, to tell the truth, did I.

Eyeball to Eyeball with Rosalynn

November 2, 1980

WEST MONROE—I was eyeball to eyeball with Rosalynn Carter in the Convention Center here Thursday night, but to tell the truth it wasn't much of an interview. In fact, it wasn't an interview at all.

It just happened that West Monroe Mayor Dave Norris steered the First Lady in my direction and suddenly there we were—face to face. Dry-throated at this proximity to history, I couldn't even muster a greeting while she launched into an explanation as to why her plane was late.

I did sort of touch Mrs. Carter on the elbow as she moved on down the line. That touch earned me a very direct backward look from a pair of sea-green eyes. A professional at this political business, the First Lady is big on eye contact.

A bunch of people had their picture taken with Mrs. Carter and everybody got that direct green look, a "hello, how are you" in that soft, slightly blurred Georgia accent, and a quick touch.

After greeting everybody at the reception she shook hands with the servers, too. Nobody was missed. She even straightened somebody's name tag.

Mrs. Carter has impressed me on television, and I still think she is an attractive woman, despite a certain shoulder-sagging weariness this night that is—given the campaign and her schedule—perfectly understandable. The First Lady has a shy, almost vulnerable smile that I liked, and she works hard.

Mrs. Carter was wearing an understated outfit of browns. Sandy Stokley of Ruston described a "dusty rose blouse, a flowered vest and a tan skirt." A friend and I observed that the First Lady was a good-looking woman. That was when Sandy observed that we were typically chauvinistic.

It was nice getting that close look at Mrs. Carter, but I almost didn't make the reception. To be honest, I wasn't invited. I kind of sneaked in with Dr. Allen Herbert of Ruston, a Carter supporter and party official.

We got turned away rather abruptly at two doors after squeezing into a parking space beside a car with a Reagan sticker. Allen was waving his $100 check for the Carter campaign and I maintained the futile fiction that I'm employed by *The Times*. (Montgomery, could you please send me that press card?)

Finally Allen recognized somebody named Mrs. Winters and we were admitted. I sneaked in beside Allen. For those who paid their money, I didn't eat any of the food. Well, maybe a canape or two. The caterer was afraid the ice figure of the Democratic donkey on the table would melt before Mrs. Carter arrived. It didn't.

Meanwhile, in another room of the center, the Monroe Suzuki group and the Northeast Louisiana University band were preparing to serenade the First Lady. An NLU student was wearing a "Reagan Youth Staff" button. "I'm in the band," he explained. He shook his head. "We have to play 'Georgia on My Mind.'"

Both the NLU bandsmen and the Suzuki kids got into a pile

of peanuts that were supposed to be decorative and, of course, make Mrs. Carter feel at home. Pretty soon peanut hulls were all over the floor. "This is awful," said one of the sponsors.

A man carrying anti-abortion posters made it into the center, but William Sumlin of Ruston, State Democratic Central Committeeman for Lincoln Parish, carefully but crisply relieved him of that burden. William made a neat stack of the signs under a table heavy with green Carter material.

The fellow carrying the anti-abortion signs wasn't mad. "I finally decide to express myself, and look what happens," he told me, looking wistfully at his stack of seized signs. "But," he added, brightening, "I'm gonna get to see the First Lady."

After that Dr. Gary Stokley, a Tech social science professor who happens to support Carter, got into a rather heated debate with some more NLU students who were wearing Reagan buttons. Gary was about to launch into one of his best classroom lectures, but his wife Sandy stepped between the combatants. But Gary got the last word: "Typical Reagan types," he snapped.

There were some political types circulating, though not that many. I talked to Jim Brown, the active secretary of state. Mayor Norris was there, of course. And Sue Huckaby, wife of Rep. Jerry Huckaby, arrived with a purse full of presidential match-folders she had swiped from Air Force One. Sue had flown in with Mrs. Carter on the presidential plane.

I wanted one of the white and gold folders—they have the presidential seal and are printed with "ABOARD THE PRESIDENTIAL AIRCRAFT." Naturally, the fellows at Shipley's in Ruston were not impressed when I passed my souvenir around.

"I hope you write something about it," sniffed Pee Wee Edwards, "two weeks of letters in your column is too much." Sonny Barnard insisted I had the matches made up. Oh, well. Shipley's is a Reagan stronghold, anyway.

No matter. The fact is I crashed the reception, with Allen Herbert's help, and got to see the Mrs. Carter. Really, it would have been nice to be photographed with Mrs. Carter. I watched Allen and the Sumlin family and Joe Colvin from Gibsland and some other people get their pictures taken with the First Lady.

But that would have been asking too much since I wasn't even invited to her party.

"Hey Boots!": Kendall Flournoy Was Back

February 1, 1981

"Hey Boots!" he will holler with the soaring good humor that is his trademark, using a family nickname with an easy familiarity that puts me entirely at ease.

Ruston's Kendall Flournoy and I have been on a close first-name basis for a long time—despite the fact that he is eighteen years old and I'm crowding forty-three. Actually, Kendall is one of my son Greg's best friends. It's just that Kendall is one of those people I'm somehow always glad to see.

There he is standing in front of his dad's Enviro-Med building on busy West California Street, that grin glowing. The traffic pushes me along fast, but I catch his lips moving. "Hey, Boots," he is hollering.

We're at a basketball game in Tech's Memorial Gymnasium. I hear that familiar, friendly voice somewhere in the multitude. "Hey, Boots!" It's Kendall again, waving and grinning.

There is something All-American about Kendall. Maybe it's the grin. Anyway, other people—kids his own age, too—see something special in Kendall. Students at Ruston High School voted him "most courteous" and "best all-around." That kind of an All-American boy. You know the type.

There are, of course, a lot of All-American boys in North Lou-

"HEY BOOTS!": KENDALL FLOURNOY WAS BACK

isiana. The only difference is that Kendall is operating with one leg and half of one lung. Kendall, the big kidder with the big grin, has been fighting cancer for almost half his life.

He has been winning, too, though the medical odds were, from the first, overwhelmingly against him. Doctors, in fact, gave Kendall only a 15-20 percent chance of living after the cancer—lethal osteogenic sarcoma—was discovered in 1972. Kendall was told those odds; that, indeed, he could die. "Let's talk about brighter things," he would say.

Brighter things were not immediately in prospect. There were five operations. When Kendall came out of the anesthetic, his leg gone, he observed, "Well, I don't have to worry about the Army now." That wasn't bitterness, that was Kendall, his father said, looking at the brighter side. Still grinning.

The chemotherapy, however saving, was almost as brutal as the surgery. Kendall's shiny brown hair fell out and, beyond the heaving nausea, there was the chance that the medication might weaken his heart.

Kendall kept grinning through it all. He came back to the eighth grade to play schoolyard goalie in a soccer game. He also made 20-foot shots for the church basketball team. During those games Kendall's crutches were neatly deposited on the sidelines. He hopped.

In the eight years after the first operation, Kendall did some things his parents frankly never really expected him to do: like driving his own car, and graduating from Ruston High and dating girls and enrolling, this last fall, in college.

He was doing fine. And the whole reason for writing about Kendall now, really, is that he gave us a scare over the recent holidays. A routine checkup in Houston revealed one of those damned, dreadful spots. Telephones rang in Ruston. The town sort of held its collective breath. Kendall is on a first-name basis with a lot of people in Ruston. "Hey, Boots!" We were scared.

Kendall wasn't scared, at least, like always, he didn't show it. The weekend before this last surgery he paid us a visit. He was

"HEY BOOTS!": KENDALL FLOURNOY WAS BACK

laughing and mostly kidding Anne Marie, those brown eyes snapping.

That night he never mentioned the operation to me. When I left the room to hit this typewriter he told Ellen about it. He was dry-eyed and decisive. "I'll be out of there (the hospital) in a week and a half, and there will be plenty of time to register" (at LSU-Baton Rouge where he is a freshman).

Then he was kidding Anne Marie again. "Re," he calls her, just like we all do. She's crazy about him, too. "Bye, Boots," he yelled at me that night, backing out of the driveway—headed for Houston and surgery and what else nobody knew.

The operation was performed as scheduled the following Tuesday. Telephones in Ruston rang on Wednesday. The news was good. The spot, the dreaded spot, was revealed as scar tissue. The town let out its breath. Greg and Ellen telephoned Kendall the next night in the hospital. They told me his voice sounded weak, but that he was kidding again.

Kendall was out of the hospital right on his schedule. He came to church a couple of Sundays ago with Greg. Ellen fixed butterbeans and ham hocks for the whole bunch of them the other night; Kendall was joking. "I expected steak, Ellen," he said, grinning a yard. He registered at LSU, too.

He's all right.

"Hey, Boots!"

Hey, Kendall.

The Curmudgeon Whom We All Admired

April 26, 1981

Mr. Hewins, you were wrong.

A solid quarter-century before he died this past winter, Kenneth F. Hewins was telling his journalism students at Louisiana Tech that "nobody will come to my funeral . . . I've made too many people mad."

Actually, a good turnout paid their last respects to the Indiana city editor who came to Tech as head of the journalism department in 1929 and stayed on to terrorize students until he retired in 1968.

If Mr. Hewins was mistaken about the eventual turnout for his funeral, it's probably because he was the curmudgeon we came to admire and appreciate only later—the curmudgeon who, in one form or another, inhabits almost every life as a stormy catalyst for learning and growing.

Mr. Hewins was my department head, adviser and teacher for four years at Tech. Once, when I failed to meet the deadline on an assignment, he informed me: "Hilburn, you don't give a damn about Louisiana Tech and I want you to know, formally and officially, that Louisiana Tech doesn't give a damn about you."

What redeemed Mr. Hewins in my eyes, even then, was that his wrath was equally distributed among the high and the low at Tech. On the high side, there was the time he hung up on a *Times* editor who inquired politely about a panty-raid—the demonstrations of those days. Mr. Hewins frowned on any negative news about Tech.

It was decided in *The Times* newsroom, however, that if Tech— or Mr. Hewins—refused to talk about bad news, then maybe the good news about the university, in the form of KFH's neat press releases, ought to be spiked for a couple of weeks.

Mr. Hewins never once remarked on this absence of Tech news, but a new president making his mark at the university—F. Jay Taylor—soon noticed that Northwestern State was getting all the college space. So young President Taylor came calling on Mr. Hewins.

"Mr. Hewins," Dr. Taylor began respectfully, standing at the door of the journalism office in Keeny Hall, "we don't seem to be getting any news in *The Times* at all. I'm just wondering if there is anything I can do to help?"

Mr. Hewins stayed behind his desk, making a rampart out of it. "You can fire me," he answered his boss.

Dr. Taylor maintained his position in the door. "Of course I'm not going to fire you . . . you've been here a lot longer than I have," the president said. Then he tried again: "I just wonder if I can help you with this *Times* thing?"

"You can fire me."

Mr. Hewins was a small man, but his desk was a bunker.

The university president tried one more time, still in the door. "Could you just tell me somebody I could call, Mr. Hewins?"

"No," replied the head of the journalism department, "but you can fire me." Jay Taylor retreated. Before long, so did *The Times*. Tech news reappeared in the paper. And Mr. Hewins stayed behind his desk.

By the time I got back to Tech in 1968 Mr. Hewins had retired, but only across the hall to an office where he advised the *Lagniappe*, the university yearbook, on a part-time basis.

When then-Vice President Virgil Orr and I couldn't pinpoint a date we needed for a news release, Dr. Orr told his secretary to get the current *Lagniappe* where the information could be obtained.

The secretary joined us, a funny look on her face. "We don't have this year's *Lagniappe*, Dr. Orr," she said.

"Why not?" the No. 2 administrator on campus wanted to know.

"Mr. Hewins won't let us have one. He said you didn't fill out the proper form," she said.

Dr. Orr's eyes flashed. "You mean the vice president can't get a yearbook. . . . " Then he considered the source of the problem. "Mr. Hewins," he said, grinning, and left it at that. "Borrow one from somebody else," he concluded.

As the campus newspaper adviser, Mr. Hewins in fact was editor, managing editor, sports editor and censor. He even edited the minutes of the Student Senate. What didn't dawn on a lot of his students, until much later, is that this was another time.

There was also the fact that only Mr. Hewins did the censoring. In that sense he established and guarded the integrity of Tech journalism. Nobody censored that paper but him; no dean, president, publications board, Student Government Association or Louisiana governor.

He was a good teacher, too, using the Ruston *Daily Leader* as a dartboard for his witty critiques. He had a physical hatred for style errors, for any newspaper errors, but his temper was lightened by a sharp sense of humor.

His *Tech Talk* was never less than professional, and his often-fired student editors performed well in the newspaper trenches. For example, the editors of both Shreveport newspapers today, *The Times* and the *Journal*, came out of the Hewins corner of Keeny Hall.

It would not have surprised Mr. Hewins, meantime, that the *Tech Talk* story on his death contained a typographical error. "The *Tech Talk* never gets anything right," he told me when I worked on the college paper.

You were wrong about the funeral, though, Mr. Hewins.

A lot of us were there.

Dr. Roane: He Knew It Hurt... and Cared

June 28, 1981

Henry Roane was dying.

But when I passed his office in Ruston's Green Clinic, where a lot of my ailments had been diagnosed, it was good to see the color picture of his family, like always, reflected in the stainless steel sterilizer.

In fact, everything in the little office had been left as it was—even though everybody knew Dr. Roane had seen his last patient there. And when he died, from the cancer he had treated in so many others, the whole clinic shut down for the funeral.

Henry Roane deserved that.

He was a good doctor and a good man; the two things merged in Dr. Roane. He wasn't a brilliant specialist. And I had the feeling Henry Roane didn't exactly bury himself in the *New England Journal of Medicine*, either.

But people said Henry Roane had experience, and they were right. What's more, he *listened*. "Uhuh... uhuh," he rasped, barely audible, cataloging the symptoms. He was always listening, and touching and probing with sympathetic hands.

You just felt better after talking to Henry Roane, even if he didn't do anything. He had this feeling for pain. That gentle touch could push back pain. He knew it hurt. You knew he knew. "You'll feel better," he'd rumble. And you did.

Things went better after you left, too, because Dr. Roane explained a course of treatment. What would come next, I mean, and things like that. When I cracked two ribs he told me, "Your side will hurt a little worse every day. You'll think you aren't

DR. ROANE: HE KNEW IT HURT . . . AND CARED

getting better. Then it starts down the other side. It'll hurt less until it's gone. That's all I can do and all I can tell you."

That was the way Henry Roane prepared people for a lot worse than broken ribs. His explanations took away the fear.

A lot of older people came to Dr. Roane, too, because he listened and he cared and he knew it hurt. He was the old people's doctor for a long time in Ruston. They loved him, and they didn't want to see anybody else. He had experience, he listened to them, and he knew it hurt.

When an editor-friend of mind with a bad heart suddenly went white with pain over lunch one day at the Holiday Inn, I took him to see Dr. Roane. He saw us on short notice. You could get in to see Henry Roane. He was like that.

Actually, there wasn't much Dr. Roane could do for the editor, who had gone through six cardio-vascular surgeries. It wasn't a heart attack but the man was hurting. Really hurting.

Henry Roane listened to the history of those operations. "Uhuh . . . Uhuh . . . Uhuh." His fingers gently tracked the scars on the editor's chest. The man relaxed. Somebody, a doctor, was listening. Some of the pain drained out of his face. "You'll be all right," Dr. Roane told him, almost inaudibly. But the editor heard him. He felt better.

Henry Roane was there when Daddy had that crushing heart attack. The doctor pulled a chair close to the oxygen tent. Daddy parted the flap and asked Dr. Roane for a cigarette. "Wiley, cigarettes helped to cause this thing," he said. But Henry Roane had his hand on Daddy's arm. Everybody relaxed.

Dr. Roane got me excused from physical education classes at Tech. "I'm not a jock and I hate that stuff," I told him. He had a deep laugh that matched his voice. "You need the exercise," he told me. But he signed the excuse.

After that Henry Roane always claimed that his name belonged on my Tech diploma. We met occasionally when I came back to Ruston. Once, on the street, he took me by the arm. "I read you," was all he said. It was more than enough. Dr. Roane had made me feel better one more time.

Not that Henry Roane was perfect—some kind of peerless Ben Casey saint or something. Dr. Roane had a lot of problems, including a brutally-short, crooked arm that never properly healed after surgery and made him wince with pain.

Maybe it was the problems and the pain that made Dr. Roane understand what hurt. Maybe it was because "he never said a bad word about anybody," as Lincoln General Hospital Administrator Frank Jerome told me. All I know is that he was a good doctor and a good man—the best—and that they were right to close down the clinic when he died.

Educating "The Barbarians"

December 6, 1981

It was a dreary December morning in the late 1950s. The scene was the peeling, underheated second floor of the Old English Building on the Louisiana Tech campus. Robert C. Snyder, associate professor, was reading and teaching from his heavily underscored copy of Plato's *Republic*.

Mr. Snyder was making a point, about the philosopher-kings, I believe, from that tattered blue-and-white paperback. He had paused, unexpectedly, full of academic truth. That was when somebody let out a whisper that sounded startlingly loud in the quiet interlude: *What time is it?*

It was a question that broke Robert Snyder's scholarly spell and set the class, except for one who let out that intemperate question to tittering. The professor slowly lowered Plato to the desk; his blazing eyes silenced the murmur of laughter.

EDUCATING "THE BARBARIANS"

"Barbarians," he finally said in a savagely measured tone. "All of you are a bunch of barbarians." He pointed to the door. "Get out," he ordered and added that "you can go tell Dr. Ropp (R. L. Ropp, then president of Tech) that I called you barbarians. You *are* barbarians."

All the barbarians came back to the next class period, of course, and Mr. Snyder returned to the impossible task of planting Plato's dialogues in North Louisiana red clay. Actually, Mr. Snyder—he'll always be "Mister" to me—never gave up on us. And we came back because he had the rare classroom chemistry that draws students, and because we never knew what he would do next.

In that same English 402 class, for example, Mr. Snyder told us that somebody down the hall was teaching Salesmanship. The idea that somebody could pollute the sacred halls of the Old English Building with Salesmanship broke Mr. Snyder's liberal arts heart.

So he would open the door of his own classroom and peer malignly down the hall toward that offending stronghold of Salesmanship. "You know what he's down there telling them?" Snyder thundered. "He's telling them to *know your territory.*"

Mr. Snyder's voice draped icicles of scorn on those last three words. "Any fool knows a salesman has to know his territory," Mr. Snyder concluded before returning to Plato.

That was the class where I met Mr. Snyder. The semester before I had folded academically, and a career in journalism—once my goal—seemed out of reach. I was discouraged. Mr. Snyder stood me up, said I could write a little, declared journalism a good profession and gave me the first of several reading lists that were to form the bedrock of my education.

In fact, Mr. Snyder became my unofficial academic adviser at Tech and I sought him out frequently in his drafty, book-cluttered little office. He was always there until five o'clock, swathed in muffler and overcoat during the winter months to combat the cold of the Old English Building and yet still sneezing with a perpetual virus.

Just before I was graduated with a degree in journalism and took a job at The Shreveport *Times*—his recommendation helped to convince Associate Editor Don Ewing I could do the job—he even told me how to get my girl back. The plan worked, and Ellen is my wife.

I moved on, and so did Mr. Snyder—to chair the English Department eventually and to make statewide speeches and to serve on governors' committees and to help build a library in Lincoln Parish. Last week Mr. Snyder announced his retirement as department head though he will continue to teach full-time.

In the interim, Mr. Snyder and I have differed, and sharply so. I came back to Tech in 1968 and those differences grew—over the role of the college newspaper, news releases and academic leadership. In fact, we got into a push-and-shove row at a meeting of the Athletic Council that caused a vice president to observe that he's never seen such a thing in thirty years of peaceful academia.

All that isn't important now. Mr. Snyder is retiring and they have torn down the Old English Building. I'm glad, meanwhile, that he will continue to teach. Because he is the best teacher I—and a generation of other North Louisiana barbarians—ever had, and I'll always be grateful for that.

"She Gave You Your First Book, Son"

March 14, 1982

"Mrs. Upchurch died," Ellen told me as soon as I came home. She knew I'd want to know. During those growing-up years in

"SHE GAVE YOU YOUR FIRST BOOK, SON"

Ruston, from twelve until Discovery-of-Girls, Bill Upchurch and I ran our dogs endlessly along the little creek behind the Upchurch's two-story frame house on the Old Monroe Highway. Mrs. Upchurch, Bill's mother, became a part of my life.

A voracious reader, Mrs. Upchurch introduced me to Winston Churchill's Second World War series—an acquaintance that remains with me still. In fact, *The Gathering Storm*, borrowed from Mrs. Upchurch's library, is still on my shelf (I have this awful habit of refusing to return books I really like). She also suggested that I take *The Caine Mutiny* home to read. That novel started me on serious fiction.

Mrs. Upchurch had a directness about her, lightened by a dry, ironic wit and a gravelly chuckle. She told me I wore my jeans too low (Bill was forced to wear his under the armpits) and often corrected my grammar and manners as well. "That was a breach of etiquette, Bootsie," she was always telling me.

I liked Mrs. Upchurch. She was gracious, intelligent, even-keeled and forgiving. She never got mad at me when Bill and I tied up in one of our fights, and we fought often. The only time she called my mother was after I shot Bill in the cheek with a BB gun. The next day she was serving me V-8 juice on her front porch.

The last time I saw Mrs. Upchurch was a year ago when Bill, now a top executive with a worldwide oil company, came home to give the commencement address at Louisiana Tech. It was a big honor. And Mrs. Upchurch was so proud of Bill. But she still took the time to ask Ellen and me about our family.

It's too late to return the Churchill book, I guess.

Another breach of etiquette, Mrs. Upchurch.

Oh, yeah. I went by to see Mr. Upchurch the other day. "She gave you your first book, son," was the first thing he said to me.

Miss Butler, Miss Pepper, Miss . . .

July 11, 1982

Miss Butler was my fifth-grade teacher. And just the other day there she was—sitting at the next table in the Holiday Inn restaurant. Gosh, Miss Butler looked just the same; everybody at the old Model School in Ruston said she was pretty. She's still pretty. Same soft voice, too. Same even, brilliant smile. It was like, well, yesterday in the fifth grade.

I told Miss Butler, right then, how good she looked. "But, Wiley," she protested, in the same low-key voice that was never raised once in the classroom, "I'm eighty years old." Okay, so maybe the best teachers in the world don't age. Miss Butler sure hasn't; the whole class in the old brick building across from the Rock Island railroad tracks would say so.

Seeing Miss Butler started me to thinking about my grade-school teachers. Like most of my generation, I can still tick off those names by the grade. Miss Gerald. Miss Washburn. Miss Pepper. Miss Butler. Miss Rogers. Miss O'Neal. Miss Cotton. They were, every one, good, dedicated, above all intelligent women who—especially in my case—labored long hours to mold something worthwhile out of our resistant red-clay hides.

Those were some of my teachers, but an informal survey in Shipley's Cafe the other day had everybody remembering and reciting, very easily, their own grade-by-grade roll of mentors. It was mostly Miss This and Miss That. And everybody, suddenly looking faraway, could relate at least one incident involving every teacher from grades one to eight. We all started comparing teachers.

I told them how in Miss Gerald's first grade class it was understood that you had to read the roster of class names posted prominently on the bulletin board before crossing the hall to Miss

Washburn in second grade. Everybody faced the ordeal individually. To tell the truth, I was next to last to struggle through that roll—the name William Larry Hart stumped me time after time—but finally it was done. And obviously the name William Larry Hart stuck with me.

There was also the matter of a mattress in the first grade. There weren't nearly enough to go around so that best sleepers, the lucky son-of-a-guns that Miss Gerald noted fell cooperatively into a deep coma at precisely 1:15 P.M., were eventually rewarded with a mattress. Of course, everybody brought a quilt from home. But it was nice to get a mattress.

In fact, apart from reading that doggone class roll, a mattress was the great status symbol of first-grade at Model School. Well, I never got a mattress—nope—because I could not and still can't take a daytime nap. I tried to fake it, but Miss Gerald could spot an eyelash fluttering at fifty paces. I made it across the hall to Miss Washburn, but because of William Larry Hart and unslept naps it was, I always will think, a very close thing.

Now in fifth-grade—fifth grade was upstairs, and that was a real promotion—the status symbol was being chosen to serve as Miss Butler's First Assistant or Second Assistant. Miss Butler's assistants managed the cafeteria line and maintained silence on the way to the library. What an honor it was to be so designated; a goal that motivated all of us and a goal that some lucky son-of-a-guns achieved many times. I, uh, just made First Assistant once and that was the first selection when Miss Butler had to pick a name out of a hat. Oh, well.

In the sixth grade Miss Rogers wore her hair in a tight bun and paced up and down the rows in hole-punched black shoes. But this lady is one of my all-time favorite teachers; she had a sense of justice and mercy and humor. "Would you like me to wham you with this ruler or call your parents?" she wanted to know after I sneaked across the railroad tracks to my grandparents' house during the noon hour. I gratefully chose the ruler. But even Miss Rogers couldn't beat fractions into my thick head.

So it went, for a whole generation of us—fashioned and fine-tuned by a legion of strong women who usually had a "Miss" in front of their name. The term "old maid" rarely entered our conversations, quite honestly, because these ladies didn't fit whatever that sad description signified; with rare exceptions we respected, enjoyed and even loved these teachers. On behalf of all of us, a belated vote of gratitude.

Meantime, most of my "old" teachers are now retired, naturally, and I don't see much of them. They are too busy, really, to visit—busy taking sea cruises, rooting for the Lady Techsters, tutoring slow math students, bossing committees, jogging, writing parish histories, playing bridge and winning yard-of-the-month contests.

But what I really wanted to ask Miss Butler the other day was to let me have a shot at First Assistant one more time. After all, I only got to do it once.

How about it, Miss Butler?

Johnny Perritt, a "Rare Survivor"

July 11, 1982

In the perilous world of politics, twenty years in office is in itself a saga of survival—especially in a small-town mayor's office where constituents call their leader by his first name and are quite willing to call him any name at any hour of the night or day when the sewer stops up or the lights go out during a thunderstorm.

So Ruston's Johnny Perritt, who did not seek a sixth term and stepped down as mayor recently after two decades in office, is a rare survivor in a time when people switch leaders like they change television channels. But Johnny deserves credit for more than mere survival. Among other things, he leaves Ruston on solid financial ground—and with a legacy of good race relations he forged in the tumultuous 1960s.

Perhaps inevitably, Perritt's last term was controversial. But Johnny, literally a suspender-popping old-line politician who made it to funerals and ribbon-cuttings on crutches—he lost both hip sockets long ago—gave as good as he got, right up to the last City Council meeting.

Now, in retirement, Johnny can strum one of his five guitars, savor his Levi Garrett tobacco, try to sing like his late idol, Hank Williams, Sr., and—as the Ruston *Daily Leader's* Nancy Bergeron wrote—pass the time with "the greatest people in the world . . . right here in Lincoln Parish."

A Fig Tree Grows in Shreveport

February 27, 1983

For years John Rodakis of Shreveport searched for what he called "the perfect fig tree." He couldn't find it, his son Steve suspected, because nothing growing in North Louisiana measured up to the fig tree of his boyhood in Greece. Mr. Rodakis had joined his brother in Shreveport at age twenty via New York City.

Then, maybe fifteen years ago, John Rodakis returned to his native Greece for the last time where, not surprisingly, he soon spotted "the perfect fig tree" which had escaped him all that time. He wrapped the cutting in a damp cloth and foil and smuggled it, inside his vest, past customs.

It took a while, but "the perfect fig tree" bore fruit from the

soil of Shreveport just a year before John Rodakis died recently at eighty-three.
   Talk about roots.
   Real, literal roots.

The Yankee-Killer Who Came Home

April 17, 1983

It is springtime in the major leagues, and some marginal arms are already delivering millions of dollars and much fame to their owners. Meanwhile, they buried Bruce Price in Antioch this spring, and the talk at the funeral was how he could have had all of that. Not the money. Because in the 1920s, when Bruce pitched, baseball was still a game. But maybe the fame.

You see, in the springtime of 1921, twenty-four-year-old Bruce Price struck out Babe Ruth twice in a row in Shreveport where the New York Yankees were in training and playing exhibition games against the old local Gassers of the Texas League. In fact, the Babe couldn't break through Price's soft, precise curves at all; he popped out to second and hit a harmless grounder to shortstop in his two other at-bats.

It wasn't the only time Ruth struck out in his career, of course, but the hulking, bulb-nosed Yankee star seemed to recognize something special in the 5-8, 150-pound Price. "Who is that narrow b------?" Ruth was heard to ask. And Ruth also told a Shreveport *Times* sports writer that "I like that little Price."

Price didn't strike out Ruth with speed and strength; it was "always control," says his son Bob. And Bruce, years later, volunteered that he "could throw a baseball and make it curve through the crook of a stovepipe without ever touching metal." Okay, that's a little much. But he had that special control, a control that allowed him to probe the outermost perimeters of the strike zone. Bruce Price was a slowballing Ron Guidry in the springtime of 1921.

But let Bruce Price tell how he handled Ruth, as he told it to his nephew, *Times* "It's Friday" Editor Larry Price, a few years ago. "I had to keep the ball off of that trademark . . . so it was inside low and inside high," Bruce remembered. He also remembered measuring Ruth's methods and adjusting his delivery. "He (Ruth) would take one step with his left foot toward me, and then bring his right foot around to swing. I'd hesitate with my throw and try to throw his timing off."

Price was refining his pitching as a rookie thrower for the Gassers that spring. Ruth, on the other hand, had hit fifty-four homers the year before—his first with the Yankees. Some observers would say later that the Babe's spectacular 1920 season saved major league baseball, which was reeling from the Black Sox Scandal of 1919. After waving at Price's curve in Shreveport, Ruth would go on that year of '21 to hit fifty-nine homers, bat .378, score 177 runs and forever establish the Yankee dynasty.

Before the '21 season started, though, Ruth and those Yankees "roared into that Louisiana city (Shreveport) like cowboys coming to town on a Saturday night," wrote Robert W. Creamer in his book, *Babe*. Shreveport was riding high on an oil gusher. A big new well had just started producing four thousand barrels a day in close-by Haynesville, and North Louisiana was going crazy. Shreveport declared a "prosperity week." The hotels were packed, and Ruth had a high time tearing around town in his new Essex.

But for Bruce Price, well, Shreveport was too big and too busy. He missed his own little community of Antioch—not much more than a crossroads—the Trussell country store and the old Methodist Church. Compared to Antioch, nearby Simsboro in north-central Louisiana was Houston. But a few people have been clinging to the iron-ore backbone of Highway 544 in Lincoln Parish since before 1850. Most of all, though, Bruce Price missed Antioch's dark-haired Maggie Dring, his adored bride. Everybody said Bruce didn't want to be away from Maggie for a minute, even to pitch baseball.

So, while Ruth went on to glory with the Yankees, Bruce Price came back to Antioch and Maggie within a month of the spring he struck out The Babe. Offers came, the family said, from the Gassers and even from the Yankees, but Bruce was happy at home in a pinewood cabin with a big front porch that still stands watch on La. 544. He was waiting on that same Maggie, pouring her a cup of coffee a few springtime days ago, when he finally got a curve too high in the strike zone. "Mama," he said, "I feel bad." And that was it.

Bruce Price lived to be eighty-six, active and healthy right down to this very last springtime, and everybody at the funeral—held at the Antioch church, naturally—knew he never had a regret about the Yankees or baseball or fame or anything else. He farmed some and drove a school bus and rocked on the front porch and loved Maggie and his kids. And everybody, it is safe to say, loved Bruce.

That's because Bruce Price was one of those rare men who had no regrets, who was content within himself, and who never so much as frowned. He was there, grinning, when I came to Antioch church a few years ago to make a talk. Talks make me nervous, and Bruce could tell I was fidgety. "Let me play you something, that will settle you down," he said. The man who struck out Ruth twice was, you see, a mean harmonica player. "You pick something," he said, shining that big smile.

I picked "In the Garden," my favorite. And there, in the back of Antioch church, Bruce turned that metal instrument into something mellow and alive. We could feel the words in his music. "I come to the garden along . . . while the dew is still on the roses . . . and the voice I hear . . . falling on my ear . . . the Son of God . . . is calling . . . "

"Feel better?" Bruce wanted to know. I felt better.

Bruce always made everybody feel better. He was just that kind of a man. Gentle. Laughing. Happy. No regrets. He never dreamed of the money those young major league arms are pulling down now, but he struck out the greatest, Babe Ruth, in Ruth's prime. And then he came home to Maggie and to Antioch.

I can see that stovepipe curve stopping the Babe. I can hear him playing the harmonica in Antioch church. Naw, Bruce Price never made any money, and he never made it to the major leagues, either. But he played for us all.

Christmas, in the Lap of Vulcan

December 25, 1983

It was Christmas Eve in Vietnam, 1968.

Nobody there knew or much cared that in Louisiana and in much of the United States the weather was cold, that the Hong Kong flu bug was biting, and that Lyndon Johnson was spending his last White House Christmas before a roaring fire.

No, in Vietnam it was hot—over ninety degrees on Christmas Eve. The mosquitos were biting. So were the Communists, even though a 72-hour cease-fire had been declared for the holidays. A dozen violations were reported in the first hour of the "truce."

Wade Baker, a Spec. 5 from Plain Dealing who now runs a Ruston-based oil drilling firm, was out prowling that '68 Christmas Eve in Vietnam—riding shotgun on a two-man mission designed to beg, borrow or literally steal a big special operations radio.

CHRISTMAS, IN THE LAP OF VULCAN

Baker's 269th Combat Aviation Battalion needed the radio. It flew the 25th Infantry Division from one hot spot to another in Hooks or the big Chinook helicopters. Wade was stationed at Cuchi, about twenty-eight miles northwest of Saigon, and his turf was the embattled Parrot's Beak, which bulged into Cambodia.

Only hours before the Christmas truce North Vietnamese troops had boiled out of those Cambodian sanctuaries, blasting the 25th with human wave attacks. Outnumbered four to one, the GIs answered with automatic weapons fire and helicopter gunships. The Communists left nearly 100 dead. It wasn't a lot like Christmas.

But things had settled down a little with the holiday truce. Before that—and after—Parrot's Beak was one long, bloody pain. Baker, with others who were there, would never forget the names and the places: Hobo Woods, Ben Loi and the Rubber Plantation.

But this was Christmas Eve, and Baker and his friend weren't looking for a fight. They wanted that special ops radio. And they found one, but the Thai troops who owned this particular radio had taken proper precautions. It was chained down.

Moving on, the pair chanced on something else. It turned out to be a track-mounted 20 mm Vulcan cannon—capable of ripping off 6,000 rounds a minute and still a classified weapon. "That thing would break up a human wave attack," Wade remembers thinking, the recent assaults on the 25th still on his mind.

They edged up closer to the new weapon, drawn to its killing power. Wade himself wore a quick-draw holster which held his own long-barrelled .38 Smith and Wesson revolver. Both men were in uniform this Christmas Eve—jungle fatigues, grunt hats and M1s at the ready.

Baker says now, thinking about it, that the Smith and Wesson was of course as unauthorized as the Vulcan was classified. But it was, in a great sense, an unauthorized war and Baker recalls that "we all felt kind of isolated from the world . . . it was crazy, just crazy . . ." It was *Apocalypse Now*, even on Christmas Eve.

Meanwhile, Wade couldn't take his eyes off the Vulcan cannon. Both he and his partner wanted a closer look at a weapon that could blow the heart out of one of those Communist banzai attacks. Wade sure wasn't thinking about Christmas. Not then.

He *was* curious about the Vulcan. The weapon was hard to see, surrounded by sandbags and stacks of ammunition. They scrambled up over the sandbags, anxious to get a closer look. Finally Wade and his friend could see right into the position.

And there it was. Close to the cannon. A little Christmas tree. Wade can still see it. "It was a little, green, coneshaped tree. Just little miniature bells on it. It was kind of neat," he remembers, his voice quiet in recollection.

"There we were," he says now. "Everybody with their guns. And that big Vulcan cannon. And the little Christmas tree. It kind of made me think. Not about home, exactly. But about Christmas. And how crazy this all was, after all. It was kind of neat, really."

The next day, fifteen years ago this Christmas morning, Wade Baker joined thousands of other American servicemen in greeting Bob Hope. He remembers that a three hundred pound ex-pro football player named Rosey Grier accompanied Hope. Miss World was there too.

But Wade also remembers the small Christmas tree in the gun position.

Christmas, in the lap of Vulcan.

It was kind of neat.

"I Don't Have a Country"

March 4, 1984

When my Lebanese friend Karim Adib came back to North Louisiana last summer, he was sadder and more subdued than I had ever seen him. While we sat at the edge of the pool at Ruston's Holiday Inn, amid happy shouts and splashes, his country was even then falling apart.

"I don't have a country anymore," he said quietly. Those words spoke tragic volumes, because in his college days at Louisiana Tech—days when we became argumentative friends—Karim was the fiery patriot of his beloved Lebanon.

He earned three engineering degrees at Tech, served on the university's Student Government Association, worked with the Tech Theatre Players, lectured on international humor and took his first job in Shreveport. Karim was at home in North Louisiana.

But he remained, at least until last summer, the proud advocate of his Arab heritage in general and his Lebanese homeland in particular. But that last time, beside the pool and then later on the campus, he did not speak of patriotism. "I don't have a country anymore," he said, again and again.

"There are only guns," he said. "No business. No schools. No debate. Only guns." Dr. Adib, who was awarded the terminal degree at Tech, was dean of an engineering school in Tripoli. He told me that July afternoon in Ruston that the shells were falling close to his offices and that a Syrian major listened in on his telephone calls.

And he told me, even then, that his country was dying. "It will be partitioned between the Syrians and the Israelis," he said in a tired, quiet voice unlike the thunderous clarion call of rhetoric—laced with humor—that had been so characteristic of him.

"I DON'T HAVE A COUNTRY"

I didn't want him to leave last summer, but Karim had family in Lebanon—he was particularly worried about an aging mother who refused to leave—and so soon he was gone again. I remember watching his family walk around the Tech quadrangle a last time that July day, just looking at the benches and the live oaks. Smiling. Remembering. It was a peaceful scene.

But he returned to Lebanon to run his engineering school, which is all he wanted to do, really. Though a Moslem, Karim is "not political." Except that he always wanted reason to prevail, and for Lebanon, as an Arab nation, to be strong and free and independent.

The last word from Karim came a few weeks ago to Jack Painter, a friend of his on the Tech engineering faculty. It was a late-night call. Painter recalls that Karim was "very subdued, almost as if he felt somebody might be listening." Still, Adib did say that he had tried to "reason" with some of the fighters. Shortly after that conversation his car was blown up—only five minutes after his family had gotten out of it.

The siege of Tripoli by a Syrian-backed Palestinian faction drove Karim and his family into an underground bunker. But when Karim's mother got sick in the stale air, the Adib family had to vacate that shelter. Minutes later it was blown up.

So it has been a series of close calls for my friend Karim, who a summer ago said his country was falling apart. Of course, Lebanon *has* fallen apart since then, and I worry about the Adibs who—Painter says—have taken refuge in the mountains.

I wish that Karim was out of Lebanon altogether, and I'm glad our Marines have been "redeployed" at sea. Unlike some other people, I think President Reagan's motive in moving into Lebanon was at once noble and self-serving and not so hard to understand.

Reagan wanted to preserve Lebanon as a nation and at the same time prevent Soviet-sponsored Syria from completely dominating most of it. That's clear enough. But I'm convinced,

"I DON'T HAVE A COUNTRY"

with Karim, that Lebanon isn't a country anymore, and that you can't defend something that doesn't exist.

Every faction, family, tribe and punk gang wants a hunk of this poor carcass of a country. So I say let them have it. Let Walid Jumblatt have his mountain and bury his ancestral bones of Druse hate. Let Habih Berri and his Amal gunmen occupy the presidential palace.

Give every gang of punks in Beirut—there are an estimated fifty different militias in that smoking ruin of a city alone—a neighborhood and let 'em target-practice on each other with their Soviet-made rocket-launchers.

Don't forget the Shiite fighters; they need a place to praise the ayatollah, pray and pound away with their automatic weapons. Give them all a hunk of Lebanon; they have all claimed, like warring cannibals, a piece of the body anyway.

All that's left, like Karim said, are the men, and often the punks, with the guns. Oh, the shooting will finally stop. Several truces have come and gone. But this will be a Syrian peace in the end—a peace of the graveyard.

As Karim prophesied, the body of Lebanon will be divided. And the Syrians, who egged on the fighting, will not be easy masters in their domains. Mr. Jumblatt will not get to keep his mountain, the Druse will not be free, and the militias will finally lay down their rocket-launchers.

The Syrians, with their powerful army and efficient secret police, will see to that. No more Jumblatt interviews on TV or with The New York *Times*. Not after the Syrians *really* take over. Damascus knows how to handle such troublemakers.

In 1982, when members of the Muslim Brotherhood—these were *Syrians*, mind you—put up a protest in the Syrian city of Hama, well, President Hafez al-Assad burned down the place and had 20,000 civilians slaughtered. Nobody is giving interviews or talking about what belongs to whom in Hama.

No, Lebanon is tearing itself apart and Syria is already picking up the pieces. "Our country is dying," begged Christian President Amin Gemayel when he tried—and failed—to put together a national reconciliation movement.

Lebanon is no longer a nation. Mobs that call themselves militias have taken over, mixing hate and religion, and making common cause with more powerful forces that will—in turn and time—devour them.

I wish Karim was out of Lebanon. I'm glad the Marines are gone. You can't save a nation that doesn't want to live. Let them all have a bloody bite of what's left of Lebanon—the Jumblatts and the Druse and the Shiites and the rest. Until the Syrians come and bury the pieces. Then the tribes of Lebanon may remember the chance they had to survive as a nation. But it will be too late then. It's already too late.

The Major Against the Mob

March 25, 1984

I came across the line in an American literature class while an undergraduate at Tech. "Consistency is the hobgoblin of little minds." It came from Ralph Waldo Emerson.

Delighted, I had the quote set in twelve-point type and pasted onto the front of Maj. Larry J. Fox's typewriter at the Ruston *Daily Leader*. The major wrote a daily sports column, "Diamond Dope," that would run for more than a quarter of a century. I was a *Leader* reporter during the 1950s.

Consistency, I knew even then, was the hallmark of the Major's life. In class at Tech where he taught sociology for thirty-five years, Larry Fox told us that—among other constants of consistency—he ran 250 brush strokes through his hair every morning. Precisely 250 strokes. Every morning.

That was the Major. I forget his reaction to my quote from Emerson, but most likely it was the same reply he invariably made to the heavy kidding that often came his way in Ruston during those days. "If they don't like it, they can line up in alphabetical order and kiss my ---."

Consistent as a columnist, the Major resurrected cliches that died with Abner Doubleday. Larry Fox never wrote about "men on base." They were "ducks on the pond." And the Major always acted as if he had somehow discovered those old baseball dinosaurs by surrounding them with quotation marks.

As a writer, the Major decided to eliminate the noun as a part of speech. It was always, "Believe the Bearcats will win tonight. . . ." And, grammar aside, the Major believed in the Ruston Bearcats and the Tech Bulldogs and the Grambling Tigers.

The Bearcats, in particular, were "lovable" even when they lost. When the Major was promoted to sports editor for a time, he specialized in 60-point "Lovable Bearcat" headlines. He was the Norman Vincent Peale of Lincoln Parish journalism, the supreme and shameless booster of Sinclair Lewis' *Main Street*.

In that same positive spirit the Major also wrote a column called "It's Your Life" that ran on the *Leader's* religion page. With his usual eye on consistency, the Major numbered those columns prominently. "Number 2,151," proclaimed a large, boldface announcement right under the headline.

In that religion column, the Major returned to his sociology roots and organized each article by "problem" and "solution." His solution was ever consistent. "Pray," he advised at the end of every "It's Your Life."

Though the Major was never a threat to Jim Murray he did anticipate the personal column most daily newspapers now feature. "Grandson Shep's" achievements in school and athletics were regularly cited, along with the Major's own battle against an expanding waistline.

"The Battle of the Bulge," detailing the Major's diet, was a regular subtitle in "Diamond Dope." At the time, Ruston grumbled good-naturedly about mentions of Grandson Shep. It was as if the Major was waving his family snapshots in the face of the whole town. And the town loved it when LJF couldn't report much of a weight loss (too many of Mrs. Fox's Boston cream pies).

But in his prime (and his prime was a long one), the Major was read—and watched. When he fell out of the end of his boat into a local pond, for once extinguishing his ever-present cigar, Lincoln Parish laughed out loud. And when the Major, who said, "sickness is ignorance," was sidelined (very temporarily) by an abscessed tooth, the town was secretly pleased.

Read or not, the Major was once fired by a young editor who wanted to do things differently. "I do certain things every day," the Major told the editor, "and that includes writing 'Diamond Dope.'" The Major unfired himself, and "Diamond Dope" and "It's Your Life" continued, along with the 250 strokes of the brush every morning.

Maybe he was taken lightly at times, but the Major gradually became a Lincoln Parish institution. Like the Peach Festival or the Hilly Fire Tower or Railroad Park or old Chautauqua. His consistency and his cliches represented certain very American values of stability and survival and strength.

It was all right for Tech and the *Leader* alumni to kid him a little. But at the same time at least two generations that had played on one of his teams (he coached, too) or read his column or participated in one of the youth programs he helped to organize began to measure memories against that finely-chiseled Irish profile. It was like he belonged to us, comma faults and all.

But what I learned about the Major only a few years ago cast him in yet another light—the light of pure courage. The Major, I was told, stood up against a lynch mob in the 1930s. He climbed on top of a pile of empty Coke cases and tried to reason with a crowd-gone-crazy.

It didn't work. The Major was shoved aside, roughly so, and the mob had its way. That wasn't the end of it for the Major. A petition was circulated demanding his Tech job. Maybe the Major unfired himself that time, too, because he taught me in the '50s. But it was a close thing. And I knew, finding out about it, that there was courage behind the cliches.

The Major confirmed that episode in his life when I asked him about it, but the subject was something he didn't want to discuss at length. Maybe the Bearcats were playing that night. Anyway, from that point forward I knew the Major didn't fit Emerson's description of a "little mind" or a little man—consistency or not.

The crowd that overflowed Ruston's Episcopal Church of the Redeemer to pay last respects to the 90-year-old Major a few days ago wasn't plunged in gloom because everybody knew that Larry Fox had lived a productive, full life. But there was sadness because a lot of the men at the funeral had, like *Leader* Sports Editor O. K. Davis said, "lost a second father."

More to the point, a lot of us had heard a bell toll with Larry Fox's passing; a bell that told us nobody, not even the Majors of this world, last forever.

A Garden in Webster Parish

April 15, 1984

He was among the last of a disappearing breed, though that statement is—of course—a cliche. But if the cliche fits, I say wear it. And Billy Grigsby fits into that category: the last of the North Louisiana generations that could *do* things.

I'm not talking about doctors or lawyers or politicians or preachers or newspaper columnists. I certainly don't include myself in Mr. Grigsby's mold; in the mold of men who can make things grow; of men who can build things with their hands.

Mr. Grigsby, you see, grew the tallest, greenest corn on the Dorcheat Road near Minden where he lived. Mr. Grigsby could also lay bricks with the best of 'em. He counted the seventeen thousand bricks that *he* laid into his own high-walled home. Heck, he *made* the bricks that went into that home. He also made his own beer until a few quarts he had hidden under the bed exploded.

Like most men who can do things with their hands, Mr. Grigsby didn't want to talk about himself. But in the summer of 1978 Randy Grigsby, a former student of mine and a good friend, invited me to lunch at his parents' home and I tricked Mr. Grigsby into the paths of his past.

Mr. Grigsby, it turned out, had started his married life with eight cents, sold the old *Louisiana Progressive* magazine and borrowed $35 to put in his first crop. He had operated a sawmill, owned a brick plant, drilled a well, and made a career with an oil company. Like I said, it all fits into a generation that did things.

A few months later I wrote about that lunch and that visit to the Dorcheat Road:

"The table is still spread out in the mind's eye: fried chicken (fried chicken that is dark and crumbly around the edges), new potatoes in white sauce, cornbread, colored butterbeans, corn on the cob, tomatoes, peas, iced tea sweetened in the pitcher and banana pudding. Mr. Grigsby raised all the vegetables and Mrs. Grigsby did all the cooking.

"The truth is, though, that I fell in love with the whole family at the front door. There was Randy readjusting his dad's jauntyangled baseball cap. And he gave Mrs. Grigsby, a petite woman with lovely brown eyes and an instant gentle grace, a special,

A GARDEN IN WEBSTER PARISH

unembarrassed kiss and ushered her off into the kitchen for a mother-son talk. I understood that, and liked it.

"Mr. Grigsby took me over at first, showing me around their big sprawl of a home, and I loved that too. Billy Grigsby, who has a grin that would put Leonid Brezhnev at ease, doesn't waste a thing.

"The dry and tough end-of-the-season corn would be shelled off the cob, taken to the grist mill and ground up to provide fresh meal for their cornbread. 'It (the cornbread) tastes just a little better that way,' Mr. Grigsby tells me with that brilliant smile.

"After dinner we talked: about Webster Parish politics and Jimmy Carter (Mr. Grigsby said Jimmy Carter "couldn't run a 7-11 store"), making it to Mars, the Bible and haunted houses. I could have talked to the Grigsbys forever.

"But they finally sent me off that August afternoon with a full stomach, two watermelons, a sack of purplehull peas and some red okra. I also left with the knowledge that a self-sustaining, God-fearing, compassionate breed of people who love their children and the land endure yet in a changing North Louisiana. I left relaxed and secure."

All that was written, as I said, some five years ago. A few days ago Mr. Grigsby died. Cancer. Characteristically, he rejected treatments that might have added a few days to the final ordeal. Randy called to tell me about it toward the end. "He won't get in the garden this year," said Randy. That told it all.

But Mr. Grigsby had a good life. And all his kids were home for this last Christmas, maybe sensing an end to something. There was a lot of laughter. And Mrs. Grigsby, with him right to the end, is holding up. "She's a country woman . . . a rock," Randy said. That told it all too.

So this spring one garden on the Dorcheat Road will lie quiet. And I wonder, again, how many Mr. Grigsbys there are left in North Louisiana to make the corn grow tall and green. I'm appreciating my dad and my wife's dad; they belong to that special breed.

I also think about what Mr. Grigsby said that afternoon in 1978 when we were all laughing in his living room. The conversation had turned easily and not morbidly to death and dying. Mr. Grigsby, grinnng broadly, allowed that he wanted a big funeral "with everybody bawling and squalling."

You got it, Mr. Grigsby.

A Quiet Theologian

August 26, 1984

Like everybody else, I experience negative emotions from time to time. Emotions like anger and fear and frustration. But, perhaps because of a singular recognition of blessings received, depression was something I could avoid.

Until late last spring, that is. Then I found myself feeling strangely unmoored. As if I were on automatic pilot. With all the sharp edges of my consciousness somehow dulled. Like I had two degrees of fever all the time. Then the realization dawned on me. I was depressed, at last. And, finally, I knew why.

It was because Curry was dying.

Curry Patton, I mean. Curry was maybe fifteen years older than I, and since I'm forty-six, well, he's the first and last big brother I'll ever have. He was older, yeah, but big, tree-tall, sinewy, ageless Curry—a Yale-educated forester—could walk me down to a stump in the woods.

That's what we did, mostly. Walk in the woods. Curry helped me gather material for *The Times* North Louisiana editorial series. That's a pignut hickory, Curry would say, or that's a Southern red oak.

We held up barbed wire fences for each other, and he opened

A QUIET THEOLOGIAN

the shiny amber pupil of a buckeye for me. "Put that in your pocket for good luck," he said. We looked at haystacks and deserted old country cabins and lost graveyards and pear trees left to grow gnarled and wild.

The last woods walk we took was when he showed me every briar-tangled foot of my mother's Antioch property near Simsboro. It was something he wanted to do. "I'm worn out, Curry," I said at the end of it. He just laughed—a unique, neighing, unembarrassed laugh that echoed through the forest.

We didn't talk a lot on those walks. Somehow, though, things got explained when I walked with Curry. He never imposed on our friendship, and though I was the one who benefited from the hikes, he always initiated them—calling me at home. "Wiley, Curry here, . . . " he always began. But everything was always at my convenience. Always.

And, like I said, things got explained when I was with him. I came home feeling better. You could ask Ellen. She liked Curry too, and liked for me to be with him. It was like he set a quiet example, and that was enough to answer questions. He was an elder in our church, First Presbyterian of Ruston, and so was I.

But Curry was *the* elder. He worked in the church. I could see that. Oh, he taught Sunday School and served on committees and raised money and led pulpit searches and things like that. But I mean Curry *worked*—down on his knees scrubbing and scraping and painting the upstairs and downstairs of our 100-year-old church.

He was a quiet theologian, really; a Calvinist who could quote with equal accuracy from the Bible or the bulky *Book of Church Order*. He knew all the verses and all the rules—he was a *Presbyterian*, morally and intellectually and in his bones—but there he was, on his knees, scraping century-old paint off the sanctuary baseboards.

Curry never imposed any of that on me; that wasn't his way at all. Curry never imposed. Theology isn't my thing, anyway, and a paintbrush, in my hands, is a dangerous weapon. In fact,

"He was a quiet theologian, . . ."

A QUIET THEOLOGIAN

the only time I ever saw Curry come unstuck was when I sneaked up to the podium and set the preacher's watch ahead twenty minutes during a break in our endless elders' ordination session.

But I saw what Curry did. I watched him, and we walked together in the woods. That was more than enough, and I waited for him to call me—usually on a Sunday night—to set up a hike during the week. It was at my convenience, again. He didn't want to impose or intrude. Not him. The telephone would ring, and he would say, "Wiley, Curry here. . . . "

Then, I think it was on a Sunday, he got suddenly sick. Cancer, they said. I couldn't believe it. Not tall, tireless, laughing Curry, the prince of the forest.

Being a very private person, and never intruding on anybody else, Curry wouldn't want me to go into the details of the struggle that followed. Somebody else had to tell me he was sick. Very sick. But he hurt. He hurt so much. And to the very end, I'm afraid.

But, down to the end, he was Curry—pain and all. "You want to lay down?" I asked him. "No, I don't want to *lay* down; I want to *lie* down," said this grammatically proper Yaleman, neighing loudly at my frown.

Every time he coughed I asked, "You need some water, Curry?" Then, late one night, in the gloom of the hospital room, I couldn't suppress a cough—thinking him sedated and sleeping at last. "*You* need some water, Wiley?" he asked, his voice full of amused irony.

Another such night, watching him, I saw that handsome smile—handsome right to the end—lance the darkness like a flashlight beam. I knew that he was soaring from that awful bed at times, and I was glad. "Where are you, Curry?" I asked.

"Spelunking in Arkansas," he said, the smile lighting his face again. "I'm enjoying it." And then: "Wiley, does a newspaper person know that spelunking means exploring caves?"

"Thanks, Curry," I said, pretending not to be amused. It was the last time I heard him laugh.

Curry died an hour and a half after I left for home on one of those long hospital nights. As I think of it now, he was not a member of my family, a boyhood buddy or a friend made in the trenches of work—the ties that usually bind closest in the South.

All I know is that I got depressed while Curry Patton was sick, and now that he's gone, well, my life just isn't exactly the same as it was before. And that is the best and last compliment that I can pay him.

A Measure of Goodness and Grace

October 21, 1984

Maybe everybody knows someone like John Ardis Cawthon, but I doubt it. He always wanted to know how *you* were doing. Know what I mean? Dr. John, as everybody called him, was that rare individual who took an unselfish pride and interest in the accomplishments of others.

Not that John Cawthon wasn't accomplished himself. He was an educator (professor and department head in Louisiana Tech's College of Education), author (*The Inevitable Guest*), and area historian (among other things, he was *the* authority on North Louisiana graveyards).

But Dr. John was always bragging about what *somebody* else had done. Oh, he was continually asked for information and readily supplied it—even when the chore took days of research. He gave a long interview on Doyline to *Times* Ruston Bureau chief Gary Walker only last month.

A MEASURE OF GOODNESS AND GRACE

He knew the names, places, families and faces of a whole region, and it was a knowledge that spanned the generations. People were forever calling him about this or that, and if he didn't know, he looked it up. "He was a community resource," said Tech history professor Dr. Philip Cook.

But, mostly, he wanted to know what *you* were doing. It was unusual, then, to find Dr. John in the spotlight. But during Tech's recent homecoming activities, he was honored. There was sustained applause when he received a fifty-year alumni diploma, but only a few knew that he had left a hospital bed to accept it.

I wasn't surprised that Dr. John was there, even though it was apparent he was ill. Very ill. He understood milestones and tradition; he *wanted* to be there for the homecoming ceremony. It was the last time I saw him. He died three days after receiving the diploma.

At the funeral everybody said the same thing about him. "He was a good man," they all said, and everybody nodded. "Good" is a general term, but Dr. John defined the word. He was humble. He was gracious. At seventy-seven, he blushed when somebody told a dirty joke. He was, quite simply, a good man who cared about what other people did in this world.

Dr. John had a sense of humor, as well, and it never failed him. Never. Surfacing briefly after the operation, he wanted to know the score. "Well, they had to disconnect some things and reconnect some things," he was told.

"I just hope they didn't make a mistake and connect my kidneys to my tear ducts," he answered, weary but smiling.

After what I've seen of cancer these last few months, I'm glad Dr. John didn't suffer long. But he is gone. And gone with him is a measure of goodness and grace that spoke so well, and so gently, to the generations of a North Louisiana Dr. John loved so much.

A "Little Ride" with Jay Taylor

July 7, 1985

The name isn't really important. Let's just call him an Important Person, at least by this world's definition of important. In fact, he has been important for a very long time now—long enough for a lot of people to take his achievements for granted.

Long enough, indeed, for people to assume the Important Person "has it made." It's a common assumption. A shake of the head and the resigned, slightly envious observation: "He's got it made." Maybe we even assume the Important Person always had it made. No problems. No grief. No sweat.

And this particular Important Person has a certain almost boyish enthusiasm about him—especially in public—that contributes to the he's-got-it-made, he's-always-had-it-made impression. No problems. No grief. Not ever.

Maybe because I know how hard he works—even after all this time at the top—my own impression was a little different. But, even though we had become friends, I couldn't really see how this man ever had that much of a problem. He's so positive. So optimistic. About everything.

Because we are friends it didn't surprise me to get a call from him a couple of days before Christmas. He wanted me to take a "little ride" with him. Typically, he apologized for calling on such short notice; he does not take people for granted. "I don't want to keep you away from your family . . . if you have plans, fine . . . I know it's the holidays," he said.

"Where are we going?" I wanted to know. "Aw, just a little ride," he repeated in a polite voice that begged me not to ask any more questions. So I went, because we have a good time together and because of that tone of voice. It was Christmas and he wanted me to take a ride. Okay then.

A "LITTLE RIDE" WITH JAY TAYLOR

The miles evaporated quickly, even on potholed old 167 South, and—like always—we relaxed and released the little boys that hide out in most men whatever their age. We laughed and joked and told our favorite stories. It was a warm December day and we let the air come in through the windows.

Enjoying the ride, I forgot about where we were headed until an old truck loaded too high with wood chips passed going in the other direction, showering us with its loose cargo. When I turned around to watch the truck recede into Winn Parish I saw the two wreaths in the back seat.

"Where are we going?" I asked then. He knew I had seen the wreaths. "To the cemetery," he said, and once again his voice implored me, gently, not to pursue the matter. He changed the subject, and I let it drop.

But I had seen the two wreaths in the back seat—wreaths made in the form of little dolls, I seem to remember. We were going to a cemetery and the wreaths back there, both of them, looked like toys for very small children.

The cemetery was a clean, piney place and the Important Person knew exactly where he was going. Like he went there often. He placed the wreaths on two small graves. Carefully. Then he stood and just looked at them, walking from one angle to another—just looking with dry but unfocused eyes.

I couldn't tell what he was thinking, of course, but I imagined that behind those unseeing eyes his mind was a movie projector, unreeling flickering, sad images of small faces. I looked at the markers. Yes, two children were buried here. One boy. One girl. Born four years apart in the 1950s. One lived for a few hours; one lived for a few days. One died on a Christmas Day. *His children*.

It came to me, standing there, that it would be a shattering experience to lose a child. But to lose a newborn—in his case, two infants—must leave great wounds, too. Because there are no real memories (we are grateful for the time we had with him or her,

A "LITTLE RIDE" WITH JAY TAYLOR

I have heard parents say about a lost child of even a few years) to fill up the black hole of grief.

He finally told me a little about the circumstances as we walked back to the car. I can't remember his exact words; something to the effect that both infants would have lived had they been born in this decade. I do remember, exactly, that he looked back once and said, very softly, ". . . that was a bad Christmas." That was all he said, and all I knew to do was keep quiet and touch him, once, on the arm.

We closed the car doors and, once again, he closed the door on the subject. I had not known; not an inkling and not a hint. Later I found that only a few people did know. I knew then that this Important Person never had it made; that he had known problems and grief and pain. And now, after that "little ride" to the cemetery, even I saw him differently.

He was his old self again as we took that old road north home—full of optimism and energy and hope. But I kept glancing at the back seat. The wreaths were gone. But, no, I thought to myself, they are not gone. There will always be two wreaths in the back seat for this Important Person. Always.

(UPDATE: The "Very Important Person" described in the foregoing, published in 1982, is Louisiana Tech President F. Jay Taylor. We have made the same journey twice since, and during the last Christmas season I asked Taylor—enroute to the cemetery—if I could add his name to the column if it was ever republished. "I guess so," he said, after some reflection. F. Jay Taylor has been president of Tech for twenty-three years. His son, Terry, is an airline pilot with Delta.)

The Minnesota Fats of Forestry

September 15, 1985

All we wanted was positive identification of a big oak tree. I suggested Lloyd P. Blackwell, the retired director of Louisiana Tech's school of forestry, as the ultimate authority. Ruston's John Calhoun, who owned the oak, agreed.

"Of course, we'll get his whole 101 forestry lecture," said Col. Calhoun. We did. Wiping the sweat out of our eyes on this wilting August day, John and I had to hear all the characteristics of a white oak before Mr. Blackwell would even look at the tree.

He brought a whole library of forestry books and spread them out on the hot hood of John's pickup, but focused on his prized 1921 edition of *The Trees*.

We even had to look at his personal bookmark. All I can remember from the lecture, understandably, is that white oaks are used, among other things, to make whiskey barrels.

Then, based on the information he had provided, Mr. Blackwell made us identify the tree in question. It was like a test. "We got the forestry 101 *and* 102 lectures," John whispered in my ear.

You get the whole forestry lecture, always, when dealing with Lloyd Blackwell, and you get it on his terms, if not on his turf.

On this late summer afternoon, it just happened that a high pasture on the Douglas Road in Lincoln Parish was Professor Blackwell's classroom and his theater.

High theater doesn't play that well in laid-back Lincoln Parish, where Mr. Blackwell's Yale diploma was also regarded with some suspicion. None of that mattered or matters to Lloyd P. Blackwell.

He handles a meeting of the North Louisiana Group of Foresters (an organization he founded) in Winnfield as if it was the opening of the disarmament conference in Geneva, and he gets better results.

In pointing out the leaf structure of the water oak, he is Edward R. Murrow, broadcasting from London at the peak of the blitz. Once briefly and unwillingly confined to the intensive care unit in Lincoln General Hospital, he was Ronald Reagan bossing the planet from Bethesda. He invents his own pronunciations, calling his beloved Kiwanis Club, "Key-wanis."

Part of this flair for the dramatic is staged for effect; part of it stems naturally from eight years of speech and drama absorbed in high school and college at Lynchburg, Va. Blackwell's masters in forestry was earned under a nationally known forestry authority, Yale's Dr. H. H. Chapman.

Still, Mr. Blackwell brought the role of a Russian prince he played in a college production to Ruston in 1946. Not everybody in the piney woods was enthralled with the idea of dealing with, as one writer put it, "The Prince of Yales."

Another interviewer pointed out that Lloyd Blackwell didn't look like a forester, either. No, to tell the truth, he's always reminded me more of Jackie Gleason, in act and appearance, than of a prince or a forester. Indeed, Mr. Blackwell makes me think of Jackie Gleason playing Minnesota Fats.

"I never knew I was fat," said the graceful, confident Gleason in a recent interview. That's Blackwell—confident to the point of arrogance, quick as Baryshnikov on his feet, and just as fast and agile with a quip or comeback. "A professional who would rather achieve results . . . than be popular," said Scott McWilliams in *Forest Farmer*.

The best example of Blackwell landing gracefully on his feet came when he took *Forests & People* writers Ed Kerr and Elemore Morgan on a tour of the Tech forestry school.

They noticed a small pile of sawdust smoldering in a corner of the student sawmill—an obvious danger. This was pointed out to Professor Blackwell.

"Oh, that," he answered in the split-second, "that's just for atmosphere. Who ever heard of a sawmill without a sawdust burner?" Eight ball in the corner pocket for the Minnesota Fats of Forestry, and game won with a couple of important guests.

"Professional forestry owes much to Blackwell," said the same national publication, *Forest Farmer*, in an ultimate peer-compliment of ten years ago.

His innovative programs, from the establishment of a land-use seminar to the creation of a Tech forestry camp in the big woods of Kisatchie National Forest, won attention.

Blackwell founded Tech's school of forestry in 1946, and got those kinds of results by playing Minnesota Fats, even when it wasn't an endearing role in Lincoln Parish. He cleared the table, graduating 625 students before he retired in 1976 as professor emeritus.

Two years ago the national convention of the Society of American Foresters, meeting in Portland, Oregon, gave him a standing ovation, impressing a fellow Rustonion who was also at the meeting—Tech President F. Jay Taylor.

Such recognition is something Blackwell frankly doesn't mind, for himself or for Tech forestry. The Russian prince, or call him Minnesota Fats, will take a bow—or show you his bookmark on a hot day.

But what always impressed me most about Blackwell, when he was heading forestry, was his chemistry with students. He worked personally, he worked hard, to get them jobs—using his national connections.

And then he greeted them on a first name basis when, ten years later, they popped into his office on the Tech farm campus to say thanks or—more likely—aid Tech forestry. And he still keeps a personal file on the progress of each.

Those students understood the Blackwell bombast, and on a trip to the forestry camp on assignment for the Ruston *Daily Leader* I learned that he could appreciate criticism or hard kidding as well as dish it out.

As we rose from lunch after inspecting the camp that day,

there was a flurry of chatter and a dark-haired youth broke for the other room.

"I don't want to get kicked out of here," was a snatch I heard. Blackwell strode off in the direction of the talk and soon the culprit was cornered and the press summoned.

"Listen to this," said Blackwell. It seems that a forestry student, one Francis Xavier Nicoletti of New York State, had perfected an imitation of his school director. "Do your best," Blackwell ordered.

The room filled up with chuckling students and Mr. Nicoletti did a leg-pumping, arm-waving, finger-pointing imitation of Mr. Blackwell as the Russian prince, with particular emphasis on various Blackwellian pronunciations and enunciations.

The students fell out of their bunks laughing. And Blackwell laughed hardest of all and, at the end of the show, shook a relieved Nicoletti's hand.

Since his retirement in 1976, Mr. Blackwell has observed the progress of his generation of Nicolettis, entered successfully into private business with his son-in-law and daughter, and played Russian Prince and Minnesota Fats to the Ruston Key-wanis Club. He hasn't slowed down.

And people still either like him or don't like him. A guy who always knocks the eight ball in the corner pocket, and calls the shot, doesn't inspire neutrality. I like him a lot. Always did. But, damn, it was hot during that forestry lecture at the edge of John Calhoun's pasture.

Constancy, Character, Cornish Hens

September 29, 1985

If Harold Smolinski made out the Tech football schedule, it would include Notre Dame, Michigan State, LSU, The Red Army (we'd play them on a neutral site, say Afghanistan), Southern Cal, the 101st Airborne Division, the Shiite Amal and maybe USL (as a breather), if the Ragin' Cajuns watched their language.

And woe betide Coach A. L. Williams if he protested against such a schedule; Williams would be told "we gotta go, A.L." and that nothing is beyond Tech's resources. As an ex-Marine, Mr. Smolinski would be willing to take on the Red Army, and besides, coaches ought not complain about anything, even genocidal wounds that wipe out whole depth charts.

Of course, Smokey—as a few intimates dare to call him—is chairman of Tech's Athletic Council (Chairman for Life, we said behind his back, thinking of Mao Tse-tung) and director of Tech's School of Professional Accountancy.

But he is retiring from both his positions at Tech on Nov. 30. It's the end of a forty-four year tenure, of an era, at Tech; the second longest career in school history. He has served as chairman of the Athletic Council at Tech for *only* thirty years.

But years don't matter to this formidable man, whose frown was sufficient to break up an impromptu card game in the Aillet Fieldhouse one afternoon years ago, scattering coaches in all directions, presumably to recruit. "I never kept up with that," he told an interviewer who asked about the long reach of his career.

No, he doesn't keep up with the years and the aging process seems not to have kept tabs on him, either. Harold Smolinski doesn't look any different now—really—than he did thirty years ago.

CONSTANCY, CHARACTER, CORNISH HENS

He's just as stubborn as ever, too. All his many accounting graduates who return for an annual September meeting in Ruston hated the Cornish hen he insisted on serving every time. He knew nobody wanted the bird. But we picked at the same Cornish hen for the last time this month.

Never mind the tough facade and the stern face, though. He's a pushover for students, hunting them jobs on his own time, fussing at them and praising them, giving them the most precious thing a professor has to offer: his time.

And he doesn't forget them when they graduate. They are always "my kids" to him. That's why they always come back in September to honor him; they love this gruff, ageless ex-Marine with the square Polish (he never minded a Polish joke) face and stiff backbone.

In athletics, he always said, "We gotta go." We all knew what that meant, translated from Polish. Play the best teams we could, and win, but win with class.

In academics, his accounting school won every game—the first such school established in the state, commended by the Regents, accredited to the national top, and top-heavy with alumni who have made good. Sure, his graduates ate the Cornish hen every autumn, even if they didn't like it.

He seemed gruff and unapproachable to me at first, but we got to be friends—good friends. I listen to him. Oh, we often disagree on the Athletic Council. "Wiley, you're wrong, wrong, wrong," he yelled at me once at a Wyly Tower meeting, startling even the Lady of the Mist down in the Tech Quadrangle.

The disagreements didn't matter because I recognized a couple of things in the man that are so rare today we refer to them as cliches: constancy and character. Here was a man I could still look up to, at my advancing age, and think that some good things, some good men, and a few good Marines, don't change.

"Take off your pack and stand at ease," he would tell me, reverting to Marine Corps talk, when I got particularly tired of some athletic problem.

CONSTANCY, CHARACTER, CORNISH HENS

"I'm tired of problems," I told him once, completely exasperated with a coach who had alienated the entire Western Hemisphere.

"The only people who don't have problems are over there in Greenwood Cemetery," he shot back at me, pointing from the top of Wyly Tower in the general direction of a graveyard on West Alabama Street in Ruston.

"Do you want to be without problems?" was his question. I said I didn't, punting on third down, past the graveyard, my perspective restored.

I don't know what Mr. Smolinski will do when he retires. Tech has been his life almost literally; Tech and his wife Jeanie and his two children, Carl and Dale, and big, square, dusty cars that go dead at every red light when you are trying to deliver a tired university president home after a lost game.

"I don't have any," he told Tech journalist Sallie Rose Hollis when, in an interview for the *Alumni News* magazine, she asked about his future plans.

Hollis allowed that big things are still ahead for Mr. Smolinski; they are naming an academic chair for him, among other honors. "This is rather awkward," he told her, shuffling some papers. "I would have preferred to have just walked off."

We can't let him do that; we still need Harold Smolinski. But after spearing ineffectively at the last impenetrable Cornish hen in September, after November, things at Tech won't be exactly the same without him—even surrounded with all the traditions that make the university special.

That's because Mr. Smolinski is one of those Tech traditions.

And by definition, you don't replace tradition, which is built on time and constancy and character and Cornish hens.

Under a Pink Dogwood

October 27, 1985

Maybe you didn't know Elliott Rabb Whitman, but chances are he knew *you*. It wasn't only that he wrote a genealogy column for his stepson John Hays' Ruston weekly, *The Morning Paper*.

Mr. Whitman lived and worked as an engineer in San Antonio, Texas, but he grew up in North-central Louisiana, his roots were here, and he was just one of those people who knew everybody.

He knew their daddies and their granddaddies, too, and when they had to go from cotton to soybeans and then to pine trees on their land. He knew who struck oil, and who didn't, and who made it, and who didn't. And most likely, why. His judgments were gentle. He made people feel comfortable.

John is the same way. Hays is what Ruston people call "different." But like his Pop—that's what John called Mr. Whitman—he knows things about the land, the seasons, the people, and what's happening to people.

But nobody really knew more about the people of this area than Mr. Whitman. His genealogical files start with the pioneering Colvins of this region and end with an unsuspecting couple who happened to get married in Lincoln Parish six months ago. Mr. Whitman's records will be turned over to the Lincoln Parish Library.

As Hays wrote in his paper, "Pop was a Louisiana Tech engineer surrounded by a sea of Texas Aggies in South Texas and he never let them forget it. He was proud of his Tech background." Sick as he was a few weeks ago, Mr. Whitman made John find out how Tech did against North Texas State.

They buried Mr. Whitman's ashes under a pink dogwood in Ruston's Greenwood Cemetery. Mr. Whitman would know all the names of the neighboring markers, just as John does. John wanted to plant a live oak on the grave, but it wasn't the right time of the year. Mr. Whitman would have understood that; he knew about growing things, and seasons just like John does.

Mr. Whitman's three-year-old granddaughter, Leslie, slept on her father's shoulder through the whole ceremony. She did rouse once, during the Lord's Prayer, and then went back to sleep. Mr. Whitman would have understood that, too, and he would have been glad.

It was a different kind of a ceremony, because John does things differently, but a lot of people came. And somehow everybody felt comfortable. Mr. Whitman would have liked that; he liked for people to be comfortable. He would have liked the pink dogwood, too, and I think his tree will grow.

John says the tree, planted sort of down a slope in the cemetery, will collect the debris and nutrients from all around when it rains, and make the soil on the grave rich, and make the tree grow. I imagine so. John knows about things like that. Just like his pop did.

PART TWO

GOVERNORS AND OTHER SUCH PEOPLE

Waggonner:
"I Like Him"

May 28, 1978

We met in the Captain Shreve one July day a long time ago to talk about a possible job in Washington. It was warm, even with the air conditioning going, and Joe Waggonner had stretched out on the hotel bed, shoes discarded, shirt open, relaxed. He was alone.

"I think I would like to write some speeches," I told the congressman. "Oh, I don't know," he said, dismissing that idea, but doing it easily. "I pretty much write my own stuff," he said. Maybe his contacts with the North Louisiana press could stand improvement. Joe shook his head. "That pretty much takes care of itself," I remember him saying.

Nothing came out of that meeting, except I wondered what an assistant to Joe Waggonner would do. But, years later, I wasn't surprised to see him turn up for an impromptu press conference with college journalists by himself, coat tossed over a shoulder, beige pants wrinkled, as relaxed as he was that day at the Captain Shreve. He perched on the side of a desk in the basement of Keeny Hall on the Louisiana Tech campus and, for the better part of an hour, quietly replied to questions from editors of *The Tech Talk.*

As the kids gradually melted away into the summery late afternoon, the basement newsroom began to fill with adults who had heard Joe Waggonner was in the building. Joe knew them all by their first names, of course, and there were times when he asked them about their daddies and their granddaddies, too. The conversation turned to the old corner drugstore in Ruston, people who had died, and why the watermelons hadn't made much that season. Joe was grinning that wide grin of his. He was relaxed, and he seemed very happy.

Finally it broke up and the congressman drifted off, still alone, down Keeny Hall; he knew his way out. As Waggonner left, the back of his pants more wrinkled than ever, one of those people with a congenital, abiding, universal contempt for politicians was watching him.

The man shook his head in Joe's direction, as if disbelieving himself, and said in a barely audible voice, "I like Joe Waggonner, I just like him."

Sam Jones, and Earl's Ghost

July 9, 1978

Sam Jones, the reform governor, was tired. And so at first he answered me only briefly in that interview of two summers ago—the last formal interview he gave, I think, before the end came this past winter.

SAM JONES, AND EARL'S GHOST

Finally, probing for the opening that might bring the man out, I began to quote Earl Long on Sam Jones to Sam Jones himself. "Sam Jones . . . high-hat Sam, the high society kid, the high-kickin', high and mighty snide Sam . . . the city slicker who pumps perfume under his arms."

It was vintage Earl, and it hit Jones like an armor-piercing shell. All the weariness and all the years were knocked right out of him. He shot up out of the chair, deserted his desk and came charging right at me, waving his arms, afire with anger.

No, he wasn't angry at me; not really. He was still mad at Earl Long, and that quote had struck home and let it all come steaming out, like a pent-up lava flow, scorching everything it touched. I couldn't believe it. He was still mad at Earl, and room-pacing, fuming mad at that.

Nearly four decades had passed since that bitter, historic electoral confrontation between the two, and Sam Houston Jones was still mad at Earl Kemp Long. I couldn't understand everything Mr. Jones was saying right at that moment, but he jerked open a drawer and confronted me with a magazine open to a picture of a log cabin identified as his birthplace.

"Is that a city-slicker?" he demanded, still steaming, back on the rear end of his campaign pickup truck, battling Earl on the stump. Another picture was summarily produced and slapped down in my lap as evidence, this one showing a young Jones among a group of waiters.

"I was a waiter," he said, outraged, and demanded again: "Is that a 'high society kid'?" The moment passed, and we went on to talk about other things but even after that Sam Jones returned three more times, with that same heat, to the subject of Earl Long.

The anger was gone by the time Gov. Jones walked me out of his Lake Charles law office. But the interview, I thought, had finally turned out well. Because of Sam Houston Jones, Louisiana's premier reformer. And because, just as much, of the ghost of Earl Long, the king of the pea patch farm.

73

The interview with Sam Jones follows. It is entitled "Sam Jones: Good Government Folk Hero" and is from The Times, *July 4, 1976:*

As surely as revolution breeds reaction, political excess breeds reform.

In Louisiana, Sam Houston Jones symbolized reform.

He still does, more than three decades after vacating the governor's office in 1944 and that is not so much a commentary on those who came before and after him as it is a testimony to Jones' durability as a kind of folk hero among good government diehards.

Sam Jones endures, and he endures in a state where the bleached bones of wasted careers, of unkept promises and broken dreams litter what has been—in recent history, at least—a political battleground of clashing interests and factions.

"I don't know about the hero business," he said from a surprisingly uncluttered second-floor office in the equally unostentatious Gulf National Bank Building, which overlooks a quiet mall in downtown Lake Charles.

But he is pleased by the idea and, in a characteristically unaffected way, admits it. "I'm proud of my record . . . glad to be considered a reformer," he says matter-of-factly.

The years have mounted; he is seventy-seven now, but the handshake is tight, the posture erect, and the blue eyes direct, fixing. He cups his head in one hand, carefully removes his glasses to score a debater's point, and—just as the photographs show him doing on the stump—points the arm and the finger to underline a remark.

And there are a thousand points to be made, for Sam Jones looks down the long, long corridor of a lifetime in the bright, harsh glare of state politics. But it all came into focus in 1939 when the Louisiana Scandals burst like a huge, poisonous boil.

It was the explosive culmination of what Edwin Adams Davis, author of the definitive history of the state, describes as "an orgy of political malfeasance and governmental graft." "The seeds of

SAM JONES, AND EARL'S GHOST

Huey Long thus bore bitter fruit . . . ," according to writer Allan Sindler.

The state buckled to its knees under a torrent of black headlines, revelations, indictments, prison sentences and four suicides. It was an early Watergate, and Louisiana was humiliated, a national disgrace, singled out for scorn.

Enter Sam Houston Jones, reformer. But even in all the wreckage, it was no cakewalk for the reformer; far from it. The campaign of 1939 and 1940 was a bitter struggle. Earl Kemp Long had emerged from the shadow of his fallen brother Huey, and many would say later that Earl was the better politician.

Earl, as always, hit hard, and the blows were personalized. "High-hat-Sam, the high-society kid, the high-kickin', high and mighty Snide Sam, the guy that pumps perfume under his arms," yelled Long, making Jones out the city-slicker.

Jones, a polished orator of quite a different sort who wore the right tie and wrote his own speeches, countered: " . . . when I sit in the governor's chair I pledge and promise you, on my sacred honor, that you will have a servant who, to the limits of his ability, will destroy the existing corruption and reinstate the form and type of government our forebears gave us."

The media backed the Lake Charles attorney, but Earl was a formidable foe. In the first Democratic Primary of Jan. 16, 1940, Long led the field with 226,385 votes. Jones was second, a distant second, with 154,936 votes. But it was the turn of reform and Sam Houston Jones, with a strong showing in his Acadiana homeland, defeated Long by nineteen thousand votes in the second primary.

Jones was true to his promises, and his was an administration of genuine reform. Considerable authority was returned to local governments, one hundred state agencies were removed from the governor's control, payroll padding and dual job-holding were dramatically reduced, and a civil service system established.

All this was accomplished without the bare-knuckle bullying

of the governor's office so typical of Louisiana politics. Jones worked through the legislative process, which he wanted to strengthen; it was a constant in his career.

The legislature, liberated from the straitjacket of Long control, was cooperative in its first session. It's nice to be asked, the speaker of the house said, in effect. A good part of the reform program was passed.

And a good thing that was for the Jones program, for after that the fire-arrows of the resurgent Long forces began to fall on the administration at every turn. Legislators balked and some parish political bosses defied Jones. "It was hell," he remembers now.

The governor has been faulted in retrospect for failing to forge a political reform machine; for failing to elect representatives friendly to him. But he had none of the dynastic ambitions of the Longs, and if that was his downfall, it was his abiding strength, too. He wanted no "hurray or applause," he said then. "I'm governor because somebody had to clean up this mess."

At the end of it he was able to say "I have kept the faith. I have fought the good fight." He had, and it was on the record. But after four years of Jimmie Davis, whom Jones had supported, the reformer wanted another try.

Denied another tenure in the Earl Long sweep that followed—reform bred reaction, as the cycle turned on Jones—he became a prophet without official portfolio, advocating educational reform, constitutional reform, penal reform. And always, always he advocated the balance of powers so central to his vision of democracy; more power for the legislature, less power for the governor.

It is a role he has played right up to this moment and one in which he obviously takes some satisfaction. Leaning back in the polished wood and leather of a chair engraved with the state symbol, he puts a rough estimate on Jones-instigated reforms that have been enacted into law: "50 per cent."

Out of all that, out of the reform legislation passed before and after he left office, Jones has an automatic, two-word response to the inevitable "proudest accomplishment" question. "Civil service," he says, and adds that it was "kicked out by Earl Long and put back in by Bob Kennon."

That brings him back to Long, and it is evident that an inquiry about the "city-slicker" accusation has rekindled an old flame of anger. He deserts his chair abruptly and opens a magazine to a picture of the log cabin in which he was born.

"Is that a city-slicker?" he raps out, and points a finger. It was thirty-seven years ago. And Sam Houston Jones is still angry. Another picture of Jones among a group of waiters at LSU is produced. "I was a waiter. Is that a city-slicker?" Twice more he returns warmly to the subject. "Is that a city-slicker?"

The conversation turns to the Bicentennial, and the future of the state and the nation. And Jones, never the doomsayer whatever his cries in the wilderness, allows that he is "pessimistic."

"When 25 per cent of the people vote . . ." he says. The firm voice rises for the first time, and then trails off. He shakes his head. "People still have not awakened to their share in government," Jones says, and now his voice is tired and disgusted.

"When 25 to 30 per cent vote," he repeats, and again adds in the thunder of 1939, "that's not democracy!" He focuses on Shreveport. "The finest people in the world," he laments, "but they don't vote."

A family member has dropped in. "Shreveport went for you, don't forget, Governor," he cautions. Jones responds quickly and significantly, and with the politician's total recall: "They did the first time."

Jones' auburn-haired, attractive wife bursts, literally, into the room. The place is energized. Mrs. Jones inquires as to the publication conducting the interview. She grins at the answer and pronounces it, with a flourish, as "the best newspaper in the United States of America." And then she is gone in a flurry of clicking heels. Jones says after her, in awe, "My God, she is busy."

Then the governor conducts a tour of his office. There is a big color rendering of Thomas Jefferson. "The best President," says the governor. Francis T. Nicholls is also represented. "The best governor," is Jones' comment. There is a photograph of Jones and Dwight Eisenhower together and Ike has autographed it for "my friend." There is also a "Dear Sam" letter from Ike, on White House stationery.

But a framed quote from Woodrow Wilson has been accorded the place of honor behind Jones' desk. It reads: "It is the discovery of what they cannot do and ought not to do that transforms reformers into statesmen." "I show that to present and future politicians," Jones observes, smiling.

Later, relaxed over strong South Louisiana coffee, he confides that "I don't feel good, not anymore." That may be. The shadows lengthen. But Sam Houston Jones is indestructible because, in a time of great humiliation and agony, he lifted Louisiana to its feet and restored the self-respect of a state.

That much done and out of office, he has since served as a prophet of reform; a living reminder of what a people, properly motivated and led, can do; what they ought to do and ought not to do.

That is why the man, Sam Houston Jones, and the record of reform endure.

Russell:
A Different Long

September 20, 1978

Russell Long, head cocked slightly to one side, was talking about taxes that summer day. But my eyes locked on a line drawing of his father, Huey P. Long, which hung on the wall of his hideaway office, only a few steps from the floor of the United States Senate.

I asked him, prodded by the picture and the remarkable resemblance between the two, about the influence of the Louisiana Kingfish in his life.

The senator, recently identified by a national writer as one of the three most powerful men in American government, gave the question some thought, chewing on his lip.

"He (Huey Long) was a dominant personality," he said. "That tends to make a child recessive." Then one of the three most important men in government closed the subject of his father with a brief sentence.

"I stutter," was what he said.

The following interview with Russell Long is entitled, "Russell Long—A Lasting Legacy" and appeared in The Times, *July 4, 1976:*

He never had the persona of Huey P. Long, who founded the dynasty and conceived something very close to a revolution in this nation before a bullet brought down the man and the movement.

He never had the bullwhip tongue of Earl K. Long, who came out of the wreckage that was the end of his political career to win a congressional election in an unlikely last hurrah that probably killed him.

But Russell B. Long may have carved out a more lasting legacy for himself and his state in that ultimately selective American aristocracy of politics: the United States Senate.

Just being elected to Congress is one thing. But in that upper chamber the basically shy, stuttering son of Huey, the nephew of Earl, is a leader among a few leaders. He has gained admittance to, and often prevails in, that ultimate legislative sanctuary where the decisions are made and the power brokered for what are still the mightiest people on earth.

Russell Long will not openly acknowledge the accumulation

of influence that national publications declare has made him, in his fifty-seventh year and twenty-eighth in the Senate, at least among the two or three most influential men on Capitol Hill; he knows better than that.

"I never know in advance what the Committee (the Finance Committee, one of the most powerful in the Senate, which Long chairs) is going to do," he jokes, and turns on that lopsided grin. "Just luck," he says of his success during a long interview on one of Washington's increasingly warm June afternoons.

He is fresh off the Senate floor, which is only two minutes away from his Capitol hideaway office, the strategic location of which is one indication of his seniority and stature in this place. His hair is mostly grayed out now, with only a hint of brown, and a long lock—hand-combed back into place—brushes his shoulder.

Long seems fairly relaxed, whatever the pace of the day. He talks in the familiar short, choppy bursts; his thoughts are out front of his words, and the sentences get squeezed up. The senator warms to the subject of his alleged power, of which *The Wall Street Journal* has commented: "Russell Long usually will be able to move the committee in the general direction he desires."

"No," he says mildly, "we get everybody's ideas, everybody has input, and then the legislation is shaped up and it's everybody's work."

But Capitol reporters agree that Russell often gets his way in the Finance Committee and on other Senate matters, and declare that the Louisiana senator has captured the allegiance of so-called "liberals" in the body.

"The liberals, some of 'em, have something to contribute," Long says, "I give credit where credit is due on legislation. There is more than enough credit to go around, and we need liberals and conservatives."

But Russell also knows how to juggle bills; how to strongarm; even how to blackmail, though he wouldn't call it that. He does say, grinning that tight grin again, "I'll vote for their bill if they'll take my amendment."

But the raw power is there, and even the President must deal with it; as when Gerald Ford was put on notice by Sen. Long that if White House budget reductions were to get any kind of reception at all, then the tax cut would have to be extended. Little things like that.

And what are the sources of that power? Long, as he says, knows how to get along with his fellow club members in the Senate. He strokes; he suggests; he gives credit to others. Then there is that name, Long; it still inspires a certain mystery.

More important is the seniority. He is still only fifty-seven, and closing in on three decades of service. The man sits at John Calhoun's desk; his father and mother were there before him. All that counts. And he is a master legislative strategist. Washington newsmen on the day of this interview were calling him the "King of Loophole Land."

He is intelligent; even his critics concede that. He has Huey's mind, if not his charisma. He has Earl's guile, if not his hill-country wit. And opponents fear him. He is unpredictable; foes are kept off-balance and confused.

This ambivalence makes it difficult to pin an ideological label on Long. He is variously identified as a liberal, conservative, populist. He is proudest of welfare legislation, but condemns and confronts welfare "cheaters." He wants more Social Security benefits, but his opposition doomed the guaranteed annual income.

"I like to think I am a liberal in the best definition of the word," is how he puts it. "Somebody who tries to improve the existing order of things, who tries to make changes for the better." On the other hand, he believes in "preserving the good things." Populist seems to describe him best, but that can come unstuck. Long talks a lot about capitalism, and he will defend oil and gas interests crucial to Louisiana to the last barrel.

"There is a time for conservatism and a time for liberalism, . . .

there are good liberals and good conservatives in Congress," he says, and it is part of a pattern of conciliation, of trying to understand if not agree, that runs through his conversation.

It is a softening that has probably helped Long overcome, as one Louisiana historian has observed, the factionalism that is part of his heritage. Most people have forgotten it now, but in 1948 young Long was elected by just over eleven thousand votes, over Judge Robert Kennon, to complete the term of the late Sen. John H. Overton.

That campaign was fought out over state issues, and it was bitter. Long may have learned from it. In 1950 he campaigned on his Senate record, sought a broad concensus, and won a crushing victory. He has not been really challenged since.

Again, he explains this success in the language of conciliation. "Most people are sincere in their beliefs," he says. "I try to see their point. I make mistakes. I admit them. Then others can say they are wrong, too." He thinks about it, chewing on an imaginary piece of gum. "I learned a little of that from Earl Long. He made friends of my father's enemies."

In fact, Long says he has no political organization at all in Louisiana. He does, of course, have a loose conglomerate of supporters who identify with a winner and who are willing to contribute, financially and otherwise, to the cause. But they do it all very quietly, and in a great sense Long is right; there is no political "machine" as such operating in his behalf.

That directs the discussion to the Louisiana governorship. The Baton Rouge statehouse has long been considered by many as Russell Long's family heirloom, his for the taking, the political birthright of the Louisiana Longs.

"I wanted to be governor," Long says, and for the first time really looks away, out of the third-story window that opens on the manicured Capitol grounds. He is quiet for a moment, musing. "It's a tough job, being governor," he resumes. "I would have had to be hard-nosed on some things."

He is talking about the office in the past tense. "If I had been governor," he continues, "I could never have been senator." He ends on that, but the question persists, and pulls him back. Would he ever consider the governorship? "I don't think so," Russell Long says, measuring out the words, and it drops.

Of course, his base is Louisiana, and he gets back as much as he can. And usually he tells people what he has done for them, for Louisiana, and they listen. That is how he campaigns now, really, and it works because he has proof—industry and jobs and Army bases—of his work.

"What's good for Louisiana is good for the nation," he is supposed to have said years ago. *The Wall Street Journal* article on Long in 1973 put a point on his pork-barreling for the home state: "Last year his finance panel rewrote the House-passed revenue-sharing formula, which resulted in the bayou state getting about 50 per cent more funds."

He can do it because, again, he is a power—maybe THE power—on the Hill. But Russell Long has had his problems, too, and his current prominence represents a considerable comeback from a difficult period in the sixties; a period when his career could have collapsed, and perhaps very nearly did.

Russell Long was drinking, and sometimes he was loud and abusive in the chamber. He lost his Senate assistant majority whip position to Edward Kennedy, something of an arch-foe, and that was a humiliation. His marriage fell apart.

Long's popularity in Louisiana was compromised, at least in the northern regions, by his unsubtle support of Lyndon Johnson when the state was going hard for the doomed Goldwater candidacy. Long seemed out of step then with the feelings of his constituents, and he sounded flat and stale in at least one home-state talk.

Now he is on top again. Intimates give a lot of credit to the new Mrs. Caroline Long. An attractive blonde from North Carolina, she knows politics, and now Long comes home from the Hill. Everybody says the drinking problem, whatever proportion it had reached, is licked. The liquor cabinet in the hideaway office is empty now.

He doesn't flinch at the mention of those days, though of course it isn't a favorite topic. "In my forties I enjoyed drinking," he says. "It became more of a liability than an asset." That ends it.

He is called to vote and, without him, the office comes into focus. It is comfortable, green-walled and spacious, with a lot of worn leather and pillows on the couch. There is a sketch of Huey and, as has been said so many times, the father-son resemblance is remarkable.

Long is back, and the Kingfish sketch has produced a question. Did Huey's career encourage Russell to get into politics? "He was a dominant personality," the young Long said of his father, the observation made without malice. "That tends to make a child recessive." And Russell finished, "I stuttered."

He goes on to comment on all the Bicentennial visitors in Washington, and his outlook on the nation's future, while not gloomy, is not optimistic either. "I was more optimistic ten years ago," he says. Long thinks the Supreme Court has made a series of "erroneous decisions," and adds that he isn't talking about civil rights.

Permissiveness is what he is talking about; permissive court decisions that have "given the criminals more rights than the victims." Long thinks the court may be moving back in the "right direction" but he feels terrible damage has been done.

Long thinks a Constitutional Convention may be necessary to repair the damage; or that the charter may have to be amended to make it mean what we thought it meant all the time . . . or make it work more effectively. "Society has to defend itself," he says.

That said, Long touched on issues of relevance. He thinks "Carter's gonna make it," but seems not all that impressed with the Democratic presidential front-runner. He views foreign policy with some resignation: "We are going to have to accept some countries, like we accept some people, the way they are."

The telephone rings.

It is J. Bennett Johnston, his Louisiana colleague, and Long is immediately absorbed. The interview is over, and he is waving goodbye, smiling, talking into the telephone, far away. The reflections are for somebody else now.

And the reflection is that, no, Russell Long has not harmed the legend or the name. Indeed, he may well have contributed more of lasting sum and substance than the father who hammered out an empire or the uncle who turned the state into a stage for his politics of confrontation.

Russell Long's legacy is in the Senate, and it is growing.

But so long as there is the possibility—even the barest possibility—that some day he may claim the mansion of his father's making, the Long Legend, in and of Louisiana, will not die.

Huckaby: From Plum Patch to Power

September 7, 1980

The weather was still sweating hot that autumn of 1975 in Bienville Parish, and then-Speaker of the House E. L. "Bubba" Henry was glad to climb down from his tractor and take a break from baling hay when neighboring dairy farmer Jerry Huckaby waved to him.

The two men, who often talked politics, found some spotty shade in a nearby plum thicket and Huckaby explained his version of a political mission impossible: he had decided to run for

Otto Passman's Fifth Congressional District seat, which had been as secure as a medieval fortress for three decades.

Would Henry help him?

Henry would, and a political alliance was forged right there in the plum patch. That same night Henry called Ruston Sen. Charles Barham, now North Louisiana's senior legislator. "Charlie," Henry said, "we gonna support Jerry Huckaby for Congress."

"Jerry who?" Barham wanted to know, though he too would support Huckaby.

The complete political novice—Jerry Who?—Huckaby departed the plum patch and took out another mortgage on his farm to launch an obscure campaign that would in 1976 accomplish what was then considered impossible: the destruction of the Passman dynasty. And Huckaby accomplished that feat before anybody ever heard of Koreagate. Then he beat off a well-heeled challenge from Republican Frank Spooner in the general election.

It was an extraordinary achievement for a thirty-five-year-old unknown making his first political try, but many observers felt the quiet, slight Huckaby had simply lucked out, and that he would be extremely vulnerable the next time around.

And so two short years later four challengers came after him hard—including formidable former State Sen. Jim Brown of Ferriday, who is now secretary of state. Brown had the endorsements of then Gov. Edwin Edwards, former Gov. John Mc-Keithen and the Monroe *Morning World*, the largest newspaper in the district.

As soft-spoken as before, gaunt-faced and nervous in the heat of that summer campaign in 1978, all Huckaby did was sweep sixteen of the district's sprawling twenty parishes and score a first-primary knockout. The Fifth District's quiet man, headlined *The Times*, had won again.

Nobody is calling Huckaby lucky now, or asking Jerry Who, and his bid for a third term in the Sept. 13 election has drawn but one challenger—L. D. "None of the Above" Knox, who, this side of a miracle, is not regarded as a threat to the incumbent.

"I don't want to seem arrogant," Huckaby said in a Monroe interview at his District office on North 18th Street, though arrogance is something the Hodge, La., native could never be accused of. "But we've had three tough races and now, well . . ." The soft voice trailed off behind a smile.

Huckaby will spend only ten thousand dollars for advertising "to let people know we have a race here." An informal *Times* survey indicates that Huckaby's confidence is justified; most people seem content with his consistently conservative voting record in Congress.

If there's a rap on Huckaby, it's that quiet demeanor again. "He's not aggressive . . . he just doesn't act like a congressman," said one long-time northeast Louisiana political observer, who didn't want to be named because he is still voting for Jerry, who—he admits—"has done his homework well."

Huckaby's low-decibel personality attracts others, however. "He's down to earth . . . he hasn't gotten Potomac Fever," said Madison *Journal* (Tallulah) Publisher Carroll Regan, who didn't mind being quoted.

The congressman himself, speaking just loudly enough to be heard and wearing conservative dark pinstripes, smiled at the widespread notion he is too quiet to be heard—politically or otherwise. "I'm not your typical back-slapping politician. But when there's a fight to be fought, I get out front—and I talk loud and clear." Three defeated political opponents would agree, anyway.

And most voters seem to agree that, personality aside, Huckaby has—like the man said—"done his homework well." "Doing your homework" means answering letters and requests, ranging from Social Security problems to veterans benefits to obtaining money from the Farmers Home Administration in this largely agricultural area. His office sends out about five hundred letters a week, and Huckaby gets high marks for what he calls "constituent service."

In fact, "constituent service" is what Huckaby identifies as his proudest accomplishment in two terms, mentioning his traveling van, district offices in Monroe and Natchitoches, town meetings and the recent publication of a Senior Citizens Handbook. "He works our tails off on service," one tired staffer said. Said Huckaby: "We try to help a lot of little people with big problems."

Huckaby is also proud of a Carter-signed but yet unfunded wildlife refuge in Tensas, Franklin and Madison parishes. In the western reaches of his northeast and northcentral Louisiana territory Huckaby is opposed to nuclear storage in Webster and Bienville parishes.

On national issues Huckaby takes familiar positions that mirror the views of his conservative constituency: He wants to balance the budget, still, but he is particularly concerned about national defense. He wants to see America self-sufficient on energy. Those are his abiding national priorities: defense and energy.

We talked for an hour, and the outside offices filled up. As usual, Huckaby relaxed when the yellow legal pad and flair pen of the interviewer were set aside. He had smoked only one cigarette—quite a contrast from the chain-smoking Huckaby of the previous campaign—and spoke warmly of a mutual friend who had joined his staff.

Jerry Huckaby would be jetting back to Washington, D.C. this same Tuesday afternoon—a long way from the plum patch of five years ago. From there, he will carry a perfect 3-0 record into the Sept. 13 election—an intelligent (he's working on a doctorate in economics), quiet, essentially shy man who remains the successful stranger among Louisiana's traditionally rowdy political crowd.

Bob Kennon, Ozymandias and the Governors of Louisiana

May 31, 1981

Percy Bysshe Shelley could have written his classic poem "Ozymandias," the story of the ancient "King of kings" whose great empire was finally buried under "lone and level sands," for the governors of Louisiana.

Raised to a summit of personal political power uncommon in America, the governors of this state rule an oil sheikdom in which they are courted with a fervor not unlike that accorded a Persian Gulf potentate by a whole spectrum of supplicants reliant on the king's favor.

Yet the plunge from that summit, occasioned by the end of a term or an almost inevitable turning of the political tide, is—with the notable exception of the crest-riding Edwin Edwards—as swift and final as the fall of Ozymandias.

And those same "lone and level sands" soon blow over monuments left by leaders as intensely powerful as John McKeithen. "How soon they forget," former Gov. McKeithen said wistfully one summer morning from his comfortable Ouachita River Elba of Columbia. Former Gov. Jimmie Davis, his literal political song scorned in a last bus-ride of a campaign, doesn't even give interviews.

Now Dr. Michael L. Kurtz, professor of history at Southeastern Louisiana University at Hammond, has blown the sands from another almost forgotten monument—the 1952-56 administration of Gov. Robert Floyd Kennon.

The still-active seventy-nine-year-old Kennon, who checks in regularly at his Baton Rouge law office, could tell John McKeithen something about Louisiana's political amnesia. A popular State Supreme Court judge from Minden, he earned a de-

BOB KENNON, OZYMANDIAS AND THE GOVERNORS OF LOUISIANA

served reputation—as Dr. Kurtz points out in his paper—for honesty and efficiency.

Seized by one of its periodic fits of revulsion for what Kurtz calls "the heavy-taxing, free-spending and devil-may-care attitudes . . . of the Longs," Louisiana in 1952 was again ready for the "reform" and "good government" represented by Kennon.

It was, then, Kennon's time in the traditional flow of Louisiana politics—Earl Long had gone too far this time, people said—and the schoolmaster-looking judge rode that tide well. Pledging a government "run according to the civics book"—the apt title of Kurtz's paper—the judge destroyed the divided Long forces, winning fifty-three of sixty-four parishes over Judge Carlos Spaht.

So Bob Kennon was a king in May of 1952, a popular and constitution-minded monarch who was especially admired in North Louisiana. And his proclamations rolled through a Legislature that came to Baton Rouge clutching those spotless judicial robes. Dr. Kurtz cites "a series of reform bills almost as extensive as those enacted during . . . the first year of Sam Jones' administration."

The state budget office was reorganized, independent "blue-ribbon" citizens' boards were established governing state universities, highways and welfare, and the first sunshine law in Louisiana history was passed. Voting machines were installed in every precinct. The state penitentiary system was improved. A right-to-work law made it through the Legislature.

As soon as Kennon was inaugurated, he asked the Louisiana Civil Service League to draw up plans for a new state merit system. The draft was duly presented, and Kennon's reform team scored what was then regarded as its most significant points.

"These measures," Dr. Kurtz says, "together with an almost complete lack of the usual charges of corruption and dishonesty, gave the Kennon administration a deserved reputation as one of the most honest and efficient in . . . Louisiana history."

Dr. Edwin Adams Davis, in his *Louisiana, A Narrative History*,

BOB KENNON, OZYMANDIAS AND THE GOVERNORS OF LOUISIANA

agrees with that assessment. "He (Kennon) will be remembered for the progress which was made during his administration in behalf of responsible constitutional government," Davis wrote.

Yet, despite an early popularity proved by strong support for Kennon-authored amendments to the state constitution, Louisiana's capricious political tide soon began to run against the judge and toward the same Earl Long who had "gone too far" in the 1948-1952 period.

"By the end of his term as governor," says the Southeastern historian, "Robert Kennon was popularly thought of as a dull, listless and even comical figure." The bullwhip-tongued Earl, Kurtz remembers, had not failed to notice the judge's prominent ears. "Kennon's ears are so big he can stand in a courthouse in Opelousas and hear a dollar bill drop in Ville Platte," Earl cracked. Now he was riding the tide.

And Kennon was caught in the ebb and flow—this time the ebb—of Louisiana politics. The state was ready for action and what writer Allan Sindler has called, charitably, the "buccaneering liberalism" of Earl Long.

There were other reasons for Kennon's eclipse, of course. His political supporters felt ignored. Perhaps to his credit, the judge made no real effort to maintain a political organization once he was elected. Kennon's driven, crime-busting State Police superintendent, Francis Grevemberg, trampled on important toes en route to the slot machines.

What sort of a permanent mark, though, did Bob Kennon leave in Louisiana's shifting political sands? Historians, as noted, generally give the judge high marks if little space. But Dr. Kurtz is skeptical. "The Kennon reforms generated little more than a ripple in the tidal wave of fraud, waste and mismanagement . . . in government," he says.

Taking Kennon's reforms one by one, from budget re-organization to the war on gambling, Kurtz finds that they were largely undone either by the Long administration that followed or by loopholes in the law. Though a genuine reformer, Bob

Kennon was also a conservative who broke with the Democratic Party and supported Dwight Eisenhower in two elections.

His stand against integration must be considered in the context of those times, but as Kurtz points out, the gentleman judge's support of rabid racists like Leander Perez and Willie Rainach was *not* an act of calm statesmanship.

Nevertheless, that same record bears out Kurtz's general conclusion that "the Kennon years witnessed a state government dedicated to eradicating . . . political and criminal corruption." If the judge only marginally succeeded in the long sweep—in one historian's view, at least—then he still deserves credit for an incorruptible effort.

For that effort, Bob Kennon definitely deserves better than the forgotten fate of Shelley's "Ozymandias."

We Sang It All Together Just One More Time . . .

November 29, 1981

You could tell it was an event because the Fleetwoods were parked right up against the pickup trucks in the parking lot of the Ruston Civic Center that November Friday night and the cars and trucks overflowed on down North Trenton Street.

It was packed inside, where the cultural conglomerate was even more evident in crewcuts and silk shirts and styled hair and cowboy boots—of course—and white socks and wingtips and $400 suits and Big Mac overalls.

I saw a lawyer and a doctor come in, but the two men behind me were talking about trapping one side of the creek and buying fur and how to skin a skunk underwater. In all, there were a lot of people in the auditorium in their sixties and seventies and eighties even, but I also saw young parents cradling babies less than six months old.

We had come to Joe Woods' Wildwood Express, a country music oasis that has been bubbling up out of Lincoln Parish's red-clay roots for years. The Wildwood Express usually plays up at the old Dixie Theater, where I watched the Durango Kid and Roy Rogers on those Saturday double-bills, but moved to the Civic Center this night to accommodate a special guest.

The special guest this night was former Gov. Jimmie Davis, and the advance publicity said it could be his last performance in North Louisiana. I doubt that because when Davis came on stage he looked, well, pretty much like he's looked for the last quarter of a century.

The more-brown-than-gray hair may have been inspired by Grecian Formula, but there is no excess in the familiar face, framed by horn-rimmed glasses. Yes, he's a little stooped now, but I saw him help move the piano.

Davis was dressed in a blue business suit, light blue shirt and striped tie that he could have worn into the Ruston State Bank across the street—and probably did after personally hawking records, albums and books during intermission.

The voice is a tad hoarse these days, but still pine-resin resonant, and he has that perfect timing yet—the timing that can jerk tears . . . "He'll come down from the skies and brush the tears from your eyes." And Davis had just recorded a number, "Heaven's National Anthem."

But the audience was waiting for Jimmie Davis to sing the old songs and he didn't disappoint them. "On your knees, you're taller than trees." A warm tide of applause, of recognition, rippled through the crowd, floating away the years. And they nodded when he singsonged his way through first sweethearts and drugstore ice cream and stew at the cafe.

"Come home, Jimmie, it's suppertime." A very old lady in the front row alternately cried and laughed as Davis worked his way slowly through to the end, making a poem out of it. "We're going' home," he finished, and the audience—old and young—was nodding, smiling, at every bittersweet word.

Still, the crowd was anticipating that last song; they were all ready for it. And when Davis mentioned his "meal ticket" the man across the aisle snapped a new cassette into his recorder and held it up high. Jimmie Davis had us all together then—crewcuts and silk shirts and white socks and cowboy boots and wingtips. "Let's sing it together," he said.

"You are my sunshine, my only sunshine." Slowly, gently prodded, the audience joined in. "You make me happy when skies are gray. . . ." Suddenly Jimmie Davis' politics didn't matter. Maybe they never did. Here was—is—a great performer, singing his song, maybe—like the publicity said—for the last time.

And we sang it with him. One more time. "You are my sunshine, my only sunshine. You'll never know, dear, how much I love you . . . please don't take . . . my sunshine . . . away."

Treen: No Spitballs. No Scandals.

January 10, 1982

Summoning reporters to the mansion for an assessment of just-departed 1981, a confident Gov. Dave Treen gave himself and his administration good grades for the year. And that report card, Treen indicated, would be widely advertised this year.

A suddenly more visible Treen can claim at least a couple of A's in '81. There was an almost last-hour settlement of a seven-year-old Justice Department suit which, in its original form, would have savaged higher education with academic amputations and transplants.

Then Treen proved that coup in academe was no fluke by resolving a decade-long dispute over the fate of the Atchafalaya Basin in South Central Louisiana. Again pulling strings in Republican Washington, bargaining tough ("I don't reverse fields," he said), the GOP governor won the day and—if things proceed according to plan—saved the last big river bottom swamp in America.

But if Treen was being graded on an old-fashioned report card, his best mark would be recorded in a little square (remember?) reserved for "Conduct." In other words, Dave Treen has not only made some pretty good grades, but also behaved himself in class. No spitballs. No scandals in Louisiana, either. So Treen is still "Mr. Clean" more than two years into Republican rule. Bullheaded, maybe, but unblemished. Prideful but pure. That's Dave, dull or not.

The absence of scandal didn't really hit home until Sam Hanna, publisher of weekly newspapers in Northeast Louisiana and one of the state's astute political observers for a generation, made the point recently in his "One Man's Opinion" column.

"Treen is entitled to respect . . . primarily because he hasn't had a single smear against him personally or his administration," Hanna wrote. While conceding that questions persist about the governor's ability to lead, Hanna correctly declared that "it's been a long time in Louisiana when there hasn't even been a hint of scandal. . . ."

Given Treen's good conduct and a growing accumulation of accomplishments, it's possible this administration—after a year of confusion—is gaining momentum. The GOP governor, often dismissed as a one-term accident of political fate, is mastering the rhythms of power.

By no means are all the portents favorable, of course. In fact, all objective betting still rests on Edwin Edwards—the most popular governor in Louisiana history—and a Cajun Restoration two years hence.

There's still speculation that Treen will step aside in favor of personable GOP Rep. Henson Moore.

The perception of Treen as a buttoned-down Republican Oliver Cromwell lingers despite his good-humored, piano-playing romps with the Capitol press. GOP true-believers are hard to please. Natural allies, like the Public Affairs Research Council and the Louisiana Association of Industry and Business, criticize the governor. Even close supporters complain of delayed decisions and detail mongering.

And the Republican Party, despite gains, is still at a twelve-to-one disadvantage in raw voting numbers. So, quite obviously, Dave Treen will need all the momentum he can muster to outdistance the Cajun cavalry. And in that home stretch, Treen may get the best mileage out of his so-far unflawed good conduct grade.

Dull Dave, you see, is also Mr. Clean. And, to a lot of people, clean isn't dull—in school or politics.

Louisiana's Political Schizophrenia

March 27, 1983

Already Gov. Dave Treen and former Gov. Edwin Edwards have gone to the mat in what *Louisiana Life* calls the "Main Event," but their onrushing autumn collision only sends us all back to the psychiatrist's couch for yet another bout with the political schizophrenia that has split this state's mind and morals for over a half-century.

LOUISIANA'S POLITICAL SCHIZOPHRENIA

Think about it. Treen is Louisiana's first Republican governor since Reconstruction, but he is also the heir of reform-minded chief executives like the late Sam Jones and Robert Kennon. Edwards, in this traditional match-up, is the ideological descendant of the legendary Longs.

Party label still isn't that important in Louisiana; it's the traditions that count. The neat, nit-picking Treen is all business, personally and professionally. The flamboyant Edwards speaks for the populism of the past and the present; his solid support among labor and blacks is part of the tradition.

Yes, sometimes the state's two political mindsets do merge. Treen has opened doors previously shut to blacks. And some business lobbyists, including imperious Louisiana Association of Business and Industry (LABI) President Ed Steimel, have scolded the stubborn, independent Treen. Edwards, for his part, will claim some business support and lose the endorsements of a few black leaders.

But, in the end, the state's personality will split along established historical fault lines. No matter how many times Treen visits Grambling State University, no matter how many blacks Treen admits to government, it is Edwards who will command the farmer-worker populist legacy which now includes the minority vote.

Treen, on his side, can legitimately claim the mantle of what is called "Good Government." He will wear the halo of integrity well. And the former congressman has respected the balance of power between the executive and the Legislature that is also a part of the legacy of conservative, business-backed reformism in Louisiana. Treen, indeed, is Mr. Clean personified, and in one compartment of this state's conscience, well, that's the most important thing.

But Louisiana never completely makes up its political mind, or takes its conscience entirely into consideration. Okay, Treen's administration is as clean as the floor of the church choir loft. And the Edwards record is as cloudy as the proverbial smoke-filled room of politics. "So what?" says a voice from the state's memory bank; EWE, insists that voice, is just a Cajun Robin Hood. He takes from the rich to provide for the poor and if a little of the loot gets lost in Las Vegas, so what?

Two minds, two moralities exist there and the same double standard can be applied to work and effort. Treen *is* hard-working; immersed in detail. He doesn't have time to call that rebellious GOP boiler-room worker in Ruston; his capitol office light burns late. Such dedication is to be admired in the Protestant ethic portion of the Louisiana mind, but there are gray areas where Edwin Edwards is seen as the master strategist, above detail, plotting a course of vision and purpose. He seems to know what is important.

That split personality divides everything. It's permissible for a populist to say or do wild things—like Earl Long rolling down the window of his car and pointedly returning the obscene sign tossed at him by a bunch of teen-agers. Or like Edwin Edwards saying, in effect, about one impropriety or another: "Yeah, OK, I did it, and what are you gonna do about it?" But conservative reformers, like a Jones or a Kennon or a Treen, must somehow reflect sobriety and seriousness at all times. Treen says his natural expression is a frown.

And there's yet another distinction between Louisiana's two political minds. Edwards, in the tradition of the Longs and their populist background, has already constructed a dynasty; he is the godfather and the grand mogul. He revels, bathes, in burgeoning government-temporarily-in-exile.

Conservative reformers like Treen and Jones and Kennon are not by nature political animals; one wounding, weary tour of the jungle is, at least subconsciously, enough for them. Sam Jones wanted "no hooray or applause." He was governor only because "somebody had to clean up this mess."

Bob Kennon, a schoolmaster of a judge from Minden, clouted a hand-picked Long machine candidate in fifty-three of sixty-four parishes in 1952. But the judge let his political machine, never much more than the reform of the moment, rest and rust. Earl Long, re-elected in 1956, buried Kennon's blue-ribbon "citizen boards" without so much as a funeral.

Is Dave Treen, despite his ringing declaration of "C'mon, Eddie, we're ready" any different from a Sam Jones, who "fought the good fight" and disappeared from the political stage? Or from a Bob Kennon, who won by 184,000 votes and then let his mandate melt away? "I don't have an overwhelming need to be . . . re-elected," Treen told *Louisiana Life*. "I'd rather do what . . . is right, and serve one term. . . ."

Yes, there are a couple of modern Louisiana governors who do not fit precisely into this mold of minds. Columbia's John McKeithen fused the Long and anti-Long factions, combined populism with a businessman's common sense, and gave the state what objective observers like the Public Affairs Research Council now see—in retrospect—as a season of turning-point leadership which met racial and economic challenges.

Yet, the magnetic McKeithen was far more liberal than conservative (he was an early John F. Kennedy organizer in North Louisiana) and owed more, spiritually and otherwise, to the Longs than to the anti-Longs. And like his populist cousins, he exited under a cloud of unproved but perceived wrongdoing.

That other exception to Louisiana's split personality, the tranquil Jimmie Davis, came from the poorest background ever (born into a family of eighteen in a Jackson Parish sharecropper's shack) to win two gubernatorial terms, literally for a song. But his course was much more traditionally conservative than populist, and Davis entered the political lists for the first time with the blessings of Sam Jones.

So the rule, the schism, prevails and it all goes back to Huey P. Long. The Kingfish linked up Louisiana with paved roads, bridged its great river, the Mississippi, and took more pride in the distribution of free school books than in all the buildings. The first Long was the pure expression, in power, of a populism that has its roots deep in Louisiana history. Huey, heaving the state into the twentieth century, forever broke the back of the Bourbons, the landed aristocrats, who had complacently ruled Louisiana for their own class.

But Huey was also the classic, violent expression of a political river over the banks—proof of the historical axiom that "power corrupts, absolute power corrupts absolutely." The seeds of absolute power so planted were reaped, bitterly, in the Louisiana Scandals—"an orgy," wrote historian Edwin Adams Davis, "of political malfeasance and governmental graft." The state buckled to its knees under a torrent of black headlines, revelations, prison sentences and four suicides. It was an early Watergate, and Louisiana was humiliated.

Enter that same Sam Jones to "clean up the mess." Re-enter Earl Long, who finished the fights brother Huey started in the Winnfield schoolyard, to establish old-age pensions and—yes—to destroy many of Jones' reforms. And so Louisiana careened from reaction to reform and back again, caught in a schizoid trap that often killed real economic and political progress. Yet, as PAR testifies, better management of the state's major resources—its soil and oil—has defined both of Louisiana's political mindsets in the last two decades or so, though the historic division still looms large.

In the inaugural address for his first term, Edwin Edwards spoke to the same common people the Longs had addressed. "To the poor, elderly, the unemployed, the thousands of black Louisianans . . . we extend the hand of friendship," said EWE. In 1928, at the historic Evangeline Oak, Huey Long had invoked the same vision and said "give me the chance to dry the tears of those who still weep here."

In some degree, which only time can measure, Edwards vindicated that vision while steering Louisiana on an oil-floated course of prosperity charted in the McKeithen years. His unprecedented popularity is beyond question. Yet, like his Long-populist heirs, Edwards has been shadowed by unproved scandal and proved opportunism. He is godfather government personified.

Dave Treen, across the spectrum, has lived up to the high standard of political reformers identified with the conservative creed that, from time to time, dominates the mind of Louisiana; he has been compared to Sam Jones, the model for reform. But, like his heirs, Treen lacks the charisma which attracts the makings of a dynasty. He, like Jones, would rather be right than governor for two terms. And the oil is running low, and, besides, it is the populist turn at the tiller; we've had the conservatives for four years.

Of course, some things have changed in state politics no matter whose tide is running. The focus of power has swung, with the population and the emergence of the black vote, from North to South Louisiana. No longer can a disciplined phalanx of north-country soldiers overcome the will of New Orleans in the late returns.

And the stump campaign, the politician—people progressions across the state, disappeared into a South Louisiana sunset with the Jimmie Davis bus and band and electoral bid in the summer of 1971. The television earthquake has swallowed the candidates and then raised them up, cloned and clever, through the tube.

Still, in sum, it's "politics as usual" in Louisiana, as stated by Tech professor Morgan D. Peoples in a recent lecture at Tech. It is, in the end, Treen's Republican Roundheads against Edwards' Cajun Cavaliers. It's the Longs against the anti-Longs, even though that family is mostly removed from intrastate politics. It's share the wealth against save the money. It's the populists against the businessmen. Liberals against conservatives. It's the main event, folks, and time for us to go crazy, crazy-schizoid, one more time.

When Big John Outshined Them All

May 22, 1983

COLUMBIA—Some things don't change.

Highway 165 South escorted me right up to Floyd's Bait Stand and the River Queen Cafe two weeks ago and then across the Long-Allen Bridge (always looking like some kid slapped it together with an erector set), the Ouachita River and into the corporate limits of Columbia, La.

The McKeithen law offices are on the second street down from the bridge (I remembered coming here for an interview five years ago) and sure enough that modest red-brick building sits in its accustomed place next to the U.S. Post Office.

Big John McKeithen hasn't changed, either. He's almost an hour late for our appointment (just like last time), wears the familiar tan shirt and pants and cowboy boots and the rugged good looks that made him an early political television hit. He has not aged a bit.

I discover that in the time since we talked last (he didn't remember the interview or the interviewer) his opinions haven't changed much, either. He is feeling more vindicated these days; the Public Affairs Research Council now sees his administrations (1964-1972) as good, perhaps even great, days for the state.

This pleases him, and he is more philosophical about his fallen political star. "I was twenty-nine years ahead of my time," he says, noting that his stands on a tax increase, forced busing and the New Orleans Superdome have been vindicated. I think he's right; time and the river, if not current politics, are riding a McKeithen current.

Personally, McKeithen is much the same, too. He paces the floor, grabs the reporter by the lapels to emphasize a point, and bellows with laughter. The brown eyes still blaze with intensity.

WHEN BIG JOHN OUTSHINED THEM ALL

And, just as he did five years ago, McKeithen stops when my Flair pen can't keep up with his flow of words. "Are you with me?" he asks.

Below is an updated and condensed version of the profile I wrote for The Times *five years ago. It's by way of introduction to the current interview in which McKeithen talks candidly about other governors—Dave Treen, Edwin Edwards, Jimmie Davis, Robert Kennon and Earl Long:*

John McKeithen came striding out of the double-doors of Shreveport's old Washington-Youree Crystal Ballroom like a starburst, resplendent in tux and tails, head slightly averted, reducing the rest of his entourage to a pinpoint in the glow of his own immense popularity.

It was early in his first term as governor, that grand and sweeping entrance, but the exact time doesn't matter. What mattered then was that John McKeithen had soared to the summit of Louisiana politics in those years of 1964 to 1968. Nobody could touch him.

He was incredibly popular, one of the most popular leaders ever. He was so popular, in fact, that a writer for *Time* magazine visiting *The Times'* editorial offices in search of a profile on the governor begged in mock despair: "Can you tell me one negative thing about this man?"

Yet, before the end of his second term, John McKeithen was a flamed-out political star, spinning almost silently toward his Ouachita delta farm near Columbia and what was—for him—an early and forced retirement from public affairs.

What happened? It is a question that has been asked before, but on this hot summer day in Columbia, John McKeithen faces it again, pacing the red carpet of his law office, gesturing, lightly tapping the interviewer on the foot to emphasize a point.

The energy, part of it pure outrage, flows out of him like an electric current. "Absurd," he says of the Mafia influence charge, which was never proved. The thought of it seems to all but choke him. "Anybody who knows me . . ." he begins, and decides not to say it.

"It was enough to make me lose my mind," he says of a *Life* magazine article which linked state government to the Mob. And, halting his circle directly in front of the interviewer, he repeats more softly: "Enough to make me lose my mind . . . it tore me to pieces nationally."

Then McKeithen suddenly relaxes. He looks away, and sees the decline in some perspective. Smiling, he cites a combination of things that undid him politically: He had to ask for taxes, never a popular move; there were problems with labor; a stand against forced busing (a stand he now feels has been vindicated) attracted the enmity of the Justice Department; the New Orleans Domed Stadium was an "albatross;" and the simple fact that "people get tired of" a second-term governor.

But he is not all resentment and outrage; far from it. Square-jawed and impressive at sixty-four, he is still the man who led combat troops in the Pacific campaigns.

Whatever the reasons for the political fall from grace, his own personal integrity survived intact. Two terms as governor set McKeithen's career high above the crowd, even if some vague national aspiration or, more likely, permanent political influence escaped him.

For the record, a good record, is there even if the applause has died away. Beyond the extraordinary popularity of the first McKeithen term are real accomplishments. Always of a mind to promote free enterprise, John McKeithen authored five constitutional amendments based on what he called "the right to profit." They were ratified by the people in November of 1965.

He wanted to expand the economy, to create jobs as well as profits, and during this period, foundations and institutions aimed at researching how to accomplish these "Goals for Louisiana" were formed. Almost five thousand miles of highway were built or improved during those first four years. Higher education gained academically and materially, and McKeithen enticed some top professionals from this area into his administration.

Segregation was still an issue then, and McKeithen today agrees that his handling of various problems growing out of school integration and the riot-prone 1960s earned him a good part of the public support that was his at the time. In Jonesboro and at Southern University in Baton Rouge he met with demonstration leaders and personally defused potentially violent confrontations. "I tried to be fair to both sides," McKeithen says.

"We did everything the good government people wanted," McKeithen maintains, looking back at those years, but the seeds of his later decline may have been planted in those heady days of victory. To sustain his programs to build Louisiana, McKeithen desperately needed more money—more taxes.

So a weary McKeithen finally heaved his tax package through a reluctant Legislature in November of 1968. "I was giving and I'm still prepared to give," he told a reporter then. Some of the political favors given at that time, not to benefit McKeithen personally but to secure passage of a needed (in retrospect) tax, came back to haunt him later. "You can't turn your back on people who supported you," he says even now. "Of course, later I wished that some people hadn't supported me."

But he was still "Big John" then. And his second-term victory was overwhelming. Before that, however, the electorate had to approve a constitutional amendment lifting the ban against a governor succeeding himself. That was done in November of 1966. It was, in all, a rare mandate, and McKeithen cherishes it still.

Yet there is from time to time still an unmistakable air of bitterness in this brown-hued, high ceilinged office. "People forget," he says at the end of it. And he repeats it, quietly, but with emphasis. "People forget."

That public forgetfulness has pricked whatever trial balloons McKeithen or his friends have floated since 1972. And so he proclaims no political plans now. And with characteristic openness, he says the support for such a comeback has not materialized.

But then McKeithen grinned broadly on that day five years ago. "I'm prepared to accept a draft . . . a genuine draft." But, he said then, still smiling, pointing out into the shimmering July heat, "I didn't feel even a breeze out there today, did you?" I didn't.

Loy Weaver:
The Best and the Brightest

August 21, 1983

He is the ultimate Boy Scout, the Baby-Blue Marine and—for real—the special FBI agent cited for bravery. A few days ago, in gray pinstripes and maroon tie, he was the picture-perfect banker. What he won't be, in a very short time, is the House member from Homer.

He is Loy Weaver, of course. Or just Loy, as everybody around Courthouse Square and in the two drugstores and over meatloaf and greens at the crossroads Linder Motor Lodge calls him familiarly. But even with all that familiarity and indeed popularity, Weaver isn't running for a third term from the 11th District.

That fact surprised everybody down in Baton Rouge and around here as well, because as a legislator Weaver has won the rare reputation of being what Pulitzer Prize-winning journalist David Halberstam identified in his book as *The Best and the Brightest* in government.

Loy Weaver is young (forty-two) and idealistic and articulate in a Southern Kennedyesque sense and, it is widely acknowledged, he had become a moral force in the Legislature and in a Louisiana political world that the state bicentennial history characterized as corrupt from its very colonial roots.

Then why get out now, Loy? He answers that question in terms of business and personal reasons. On the personal side, it's a fourteen-year-old son that he wants to watch grow up. "I've considered it (retirement from politics) before," he tells me from an eagle's nest of an office in the high-ceilinged old Homer National Bank where he's now a vice president.

That same Homer National Bank is the business reason. Outside in the green and shimmering upland heat of August, a couple of Weaver's constituents have another reason for his decision not to run. "He's just done about everything he said he was going to do," they say in almost the same words.

For Claiborne and Union parishes, and a part of Bienville, Weaver has made good on his two prime goals: a better economy and better roads. The Wade Correctional Institute, established only after a sharp fight, has become a model for corrections and a mecca for the area economy. And every major road in the district has been rebuilt or repaved.

Weaver, modest to a fault, lets somebody else talk about that. He says the passing lanes haven't been done yet and lets it go at that. "I don't consider myself a politician, anyway," he says, dismissing discussion about his political achievements. "I investigate politicians," he explains, with a slow-spreading grin.

Weaver investigated former State Agriculture Commissioner Gil Dozier in 1979 because, the former FBI man said, Dozier was trying to extort money from his constituents. "I didn't set out to investigate him but then I didn't back down," Weaver said.

In the end, Dozier lost his re-election bid and was convicted by federal authorities on racketeering charges. Weaver says he "didn't take any pleasure" in what happened, but that he would do it again. Indeed, Weaver has pushed hard, and in vain, for a

Louisiana Bureau of Investigation to police white-collar crime and public corruption.

He feels, it is evident, a quiet but intense outrage about crime and corruption, and especially about propriety in public life. Weaver, a floor leader and top legislative strategist for Gov. Dave Treen, sees his own record on propriety and trust as his "proudest accomplishment" in Baton Rouge.

"I don't want to sound self-serving, but nobody ever called me a crook," he says. "Even people who disagree with me, strongly disagree, say, 'Well, you did what you thought was right.'" In that spirit, Weaver still admires the late and now de-mythed J. Edgar Hoover, his one-time FBI boss.

"He (Hoover) set a standard of dress and weight and hair length," Weaver said. "Mr. Hoover didn't think it was enough to be right; he said you had to look right." Weaver looked down out of his office eyrie, thinking about Hoover, obviously. "We don't have enough heroes now," he says wistfully.

Flat-stomached (making the interviewer want to suck in air) with only his thick brown hair maybe just a shade longer than Hoover would have liked in his heyday, Weaver still looks the part of the FBI man who does what is right, regardless.

And for eight years, he has acted the part in the Legislature. Reporters, covering him in Baton Rouge, can't find a flaw. Except perhaps that "he's just too damned good," said one writer, a little irritated at the lack of scandal.

Again, Weaver thinks he should be "too good." In government, "people's conduct and demeanor ought to be a cut above," he says. "I tried to do what was right, with a minimum regard for politics. If I have a regret, it's that I didn't try even harder."

Given that philosophy, it's not surprising that Weaver was a Treen leader and now, with the governor's race quickening, a Treen supporter. "I believe what he (Treen) tells me," says Weaver. And he adds: "He (Treen) wouldn't take so much as a ham or six golf balls."

Weaver thinks people are aware of Treen's honesty and in-

LOY WEAVER: THE BEST AND THE BRIGHTEST

tegrity, and that when they get into the voting booth that awareness will count. "I definitely think Treen can win," he says, citing in addition "some movement in the black vote."

What Weaver sees in Treen and in himself—a basic willingness to "do what's right"—motivated Weaver's one political expedition outside North Central Louisiana. That was the Fourth Congressional District race in 1978, and that September for a brief and shining hour Claiborne Parish was Camelot.

Given no chance at the start, Weaver didn't get far until he fired a high-priced public relations consultant and, with some of his close supporters in a Shreveport meeting, came up with a slogan and a set of colors that captured his personality and his philosophy: The Weaver Believers, in all-American red, white and blue.

That slogan was Weaver's Excalibur, and for a few moments it was a magic wand.

Suddenly, every bumper in North Louisiana seemed to wave "I'm a Weaver Believer" like a red, white and blue flag. Speculation was that Weaver was second in the race; maybe even first.

Of course, Camelot collapsed and political reality prevailed in the end. Not one to alibi, Weaver still feels that a poll publicized in the last hours of the campaign showing him far behind—"it did not capture my momentum"—convinced voters that nice guys finish last or, in Weaver's case, next to last.

Yet, Loy Weaver, win or lose, *is* a nice guy who was also extremely effective in state government, and the writer—finding no proof to the contrary—wonders about writing the puff piece nobody believes. But the thing is, people do believe in Weaver.

Maybe that's because he "treats people the way I like to be treated . . . that is, I told the truth, even when it may not have been what they wanted to hear, and never, never talked down to them." Unpolitical in a way, Loy Weaver never hustled newspaper writers or funerals, but he was "courteous to everybody."

That last trait alone will be missed in the often-arrogant (except at election time, of course) posture of Louisiana politics. But, at the end of the interview, Weaver was careful not to rule out a re-entry. "I don't consider myself out of politics," he says.

But when his hill-country power base is gone, as it will be shortly, Loy Weaver will discover that he is out of politics—that the prerogatives and many of the patrons will fall away. It doesn't really matter, though.

Because for eight years the big Boy Scout from Homer, the quiet-spoken FBI man who never forgot Hoover, was among the best and the brightest in Louisiana politics. And who knows? Maybe the Weaver Believers will wait for him.

Edwards: History's Main Chance

March 11, 1984

The Cajun Restoration.

It arrives formally tomorrow with the inauguration of Edwin Edwards, but appropriately enough this son of a sharecropper from French Louisiana had already been restored to Louisiana's Imperial Governorship while in Versailles—the historic seat of French kings.

In a journey abroad so uniquely and daringly Edwardian that it disarmed even the most pious of critics, Edwards canceled his campaign debt, lavishly repaid the most exacting of his courtiers and took the accompanying press sweet hostage in Paris.

But Edwin Edwards was never really gone from Baton Rouge—not even while Dave Treen occupied the mansion. Edwards was always, from Treen's first day in office, the closest thing to a gubernatorial inevitability in American politics.

The Republican interregnum, well-meaning and honest, was

a constitutional and political accident that lacked vigor and vision. Edwards declared, in so many words, that he would win, alive or dead or in jail. It was almost that certain.

Edwards, in the end, captured sixty-two of sixty-four parishes in that preordained election, storming even the staunchest conservative castles in northwestern and north central Louisiana. His was the classic dictionary definition of the word mandate:

"Authoritative command or instruction . . . The wishes of a political electorate . . . Order issued by a superior court. . . ." (*American Heritage Dictionary*.) Edwin Edwards, then, was wished by the Louisiana electorate; nay, he was commanded—ordered—by that electorate.

So it is time for even those who defied that hurricane of a mandate to take note of what wind blows. For starters, Edwards is smart, pure and simple. "Brilliant . . . the quickest political mind I have ever experienced," says Gus Weill, who has advised the last four Louisiana governors but was in Treen's corner last time.

"A can-do guy . . . positive," echoed two of Edwards' closest supporters in a no-names-please discussion last week. "By the time you get the question out, he's answered it," one of the men said. In other words, Edwards is decisive. A leader. An able administrator, says another source.

Nobody can question the political charisma, either. "Mesmerize is a word one of our sources used three times to describe the Cajun campaigner's effect on a crowd. And in the last election, Edwards proved he could mesmerize just about everybody and not just his bedrock constituencies of Cajuns, blacks and labor.

There is also merit in Edwards' previous eight-year tenure—merit his flamboyance often masked. He crafted a new constitution for Louisiana, hitched state oil income to a percentage rather than to a flat rate and presided over approval of the right-to-work law. Legislative landmarks all. And there were others.

But, yes there is a darker side. Edwin Edwards skirted the ragged edge of scandal and flaunted it. He ignored environmental dangers. And the same close supporters who praise his warmth in a crowd admit that, personally, he's a cold fish. "He appears bored," one said. "No chitchat." No polite small talk. Weill said it for the record: "Edwards is a cold man . . . a loner."

The blacks and the poor, however, find compassion behind the one-to-one coldness and apparent lack of social grace. And, in this sense, Edwards is unabashedly the Last Populist—the heir to Huey Long's share-the-wealth philosophy. But the gusher that fed Huey's legacy, and those led by it, has been capped by the oil glut.

So, lacking that fuel, Edwin Edwards is proposing to run the state on a $750 million tax increase. That increase, he says, will be used to balance the budget, to strengthen state retirement systems, to clean up the environment, to encourage high-tech development and to support higher education, among other things.

Few could honestly deny the need for a tax increase if Edwards, in his Kennedyesque terms, is to "get the state moving again." But even those who don't oppose Edwards worry about new taxes discouraging industry the state needs to create new jobs. They worry about the growth of state government and what it bodes for the future, period.

Whatever the hopes and the reservations, there is the feeling among Edwards' supporters like the two I interviewed that "if this son-of-a-gun can't do it (get the state on its economic feet), nobody can." We shall see. But let nobody deny that Edwin Edwards has earned the chance to do it; let nobody dispute the mandate, nor the brilliance.

Edwin Edwards understands the chance and the choice. He knows that this time the eye of history is on him. "He knows he needs the press and all the people this time . . . he's dedicated to improving his image," said one of the Edwards intimates interviewed. "He wants to go into the history books as a great governor," the supporter said.

Again, Edwards, whatever his most unforgiving critics say, had already accomplished much. Yet, in the tumult of political give-and-take, he could miss that main chance to bring all of Louisiana into a new era of progress.

If that rare opportunity afforded by a mandate seized at floodtide is somehow missed, Edwards will be remembered as an extraordinarily popular if controversial governor. But he will also be marked as only another manifestation of a political schizophrenia that has seen the state swap a Long for a Jones or a Kennon for a Long or an Edwards for a Treen.

But with the eye of history on him, Edwards may find the economic, political and moral restraint that will complement his undisputed brilliance and charisma. If *that* happens, move over, Huey, and make room for Edwin Edwards and the Cajun Restoration.

On "Discovering" Jim Brown

April 21, 1985

When Jim Brown was born forty-four years ago, I bet his father handed out Jimmy-for-governor bumper stickers instead of cigars. Jim suffered from PPCB—premature political crib birth. It's a lifetime affliction, as common in Louisiana as flu, flea markets and grand jury investigations.

That's why it is somehow odd to read that, hey, old Jim is running for governor. *Of course* he is. He has been running for the

ON "DISCOVERING" JIM BROWN

Big Job, pretty much by his own admission, ever since starting to practice politics and law in Ferriday some seventeen years ago.

The difference is that, with Gov. Edwin Edwards and Lt. Gov. Bobby Freeman being investigated by federal grand juries, the press pays more attention to our secretary of state. He's just a couple of heartbeats away from Huey's house. It could happen in a true-bill second.

Not that Jim Brown is taking any pleasure in Edwin's pain. Not much, anyway. Brown has been investigated himself. But the secretary of state is telling the absolute truth when he says, "I'm not doing anything differently."

Brown has been blitzing the whole sixty-four parish ball of wax ever since he was elected to the No. 3 state position in 1979. He freely, joyfully admits it. "I was acting the same way when Edwards was at the peak of his popularity," Brown says over the telephone.

It's the same rapid-fire, Yankee-tinted voice that I first heard during the Fifth District Congressional campaign of 1978. But now Brown is talking from Baton Rouge, saying that "I'm not calculatedly using my position for political purposes, but my job happens to be a political plus."

Again, Brown says his activity isn't aimed at Edwards. "I discount rumors (of indictment) against him." But he candidly leaves no doubt about his desire for the Big Job.

"I happen to be an active secretary of state. I am doing my job, but it's a good scenario if you want to be governor. I can't help it if Henson Moore (Republican Congressman from Baton Rouge, also rumored as a gubernatorial candidate) is in Washington." I suspect a smile in the secretary of state's voice.

It's a voice easily recognized, again, from the '78 battle between Brown and Jerry Huckaby, which I covered for *The Times*. Brown told me even then, with no reluctance at all, that his eye was fixed on the Mansion "in the proper time frame."

There was a detour when he underrated the low-key but lethal Huckaby that hot congressional summer of '78 and got hammered. However, the hard-running Brown was soon back on track as secretary of state, elected in 1979 and unopposed in 1983.

Now the "proper time frame" for the unforgotten gubernatorial bid may have arrived. But that ultimate goal, never a secret with this tall, lanky former long-distance athlete (he's still a fitness nut), makes some people mad. And I'm not necessarily talking about Edwin Edwards.

While covering the Brown-Huckaby race, I often heard that Brown was egotistical, pushy and ambitious. I've never exactly understood that criticism of Jim Brown. For if political ambition is a sin in Louisiana, then this state will require the largest dispensation since Babylon burned.

Brown is ambitious. He's also aggressive, articulate and—even his detractors admit—damned smart. I never found him arrogant. And I think he's performed well at the legislative and administrative levels, ambitious or not.

While representing his state senatorial district, a huge sprawl of six parishes, Brown authored the Louisiana Open Meetings Law and the Louisiana Architect Selection Act—both important pieces of reform legislation.

Brown *is* a busy, efficient and effective secretary of state. He has computerized the office, unclogged the election-night information flow, and given Louisiana a chance to save its disappearing heritage with an Archives Building and oral history programs.

In the jargon of journalism, Brown is a good interview; straightforward, accessible, engaging if somewhat programmed. He wouldn't want me to say this, probably, but there is something Kennedyesque about Brown. Maybe it's those literature courses at England's Cambridge University that came before the law degree.

He was, after all, an English major. Charles Dickens, he told me during the congressional campaign, is his favorite author. Besides Cambridge, he has been schooled in the Midwest, at the

ON "DISCOVERING" JIM BROWN

University of North Carolina and at Tulane. He reads; he wants to write a novel.

But Brown acknowledged all this, in that lost race of six years ago, with a reluctant, almost rueful smile. Louisiana, he knows, is more attuned to *Tobacco Road* than to *A Tale of Two Cities*. A slightly Yankee inflection won't impress Claiborne Parish.

Brown almost physically pulls away from the word "liberal," though it comes to mind when I think of him. He prefers to be called a "practical progressive." Populism Louisiana can swallow—or could, when an ample oil chaser was available. "Liberal" is a castor-oil word around here.

I don't know for sure if Brown is a liberal, a "practical progressive" or another populist, but these are my impressions of him—gathered mostly while covering one brief congressional race:

He was relaxed during those times; so relaxed that, during an interview at his Monroe headquarters, he fell out of an improvised couch of three chairs and busted his tail. "Don't put that in *The Times*," he said then.

The casual if calculated Brown, sleeves rolled up to the elbow, tie at half-mast, hair fashionably shaggy, contrasted with the tense, chain-smoking Huckaby in the summer of '78. But Huckaby, as noted, far outpaced Brown in that race—a defeat in Brown's supposed North Louisiana stronghold that potential supporters will eventually remember and question.

Still, Brown is the indefatigable long-distance runner who made the United States track team in 1962; the finish-line for him stops only at the Mansion. If a grand jury does a Zola Budd on Edwards and if Freeman falls down too, Cambridge could jog right on into the big house and the Big Job.

Naturally, Brown says—one more time—that he wishes no federal foot on Edwin's heel. But he's running anyway—for 1987. By that time, in the Brown scenario, Edwin will be sixty years old and tired of ruling. The track will be open for Jim Brown, who has stayed in shape for the great Louisiana marathon that is the governor's race.

We shall see. Meanwhile, I agree with New Orleans *Times-Picayune* columnist Iris Kelso that "should Brown ever become governor of Louisiana, he would be a completely new kind of governor—an intellectual, sort of, a fitness buff, a loose and easy kind of politician."

Huey's Ghost: Where It Led

September 8, 1985

The fiftieth anniversary of Huey Long's death arrives Tuesday. In researching the Kingfish for an earlier perspective in *The Times Sunday Magazine*, I was struck most by the Great Schism still dividing Louisiana after all this time.

Was the First Long a hero or an early Hitler? The question remains unresolved, the schism unbridged, even in the cooler hindsight of a half-century of historical speculation.

Indeed, the state remains haunted by a Long shadow of populism and polemics that extends beyond this hour—even as Huey's extraordinary political family exits the stage with son Russell Long's honored retirement from the United States Senate.

But back to the question of the original Long: Hero or Hitler? Polar extremes of judgment are involved here, and Huey is buried somewhere in between—the easy answer, of course—with his lively ghost standing, gesturing, at every looming political crossroads in Louisiana.

My own assessment is that Huey was no hero; that he planted

HUEY'S GHOST: WHERE IT LED

bad seeds that were to bloom darkly in what was called the First Hayride; that unharvested retributions, the legacy of his rule, still face the state under perhaps its last populist.

But Huey Long was no hill-country hick, mind. "A native political genius," a New York *Times* writer called him in retrospect. And for a time this Louisiana original stood a hungry nation on its ear and made a powerful president called FDR take heed.

Well, then. Well, he was a promethean politician—no denying that—who heaved Louisiana bodily into the twentieth century, bridging rivers and building roads and breaking heads to do it.

And while he was at it, he broke the back of a mint julep and magnolia establishment, a largely unmalicious but uncaring overclass of planters who had overseen Louisiana like a sugar plantation.

Those aren't my judgments; the historians of this state pretty much agree that Huey Long blew up the ruling Big House of the time—"I'm a dynamiter, I dynamite them out of my path," he said.

Then he wanted to Share the Wealth of his Louisiana vision on a larger stage. Most of those same historians don't think Huey could have beaten FDR, but FDR heard Huey out, and the man from Louisiana didn't even take his hat off in the patrician presence.

"He expanded opportunity," his son Russell has said, and I think that is true—in Louisiana and maybe in the nation. I'm not quite convinced Huey is the father of social security, but it's something to think about.

Then comes the dark part, and the cloud—in my view—holds more of the Louisiana sky than the light where Huey is concerned. That's the part about state cops invading the legislative chambers and the National Guard occupying the registrar of voter's office.

It happened, and that's the part about arrogance, about the corruption of power, and about Huey telling even his support-

HUEY'S GHOST: WHERE IT LED

ers to shut up and let him do all the shouting. That's the dark part. That's the Hitler part.

Even distinguished biographer T. Harry Williams, whose portrait pulled Huey up from hick-Hitler to hero, from the venal Willie Stark of Robert Penn Warren's novel to savior of the masses, saw that dark side of it.

"He was led on to grasp for more and more power, until finally he could not distinguish between the method and the goal, the power and the good," Professor Williams wrote.

The Big House of the planter aristocracy was gone. Huey brought the house down, in more ways than one. But then, more and more, Huey became Tennessee Williams' Big Daddy, if not a little Hitler, and he ruled the new plantation with absolute power.

That was fifty years ago, but we are talking about a Long shadow. Sure, the old line in the dust between Long and anti-Long is mostly a memory. But the Kingfish legacy lives on in Louisiana politics, an unquiet ghost, still spreading more darkness than light.

It's a legacy of political polarization, with the populists undone by their own excesses and the "good government" guys—"the little boy blues," as Huey's brother Earl called them—unable to govern.

Divided, polarized Louisiana has spent Huey's petrodollars without direction, failing to secure its financial future, falling from "the embarrassment of riches," pronounced by one legislator, to near poverty.

So we have, long after Huey, a legacy of great stirrings mixed with scandal, of wild popularity and sudden disgrace, of kingly glory and grand juries, of an expensive oil and gas habit that made the state safe for populist excess—until now.

Now, the well has almost literally gone dry, leaving economy and education stranded and shaky, and Louisiana's last populist—I imagine—is conjuring with Huey's ghost, and wondering where it led him, and where it led all of us.

Earl: "Boy, I'm Gonna Give You a Scoop"

April 6, 1986

(Here is my own view of Earl Long. A green cub reporter, I talked to him at the Ruston home of Mrs. Stewart Hunt in July of 1959. Using notes taken at the time, I wrote an account of that interview and a later talk with Long for *The Times Sunday Magazine* twenty years ago this month. It still sums up my feeling about Uncle Earl).

For days Earl Kemp Long had been dodging flying squads of newsmen on dusty North Louisiana roads, even out-scrambling one carload of journalists in a tire-burning encounter in the middle of Winnfield that had his honor, the governor, stretching half out of his car window yelling insults at his pursuers.

That was early spring of 1959, only days before the governor smashed his nerves and his gubernatorial hopes against a rebellious Legislature. But that was in the future. Those early spring days Uncle Earl was telling everybody but newspaper reporters that he was going to run for governor again in spite of the state constitution, which at that time forbade back-to-back terms.

On the fifth day of May, 1959, still ahead of the newshounds, the governor zoomed into my town, Ruston, to ride in a parade. There were plenty of people around because Ruston was celebrating its 100th birthday. Uncle Earl had seen the festival as a chance to do some early stumping and came a-running.

I was sneaking a nap in the cool of the photography darkroom when the city desk telephone rang that day. The caller had wonderful, sleep-killing news. Earl Long would speak privately to a reporter (I was the only one around and I was only a journalism major on summer duty on the *Ruston Leader*) at the home of his sister, Mrs. Stewart Hunt.

EARL: "BOY, I'M GONNA GIVE YOU A SCOOP"

It was the kind of a break green young journalists dream about, and in something less than three minutes and a couple of violated red lights I could make out Mrs. Hunt's fine white home, standing amid magnolias and oak at the very end of Ruston's North Vienna Street.

Somewhat trembly in the legs, I alighted and looked over the governor's parked car, a long, black Cadillac covered with red dust accumulated on hill roads. Husky-looking men in black suits, bodyguards for the governor I guessed, prowled the oak-shielded backyard, telling dirty jokes and drinking whiskey out of paper cups. One of them went into the house and told the governor that the "press" had arrived.

Earl Long came out of the back door in a shambling walk, dismissed his entourage, and motioned me into the Cadillac. He looked younger to me than in his pictures, with fat, pink cheeks and a prominent middle.

His white suit was slightly soiled. It came to my undergraduate consciousness that this governor of Louisiana might have stepped right out of a William Faulkner novel—or, more accurately, out of Erskine Caldwell's *Tobacco Road*.

As he turned to look at me the governor's eyes had the politician's unseeing glaze, but they focused when he realized his interviewer was a nervous kid in T-shirt and khakis. He slammed the car door shut and relaxed, putting his feet up on the dashboard. His untied shoelaces dangled.

I was tongue-tied at this first encounter with a governor, not just any governor, but Earl Long, and there was an interminable silence as he yawned while I fidgeted. He spoke first:

"That paper you work for, kid (he was talking about the Ruston *Daily Leader*), you know I could hold that thing up just chest-high and drop it and before it hit the ground I could read everything in it."

I didn't know exactly how to take that, but the governor cut loose a thunderous laugh and gave me a real belt in the ribs. Then I laughed, pencil still poised.

"Uncle Earl."

EARL: "BOY, I'M GONNA GIVE YOU A SCOOP"

To establish my identity with this larger-than-life character, I ventured that C. E. (Cap) Barham, former lieutenant governor and a man Long was sure to know, was my uncle. Uncle Earl thought about that for a moment and then said quite seriously that he wanted me to tell him something.

"How does your Uncle Cap manage," he said with just a trace of a smile, "to talk out of both sides of his mouth and whistle out of the middle at the same time?" He followed this blast with another whack at my mid-section.

The governor was talking about a much-admired uncle of mine, but somehow I couldn't take offense the way he was grinning at me. And besides, he was the governor and I was in his car.

But at the moment all I had for this interview that was going to shake the world were insults for my uncle and my newspaper and some aching ribs—none of which was going to thrill the wire services. So I steered the talk to politics.

Was he really going to run for governor? Yes, he definitely was going to run. He was running now; Ruston today was the start. But what about the state constitution? Long waved his finger in my face.

"Don't you ever let anybody tell you that Uncle Earl doesn't have the right to be governor again," he roared, looking like a rumpled, overweight eagle. "I'm gonna fix that second-term law," he said, with conviction.

What he had in mind was resigning before his second term ran out and getting around the constitution that way. It wasn't going to work out, but neither of us knew that then.

All of a sudden the governor grabbed my arm in a vise-like grip. "Boy," he said, "I'm gonna give you a scoop. You know what a scoop is?" I nodded, notepad at the ready, and took another shot to the ribs without flinching.

The scoop Uncle Earl had for me, which was pretty good news at the time, was his proposed ticket for the 1960 election. He named Sidney McCrory for commissioner of agriculture, C. J. Dugas for auditor and A. P. Tugwell for treasurer.

I mentioned then that there was a lot of anti-Long talk in the state and named Leander Perez, the Plaquemines Parish political boss, as one of his announced critics. Uncle Earl's mouth turned down at the corners. "Leander Pe-rez," he pronounced, with consumate scorn, looking genuinely cross this time.

"Pe-rez" he went on, "is the sorriest, no goodest, most unscrupulous grafter in the state." This seemed to take some of the steam out of the governor, and he reached into his coat pockets and came out with stacks of silver dollars.

Lining the cartwheels on the dashboard like soldiers, the governor remarked that the crowds liked getting these dollars better than candy. "I'd scatter 'em," he said. "And they grab 'em."

I wondered if he was going to give me one. I would have thought of it as a souvenir. But he didn't offer.

"How about segregation?" I asked. Some of his opponents were saying that he wasn't a strong enough segregationist. "I am 100-million percent segregation!" It was a shout aimed out his window at nobody in particular.

"But," he said in a softer tone, grinning at me, "I am also the best friend a Negro ever had."

"We won't have any problems," he said, "if the smark alecks, the NAACP and the Communists will just leave us alone." Then he commanded me: "Write that down. Get that down about the NAACP and the Communists." I complied.

Then he addressed a question to me: "Do you think I ever did a dishonest deed?" His eyes glinted. I didn't know if he wanted me to answer or not. The governor answered for me, eyes raised skyward.

"If I ever did a crooked thing may God strike me down right here, right now, in this car." Eyes cocked, grinning at each other, we waited a moment in silence.

The governor then ended the interview on an odd note. He simply leaned forward, putting all his weight on the horn and

EARL: "BOY, I'M GONNA GIVE YOU A SCOOP"

closing his eyes. The noise blasted through the quiet spring air and black-suited men came exploding out the back door. Then Earl Long was gone, headed south, waving at me from the back seat.

That was not the last time I saw Earl Long, though later I was to wish it had been the last. It was much later. He had been in and out of a state mental hospital, lost a race for lieutenant governor, and made national headlines with a really wild-west vacation.

I caught him as he emerged from that same house in Ruston. "I thought all you reporters was gone," he said wearily, not breaking his stride toward the waiting black automobile. The former governor's face had the pallor of clay; his cheeks were sunken; his collar flapped around his neck.

Suddenly he took me in. "How are you, Hilburn?" he said. He remembered me. He won a vote there, too, if I'd been old enough. But I wasn't ever going to get the chance.

"How do you feel?" was all I could ask. Still walking, he replied: "Fine, fine. But tired."

He looked very tired. Nobody could tell me that last time I saw Earl Long that he could ever manage another political campaign. But he did, and he won a seat in Congress. That victory killed him. But I can still see him, on the road, waving at me from the back seat of his Cadillac.

PART THREE

SOME PERSONAL THINGS

Mr. Bronson:
Rights and Wrongs

July 2, 1978

William Bronson, president and publisher of The Shreveport *Times*, is gone now. But that day, maybe a dozen years ago, Mr. Bronson was very much alive. I had been summoned to his office, and the omens were not good.

An attorney by profession, a publisher in daily practice, Mr. Bronson made himself understood with a scalpel-like economy of words that would have been the envy of any professor of journalism.

He motioned me into a chair, tossed over a page proof, and pointed in the direction of the masthead of the newspaper—a sort of statement of purpose, together with the officers and editors of *The Times*, which was then located in a corner of the editorial page.

"Read the masthead," Mr. Bronson said. I read it. Nothing registered wrong. It was the same every day. I looked up. Mr. Bronson was capable of a face-splitting smile. He wasn't smiling. Another bad omen.

Approaching the ragged edge of desperation, I read the masthead one more time, concentrating mightily. Then the offending phrase hit me like a stiff right uppercut to the chin.

"*The Times*," it read, "supports what it believes to be wrong and opposes what it believes to be right."

My mind reeled; the phrase, a reversed statement of *The Times* editorial credo, could have been running for days, even for weeks. Then I noticed Mr. Bronson was leaning back in his chair, watching me. That broad smile was beginning to assert itself.

"This is almost as bad as the time you identified Winston Churchill as 'first lord of Irish Potatoes' in our 'In Past Times' column." Mr. Bronson knew I was responsible for "In Past Times," but I didn't think he had caught that transposed boner. He had. My only life raft was the smile. It was growing.

He came back to the masthead reversal. "I always thought our masthead was a little pompous," he said. The grin widened, "And some people, when they read this, will probably think we are finally telling the truth about ourselves." The grin was almost full-masted now.

"But I don't believe this is the way we want to change it," he said. "Do you?" I assured him I didn't. That afternoon *The Times* masthead was cast in zinc. If a large stone had been available on Lake Street, that masthead would have been carved into it, too.

End of
The World—Almost

August 13, 1978

It was the time *The World* almost stopped—in Monroe, at least. It started when I oversold myself to The Monroe *Morning World*

END OF THE WORLD—ALMOST

newspaper. I had to have that job. So I told them I could do anything on a newspaper. Anything.

Married on Friday night, I took on the "anything" the following Monday. The message was that the managing editor and wire editor were on vacation. So the big middle desk up front in the newsroom was mine. It was, for all practical purposes, my job to get out the paper.

At first everything went well. Or so it seemed. My front page looked nice. Early reservations melted. The ax fell around 11:00 P.M. when the composing room foreman called and asked with a casual malice how I proposed to fill up about twenty open pages of a forty-page newspaper in a half-hour or so.

All the local copy was gone—edited, slugged and gone. The wire service flow had died down to a trickle, and I had killed out the surplus, which was on tape. I wanted a neat desk, and that tape kept piling up. So. Thirty minutes to fill up half the paper, and nothing to fill it with.

My first thought was to dump it all and flee, right at that moment, to Florida. I don't know why I thought of Florida, but I did. Then I remembered my new bride in that garage apartment on North Fourth Street. My arms began to ache terribly. I was sure it was a heart attack. For the first time in eighty-five years The Monroe *Morning World* was not going to publish, and I was dying, ruined professionally, at that desk.

The total panic and paralysis must have lasted about two minutes or, for me, a lifetime and a heart attack. When the shock lifted a little, I began a furious search for something to fill up half *The World*. Every reporter's desk was searched; every editor's drawer emptied. Zero.

Finally, in a corner of the room, I found a huge pile of recipes. In a matter of minutes, I packed whole pages with them. We got the paper out. Then I went home and told Ellen to pack; that the next morning's *World* was mostly beef stroganoff and lemon meringue pie and a hundred other things; that I would be summarily fired, if not executed on the railroad tracks outside the paper, the following day.

The next day I entered the side door and immediately encountered Jack Gates, who was then the executive editor. Here it comes, I thought. "Well," Jack greeted me, "you came to us on good recommendations, but to put out a special cooking edition your first day on the job . . . and nobody told you to. That's enterprise."

I caught my breath. "Well, uh, I thought it might be a little change, you know, uh . . ." Later, of course, I confessed. Much later. And the other day when I walked into *The World* newsroom, fifteen years after that arm-aching night, veteran managing editor Jimmy Hatten pointed to that middle desk. "That's the cooking editor's desk," he said. For me, it was the night *The World* almost stopped.

Football: For the Losers

August 27, 1978

It's happening on a thousand sun-blistered high school practice fields. Though the temperature would deny it, that autumnal madness known as football has already seized the season. Some of the freshmen, though mainly new to the game, will seem born to it.

Already, in the last of the pre-season drills, they leap gracefully for the errant pass and drill home tackles and blocks on driving legs. It is not easy for them, this elite; they grunt and perspire and the coaches growl at them. Yet, they still slide al-

FOOTBALL: FOR THE LOSERS

most effortlessly into the violent cadence of the sport; this is, literally, their turf.

This column is not for them.

This column is not even for the athletes who, while not greatly gifted, will still achieve the marginal reward of varsity status and even actually wear the prized letter jacket in high school halls.

This column is for the losers.

It is written for the non-athlete who for some desperate reason "goes out"—that's what it is called, "going out"—for the team. I know about that. I was a loser—the ragged fringe of the fringe, the worst of the worst. Of course, I knew that long before the first practice.

And how do you know that the skills are lacking even if the will is there? You know. Oh, you know. Kids start "choosing up" for recess games in the first grade; I was always chosen last. "You get him," somebody would always say.

In kid league baseball, the coach invariably put me in right field. If your kid is playing right field in Little League, don't bet on a college baseball scholarship; there isn't much activity out there. The budding baby stars pitch and play the infield. I lived in right field for a half dozen uneasy summers.

I weighed 119 pounds throughout high school. I got sick of writing that puny "119" into all the health forms we had to fill out; sometimes I lied and upped my weight to 140 pounds.

Given this background, the next question is why I even attempted high school varsity football. The answer is simple. My dad was an athlete, and a good one. He was all state in football, and his friends would inevitably remark on that to me, "Hey, a chip off the old football block," they would say.

A lithe 180-pounder, Daddy scored six touchdowns in one game, got his name written on the side of a new stadium for his exploits, and once led Ruston High School into the State Championship game against Byrd in State Fair Stadium.

Actually, he didn't care if I "went out" for sports or not. But I only learned that later. Like a lot of kids, I made the wrong assumption. So there I was the fall of my freshman year—stumbling and staggering around the cratered moonscape, the converted gravel pit Ruston High uses for a football practice field.

It was unmitigated hell. The athletes had sixth hour study hall free for football and during fifth hour I never failed to develop what felt like two degrees of fever. I was so uncoordinated that even getting into all the paraphernalia of the uniform was a problem. My pads stuck out in all the wrong places like cancerous growths.

The hitting wasn't bad, but on impact I went down like one of those dynamited buildings on the television commercial: total, sprawling, bone-shattering collapse. Once I actually tackled Reggie French, a naturally talented halfback, but he dragged me far downfield. When everything went black I imagined concussive blindness but as it happened Reggie had only jammed my helmet down over my eyes.

Using the Notre Dame box, an offensive formation as archaic as the Holy Roman Empire, L. J. "Hoss" Garrett and R. W. "Moose" Phillips had produced a legend of victories and championships at Ruston High. Alas, my slow-moving 119-pound body was beyond even their fundamentalist redemption.

It took the ultimate humiliation, however, to decide me on a life without football. As a freshman, I was eventually assigned to the "pee-wee" team. We played one game, won it something like 82-0, and I was the only player (I swear) not to make it into the slaughter.

Actually, one of the coaches lifted my head and asked me what position I played. It was near the end of the game and by that time I had receded into total depression. I couldn't think of my position (it was right guard; I was a 119-pound right guard).

The dressing room after that game was a cauldron of noise, and my clean uniform was a badge of total dishonor. I would have sacrificed four years of my life for a grass stain. I didn't shower. I didn't deserve a shower. No sweat.

I sneaked out of the locker room and kept to the back streets en route to my grandparents' home on Alabama Street. I was afraid headlights from some car departing the game would illuminate me and the people inside would shake their heads and say: "There is that poor little Hilburn kid, the only one who didn't play."

I lied to my folks that I had gotten in for two plays, and lasted out the season. It turned out, as I said, that Daddy knew all the time I wasn't Olympic material—some kind of genetic skip—and he didn't mind a bit. That knowledge helped.

Later revelations, such as the fact that even non-football players could occasionally get a date, further eased the pain. Later in high school I wrote sports for the Ruston *Daily Leader* and even the big stars spoke respectfully to me.

Of course, I never got that letter jacket, and what ABC describes rather hysterically as the "thrill of victory and the agony of defeat" remains something of a mystery to me. But I do serve today on the Louisiana Tech Athletic Council where Bulldog Coach Maxie Lambright has the opportunity to ask me for advice. (So far Maxie has passed up that opportunity.)

But cheer up, losers. I survived the ultimate humiliation, and my Dad's genes leaped me to land on my son Kevin. Kevin, to my amazement, makes leaping catches and has escaped the queasy oblivion of right field.

State Fair: The Four Bears

October 22, 1978

The State Fair in Shreveport was, in a way, the highlight of our high school year. The Lincoln Parish school bus was full for the

"Soon, Ellen was loaded down with four incredible teddy bears."

STATE FAIR: THE FOUR BEARS

slow, curving route down old 80 to what was for us the big city on the river. As usual, it was hot in October, but nobody cared. Some of us were in love.

The bus vibrated with laughter and catcalls and "80 Bottles of Beer on the Wall," and we rolled the windows down from the top to let the autumn air blow down the aisle. The stags played stud poker in the back. Ellen and I sat in the front. She wore a white blouse, a skirt, and loafers and white socks rolled down to her ankles. It was our day.

But nothing would be complete for any of the guys with dates unless we could win our girls something big: specifically, one of those huge teddy bears. Billy and Linda sat near us. Billy was good with girls—he could sing and play the guitar—and besides he had twenty-one dollars to win that teddy bear.

The midway broke on us in a rush: The Ruston group made one full round just staring at people. Then it was down to serious business: One of those booths hung from end to end with monstrous teddy bears. The idea, at this particular place, was to roll so many balls into a chute.

Before we even started, one of the ladies running the booth called me aside. Dark hair clung to her face; she was hot. "Would you please get me a Coke?" she asked. "I can't leave this place and my throat is parched." The lady looked formidable to me; all bone and sinew and dyed hair and dirty jeans.

So I said yes to the woman—my mind screaming no all the time. I had to leave the line and walk what seemed a half-mile to get the Coke and pay for it with my own money. The lady had not offered to pay and it didn't seem gentlemanly at the time to ask. But I was boiling mad—at her, and even more at myself.

"Well, Hilburn, you weren't at the Shreveport fair for five minutes before some old carney lady fixed on you as country sucker bait," I thought furiously to myself, bringing the Coke back down the dusty midway. "Nobody at this whole fair would be so stupid," I told myself, seething. "Not only do you let them take your money. You buy them Cokes. Fool!"

STATE FAIR: THE FOUR BEARS

Returning, I thrust the Coke into the lady's hand. "Let's try here," I said, hoping nobody had noticed my fool's errand. Nobody had. The game at this booth looked impossible, but on the very first try it developed that I had an instinctive, athletic (quite unusual for me) skill at this thing of rolling balls into a chute.

I took careful aim, and the balls plopped right into the winning receptacle. I won a teddy bear! Billy, losing, looked at me with a new respect. Ellen was thrilled. Then it was as if I had caught fire: a pitcher throwing a no-hitter; a quarterback hitting completion after completion. Before long I won a second teddy bear.

People began to gather around the booth to watch this new Ruston High School phenomenon. I aimed, feeling a great and growing new power, and the balls flew home into the winning chute as if guided by radar. I swelled and swaggered. Two people asked me to try for them. I refused—imperiously.

Billy had given up and gone to the next booth. He was mad at me and losing money fast. His date looked impatient and disappointed. My ability at this game seemed to mount. I imagined myself a Sandy Koufax. Ellen was hugging my arm, congratulating me. It was a heady experience for somebody who always came in last, even at miniature golf. The third teddy bear was deposited in Ellen's arms. She was going crazy.

Old Billy had disappeared down the midway. His girl was empty-handed. Later I was secretly delighted to learn he had blown the entire twenty-one dollar wad and all Linda had to show for it was a tiny plastic duck. I had invested less than two dollars and already Ellen had three glorious teddy bears. People watched me with amazement and tried to copy my style. Once more I guided the ball into the winning chute. Soon, Ellen was loaded down with four incredible teddy bears.

It was only on the trip back to Ruston, with Ellen hanging on to me and four teddy bears, and Billy and Linda sulking in back of us, that it dawned on me that the lady for whom I had purchased that Coke had tossed me a look, just a slightly upraised eyebrow, as we left her booth—rich with four teddy bears.

So that was it! It didn't matter much that I wasn't a Sandy Koufax after all. I knew that anyway. The important thing was that the Shreveport State Fair had exceeded my wildest expectations. I had Ellen and four teddy bears.

Anne Marie has the teddy bears now, but I've still got Ellen. I'll always think I won her as well as those bears right there at the Shreveport Fair. As a matter of fact, I still like the State Fair.

See you there—and if a lady at one of those booths asks you for a Coke . . .

Ange, Barn, Op and Aunt Bee

March 4, 1979

The lecture, I thought, was going well. Caught up in a totally unwarranted sense of power, I pranced up and down in front of the class, jangling my pocket change and feeling very professorial—before tripping over a chair.

Recovering, embarrassed, taken down a peg, I pointed to myself and said to the students: "Meet Barney Fife!" The class cheered. They understood. They KNEW Barney Fife.

Indeed, generations of people identify with Andy, Barney, Opie, Aunt Bee, Otis, Gomer, Goober, Thelma Lou, Helen, Floyd, Juanita, Clara and the whole cast of characters of the old "Andy Griffith Show."

Actually, the show was a hit more than ten years ago, but it has survived—and won its college recruits—through re-runs on several area television stations.

It was Griffith's show, of course. But Don Knotts as Deputy Fife quickly established himself as one of the supreme second bananas after Griffith's broad "big orange drink" characterization failed to generate much momentum in the early episodes.

Not that Griffith was bad as Sheriff Andy Taylor. Sensing something was happening, he became more serious, narrowed his range, and provided the perfect, low-key straight man for Knotts. In fact, Knotts' talent was burned up in the total spotlight turned on his frail frame by directors of his later movies.

Anyway, Barney (Knotts) made the TV series with his plastic face, incredible ego and enormous insecurities. Easily inflated, just as easily punctured, terribly opinionated and just as vulnerable, Barney was the everyman—the child—who resides somewhere in every consciousness. That's why Mayberry, the fictional North Carolina town that was the setting for the show, remains remarkably fresh in syndication today while other sitcoms are hopelessly dated.

Two segments, while they don't make it in print without Barney's pinched mouth and bulging eyes, suggest something of the theme and tone of the show.

Barney is explaining to little Opie, at first very confidently, the fate of dogs turned loose in the country during a severe electrical storm:

"Now, Op, you don't have to worry about those dogs. They know how to take care of themselves. And that little pup, don't you worry about him. They'll take care of him."

There follows an enormous crack of thunder, and as usual Barney's certainty begins to falter a little.

"And lightning. You don't have to worry about that. Dogs are low to the ground, so they never get hit by lightning. They're not like giraffes. Giraffes are tall. They're really up there. But dogs—they're short, so they never get hit. And that little feller. They'll take care of him. Dogs take care of their own. They're not like giraffes."

There is another crack of thunder, a pause, and Barney cracks. "Giraffes are so selfish, always looking out for old number one."

Something about the show also reminded me of the movie *Marty*. As when, sitting on Andy's porch, Barney yawns and says: "Know what I think I'll do?" He doesn't wait for Andy to answer.

"I think I'll go down to the diner, get a little ice cream, take a walk over to Thelma Lou's, watch a little television, then go home and go to bed."

"Yep, that's what I'll do, all right. Go down to the diner, get a little ice cream, take a walk over to Thelma Lou's, watch a little television and go home and go to bed."

Yeah, we are all Barney at times. It happened to me again just the other day. A student stopped me on the Tech campus. "Yes," I answered, wondering what this was all about.

"Well," he said, "I read your column every Sunday in The Shreveport *Times*," and went on to say some generous things about "Fragments." As he talked, I began to get very serious, swelling, feeling very important.

In fact, I was Barney Fife half-way across to Keeny Hall before nearly toppling into the Lady of the Mist fountain and returning, with a laugh, to reality.

Watch it, Barn, I told myself.

Come, Let Us Reason Together

July 29, 1979

Maybe it was because Lyndon Baines Johnson, in his pre-Vietnam presidential prime, was forever saying, "Let us reason together." Anyway, I joined a group of men, uninvited, in a Shreveport tavern because they were talking about an editorial I had written.

They had that morning's Shreveport *Times* editorial page spread out on a table and, from the tone of the discussion, it was obvious that they did not agree with what was printed there. The temptation to clarify, to explain whatever objections they had to the paper's position was irresistible.

I should have known better, though, no matter how strong the temptation. This place was an occasional stop on my way home from the *Times* Building because it was convenient. Nobody ever spoke to me there except a thin-faced man who usually sat in a back booth. We were both outside the circle—whatever circle it was—that came to this place regularly.

It wasn't much of an establishment, to be honest. The grafitti in the men's restroom would attest to that. "Has there ever been a good-lookin' woman in this place?" implored one scrawl. Another writer had crayoned "Medicare Bar" on the wall.

But I shouldered into the group, forgetting my non-person status for the moment. After all, they were criticizing my editorial. It was one of a series running at the time on railroad featherbedding: the practice of unions adding more men to the crew than actually were needed. *The Times* was against it, and I wanted to explain that stand to these fellows, whoever they were.

However, it became swiftly apparent that this was not to be the sort of friendly seminar I had engaged in during LSU graduate school days or even an informal debate where both sides offered up their points. The opposition shouted down my arguments, and when I inadvertently let it slip that I had actually written the offending piece (editorials represent the opinion of the newspaper and so are not individually signed), things got out of control.

A beer mug cleared my ear by a fraction of an inch. The table, summarily rejecting *The Times* editorial page and assorted glasses and cans, began to rise up hugely in my face, as if in slow motion. Angry red faces loomed out of the semi-darkness.

It was at that point that the bartender and the thin-faced man hustled me away, indignity of indignity, to the women's restroom and I was locked out of the battlefield. "Didn't you know this is a retired railroad men's hangout?" the thin-faced man threw at me as he secured the door.

Hearing sirens a moment later, I peeked out to see a couple of Shreveport's finest escorting one of the men out of the tavern. He saw me looking and yelled: "And don't even put my g-d obituary in your g-d newspaper."

So much for reasoning together. So much for Lyndon Johnson. And as far as I'm concerned, they can run the railroad any way they please.

Saturday Afternoons at the Dixie

August 26, 1979

The undersides of the seats were ridged with generations of totally chewed-out Double Bubble gum and Dentyne. The sloping floor was slick with spilled Cokes and Pepsis. The incongruously magnificent chandelier, dangling from the high ceiling, seemed to sway dangerously in a non-existent draft and nobody would sit under it.

But that didn't matter. This was the Dixie Theater in Ruston and most of us grew up in those dark confines on Saturday afternoons that seemed to never end. We cheered Roy Rogers and hissed the sinister-looking, white-haired man who always played the villain.

SATURDAY AFTERNOONS AT THE DIXIE

Republic Pictures used the same ranch house in every picture and even the same interiors, too. We hated it when Roy sang "Tumbling Tumbleweed" in front of a fake fire or flirted circumspectly with Dale Evans.

Even the trails and boulders and trees were the same in every cowboy movie, but we didn't care. The actors did change and we had our favorites. Roy and Gabby Hayes topped the list for a long time, but my favorite down at the Dixie was the black-clad, masked Durango Kid (played, I think, by somebody named Charles Starrett).

In the shoot-'em-up Western pecking order, Johnny Mack Brown was considered a star of the second magnitude because he had a noticeable paunch. It was rumored that Brown had visited Ruston once, but that didn't make any difference. He was fat. Lash LaRue also came to Lincoln Parish once, but he wasn't very high on my list either. For some reason I never could trust Lash.

We had sort of a pecking order, a Dixie caste system, ourselves. The rich kids went to the bakery located right next door and came into the movie with grease-spotted white sacks filled with delicious-smelling doughnuts.

The others survived with a sack (ten cents) or a box (twenty cents) of popcorn. It only cost nine cents to get into the Dixie then, and even if all you had was a dime there was a penny left for a single caramel from the big glass container in the lobby.

Doughnuts or popcorn or single caramel, nobody wanted to be late for the ceremonial curtain-raising (they always started the movie before the curtain went up and we all thought that was real class) because the serial was *The Purple Monster*. Invariably the hero had been left presumably buried in a monumental rockslide (on the same Hollywood hills where the Western actors rode).

As the Saturday afternoons passed, we graduated to the Seventh Cavalry, noble Indians (Cochise was played by Jeff Chandler) and a thriller called *The Thing*. It was costing us forty-one cents now, but there was some smooching up in the balcony to make up for inflation.

Later it became a rite of passage to strip down to your undershorts, sneak down the alley by Grady Harrison's filling station, and enter the cobwebby exit door at the side of the Dixie—from there to run, whooping and yelling, across the back of the screen while the audience applauded wildly and the manager called the police.

We always emerged from the theater, blinking in the Saturday afternoon sunlight, bleary-eyed, most of us walking home afterward, not even dreaming that the old Dixie was a part of growing-up that our own kids would never share—and not caring either.

He Fired Me Three Times . . . and I Deserved It

January 27, 1980

I held the telephone away from my ear. The engineer from the State Department of Highways was screaming. "This road is not supposed to be open for six months yet!" Then he was yelling at somebody outside: "No, please, lady, the highway isn't open . . . watch that sign!"

Then the engineer was raging at me again. "I've nearly had three men run over here this afternoon and you . . ." He put the telephone down again. I could hear his muffled voice: "Don't tear that barricade down . . . this road is not . . ."

I had announced in the Ruston *Daily Leader* that afternoon the

HE FIRED ME THREE TIMES . . . AND I DESERVED IT

opening of a twenty-mile strip of Interstate 20. It was my mistake, and a bad one. The road, as the harassed engineer had informed me, wouldn't be open for six months yet.

Of course, *Leader* publisher Clarence Faulk fired me for that disaster. He was to fire me twice more in my cub reporter career at the hometown daily newspaper, and in all three cases I richly deserved it. In each instance, however, I was rehired within hours, partly because Mr. Faulk couldn't find somebody else that quickly and partly (I have always thought) because Mrs. Faulk intervened on my behalf.

What brings these first-job impressions to mind is a recent article in *UPI Reporter* where senior editor H. D. "Doc" Quigg marked fifty years in journalism with reflections on his initial employment at a small Missouri daily.

"We had one reporter, one city editor, one secretary who in addition to her regular duties took down in shorthand the telephoned news report from United Press twice a day, three linotypes, and one flatbed press," Mr. Quigg wrote.

That was approximately our situation at the *Leader*. We printed on an unpredictable flatbed press, got our national news from an antiquated United Press wire, and I was the one reporter.

Mr. Faulk, my publisher, combined a shrewd business sense with a sharp eye for community news. A University of Missouri journalism graduate with a long family publishing background, Clarence Faulk didn't miss much that happened in Lincoln Parish—and daily tortured me with little items I had failed to get into his paper.

It was a learning experience for me in the truest sense, and the Faulks—Mrs. Faulk was also a Missouri journalism graduate who wrote a popular column called "Grapevine" for the *Leader*—were excellent if tough teachers.

He was, as I noted, to fire me twice more. Once I completely blew all the obituaries in the old Thursday weekly *Leader*. He literally escorted me out of the newsroom by the ear, telling me en

HE FIRED ME THREE TIMES . . . AND I DESERVED IT

route that a death notice deserved more attention and care than a so-called major story.

Then, toward the end of my college years at Tech, I begged Mr. Faulk to let me edit the whole paper during the summer months when a vacancy occurred. He said all right, but it so happened that the first morning as *Leader* editor my parents were out of town and—with nobody to wake me—I overslept.

I awoke to a tap-tap-tap on my bedroom window. My publisher was standing outside, and he looked very unhappy. I couldn't hear what he was saying outside my window, but my sleepy mind easily lip-read the message: "You . . . are . . . fired." Actually, he let me come on down and get out the paper that day.

Oh, we had some times at the old *Leader*. There was the poor editor who was overwhelmed by asthma as each deadline approached; he lived with an inhaler. Distracted by the door-slamming comings and goings of a big and intimidating composing room foreman, the asthmatic editor finally hung a sign on the glass panel: "Please do not slam this door."

Within moments the foreman banged in to check on some copy and headed out, stopping thoughtfully at the editor's sign. He read it carefully, smiled evilly, and then slammed the door so hard the glass panel shattered. The editor grabbed his inhaler and disappeared out the front door.

Then there was the editor, supposedly mentioned for the Pulitzer Prize for West Texas reporting, who turned the *Leader's* page make-up upside-down. I suggested to Mr. Faulk that this man, whatever his credentials, seemed a little strange to me. The publisher demurred, telling me three stories I had missed that morning.

But when the Pulitzer Prize-mentioned editor joined the Ruston High School huddle in the middle of the game, camera and notebook in hand, Mr. Faulk agreed with the startled football players, the police and two thousand spectators that, yeah, this guy was strange.

Yes the *Leader* was a good experience for me—thanks to the

Faulks, who are now out of the publishing business but just as active in real estate. In fact, Mrs. Faulk has her own urban renewal program going in Ruston.

And I did deserve to be fired all those times, and this will serve as a written apology to the State Department of Highways for opening Interstate 20 six months early.

Was It Only a Post-Operative Hallucination?

February 10, 1980

In that deceptively euphoric moment after minor surgery there is the fuzzy comfort of having survived the operation. The inevitable pain lies somewhere down the road—not to be even considered in a recovery room bustling with attentive nurses.

That was my situation when one of the nurses came over to me. She looked at the white hospital wristband while checking my pulse: Hilburn, Wiley W., Jr., it said. I waited serenely for words of encouragement.

"I hate your guts," she hissed in my disbelieving ear.

"This must be one of those post-operative hallucinations," I told myself. "The nurse did not say, 'I hate your guts.' Hang in there, Hilburn." I closed my eyes to let the vision subside and then looked around the recovery room. I waved the nurse back.

"Pardon me," I said. "It must be the anesthesia, but I thought you said . . ." Before I could finish the sentence the nurse looked me dead in the eye.

"I hate your guts," she said. This time the nurse did not hiss.

WAS IT ONLY A POST-OPERATIVE HALLUCINATION?

In fact, she said it pretty loud—loud enough for a couple of other patients to look my way.

Checking to make sure that no life-support systems had been severed, I waited out my time in recovery, no longer serene. As they wheeled me out, I made one last effort to reach the nurse.

"I know, you hate me," I said resignedly.

"You newspaper people don't care who you hurt," she said, and her eyes said it again: "I hate your guts."

So that was it. Something I had written somewhere. Once safely liberated from Lincoln General Hospital, I tracked down the details. It had started fifteen-odd years before when a chartered plane crashed in Lincoln Parish.

The only survivor was a thirteen-year old yellow-haired girl named Virginia. A reporter for the Ruston *Daily Leader*, I was with the searchers who found her—miraculously alive and still strapped into a seat which somehow stood upright in a patch of swamp grass.

Nobody thought Virginia would live, but she fought hard, and soon it was evident that this little girl would survive. The town took Virginia to its heart after that, but Lincoln General wouldn't let her talk to reporters.

I breached hospital security, however, by swiping Dr. Henry Roane's white coat and stethoscope. That disguise got me into Virginia's room, but the nurse in charge there immediately recognized me as a reporter in doctor's clothing.

"Get out of here," she insisted.

"All I wanted to do is let my readers know Virginia is all right," I argued. "No big deal. Just a couple of paragraphs in the *Leader*." About that time Virginia spotted me. There wasn't much difference in our ages, really.

"Can you hold my hand while I take this shot?" she practically begged.

That did it. The nurse let me stay. But the "couple of paragraphs" were transformed into a very long story that not only made the *Leader*, but also turned up in *The Times* and the Monroe

WAS IT ONLY A POST-OPERATIVE HALLUCINATION?

Morning World—papers for which I also worked as a correspondent.

I never forgot Virginia, but in the news business you always go on to other stories. What I never knew, in that rush of events, was that the nurse in charge of Virginia nearly lost her job because she let me stay in the room that day.

No, I never knew what the nurse went through because of me—until fifteen or so years later when she looked at the wristband in surgical recovery and saw a name that had caused her a lot of trouble. That nurse had not forgotten nor forgiven—she hated my guts—and I don't really blame her, to tell the truth.

Edwin and Dave: I Hardly Knew You

March 9, 1980

The telephone rang in my office in the basement of Louisiana Tech's Keeny Hall. It was President F. Jay Taylor's secretary.

"The governor wants to see you in Dr. Taylor's office," she said, her voice edged with a new respect.

"But I don't know the governor," I protested politely.

Edwin Edwards was visiting the Ruston campus that day some eight years ago, but I couldn't figure out why the man himself would want to see me. We had never met, even casually.

The president's secretary was clear on the matter, though. The governor wanted to see me and so—this was very clear—Dr. Taylor wanted me to see the governor. At Tech, this is what is known as being summoned.

So I answered the summons. Sure enough, the governor was standing in the presidential office, talking to Dr. Taylor. Edwin

EDWIN AND DAVE: I HARDLY KNEW YOU

Edwards was wearing something dark and sharkskin-looking, I recall, and his face was so shiny it reflected the room's overhead light. The whole area around him seemed filled with a sort of electric radiance.

I was impressed. Jay Taylor, seeing me, stepped forward.

"Governor, this is Wiley Hilburn," Dr. Taylor said expectantly.

Edwin Edwards' eyes flicked over me, registering no sign of recognition.

A worry line furrowed Taylor's brow.

"Governor," the university president said, clearing his throat, "Wiley is chairman of the journalism department here at Tech."

The governor's eyes remained flat and noncommittal. Dr. Taylor chewed his lip but continued the struggle.

"Wiley," he told the governor, enunciating every word, "is also director of our news bureau."

It was obvious, after that, that Edwards had never heard of me—and, what's more, that the governor was wondering rather impatiently why he had been matched up with a total stranger. Only a few seconds had elapsed since I had ventured into The Gubernatorial Presence, but it seemed an eternity to all concerned. The room was quiet.

Dr. Taylor gave it one more try, his voice a desperate question-mark: "Wiley writes editorials for The Shreveport *Times*?"

That last shot not only failed to establish an identification but seemed to annoy the governor, who has never cared much for editorial writers—even those he doesn't know.

At that, President Taylor abandoned the whole project and I was dismissed to the basement of Keeny Hall. It was like I had told Taylor's secretary five embarrassed minutes ago: I didn't know Edwin Edwards and he surely didn't know me.

As it turned out later, I did know the governor's press secretary of that time—Dale Thorn, who is now associate commissioner for the State Board of Regents.

We were friends, and Dale had mentioned to somebody that

he would like to see me. It somehow got misconstrued that the governor desired my company—and the rest is another worry-line in Jay Taylor's brow, a column for me on the next to the last day of the First Edwardian Era, and absolutely nothing to Edwin Edwards.

Unfortunately, my acquaintance with incoming Gov. Dave Treen is even more remote and removed than that fleeting confrontation with the departing Edwards.

Oh, I have a lot of second-hand impressions of the new governor. Treen's boiler-room crew in Lincoln Parish (Roy Fitzgerald, Rolanda Howe, Alice Herrmann and other members of the Republican Expeditionary Corps hereabouts) have a Goldwatery vision of the man: namely that he was cloned, all silver-haired, from a genetic conglomerate of George Washington, Winston Churchill and Robert E. Lee.

My own perception of Mr. Treen is more limited—confined, as it is, to one long-distance call in which we never spoke to each other. In fact, I almost did not recognize him, and I'm hoping he never caught my name.

As it happened, Shreveport *Journal* Editor Stan Tiner and I were talking shop on the telephone. All of a sudden Stan interrupted the conversation to say: "Wiley, the next governor of Louisiana just walked into my office."

"Who?" I asked over the long-distance wire. This was early in the first primary, and it was anybody's race. "You guess," came back from Stan's Shreveport office.

"Bubba Henry," I blurted from the basement of Keeny Hall. It was a statement from the heart rather than a declaration of cold political logic.

"Wrong," Stan said. "Guess again."

"Jimmy Fitzmorris," I said, going this time with the current front-runner in the polls.

In sum, it took me six names to say Treen and identify Stan's office visitor—a measure of my political unwisdom, I guess, and Tiner's ability as a seer.

"Don't tell him who I am," I said at the end of the conversation. "Too late," Stan said, laughing wickedly. "I guess Tech won't be getting much money in the next appropriation," he said.

Sorry, President Taylor. I blew it for you with two governors. And, dear readers, don't expect any scoops from this corner of *The Times* on politics at the very top: Edwin, I hardly knew, and Treen I know not at all.

Oh, well. The boys at Shipley's have all the answers, anyway.

"Uh, It Sounds Like the Tappets..."

April 13, 1980

The car was making a strange, clattering sound. But the driver crisply dismissed the problem. "It's only the tappets," he said with a magnificent certitude that amazes me now as much as it did then—some thirty years ago.

Ever since then, feeling a staggering ineptitude when it comes to all things mechanical, I have had something to say when a car engine falters: "Uh, it's only the tappets."

American Heritage Dictionary defines tappet as "a lever or projecting arm that moves or is moved by contact with another part, usually to communicate a certain motion, as between a driving mechanism and a valve."

Fine, but I still don't know the difference between a crankshaft and a tappet. Nevertheless, when any motor misses I say very knowledgeably that "it's probably the tappets." It sounds good and people nod. That guy knows what he is talking about, they think.

I don't. And it isn't only cars that confound me; it is, as I said, anything mechanical. At first this failure of mine irritated Ellen; her dad could construct one of those homemade nuclear bombs, given the directions.

It took Ellen a few months of marriage to plumb the depth of my ignorance. At first she would call me when the dryer or dishwasher broke. "Come and look at the dryer," she would say.

Facing the hard truth, I would dutifully stand in front of the ailing dryer and give it a long, searching look. "OK, I've looked at it." Then I would disappear. At first Ellen was amazed. Now she fixes whatever is broken (genes from her Dad), calls her father (he still brings a toolbox when coming to my house) or telephones the repairman.

Some charitable people say my mechanical ineptitude is only a mental block; that, if forced to do so, I could function with wrench and screwdriver. It just isn't true: Why, I can't even unlock doors.

Maybe its genetic. My own dad swears he can fix things—and truth to tell, he's better at it than me. But I remember when Mama complained that the water ran too fast out of the kitchen faucets.

With his customary self-confidence, Dad disappeared under the kitchen sink and we heard various grating noises for two hours—after which he emerged, grease-smeared and water-spattered, and boldly ordered Mama to turn on the water.

She turned on the cold tap full-on while Dad beamed. There followed this great, scraping groan which seemed to come from the very bowels of the house. Finally, one little drop fell from the faucet. Then, nothing. No water at all. I sneaked outside and fell down laughing.

Another time Mama complained that the front door handle was loose. Characteristically undeterred by the plumbing fiasco, Daddy attacked the front door. Soon he sat in the living room, surrounded by tiny screws and things, and totally confident.

"It's fixed," he announced two hours later, though I noticed

"UH, IT SOUNDS LIKE THE TAPPETS..."

he had thrown a couple of pieces of something into the hydrangea bush beside the front porch.

About that time Daddy's brother-in-law entered the living room with an amused look on his face and the whole front-door handle in his hand. Daddy left immediately, saying he had urgent business "up town."

So, maybe my mechanical disability is inherited. But only a few days ago, Ellen will have to admit, I fixed a flat tire in the carport. What she doesn't know is at first I had the jack propped up in the wrong place and that it came flying out like a projectile and nearly decapitated me.

Nevertheless, the fact that I finally did fix the flat (Ellen did stand around and offer a few suggestions) is proof that maybe it is all a mental block.

Meanwhile, if you, too, can't unlock doors, get flashlight batteries in the right order, or start an outboard motor, try saying "it's probably the tappets" the next time the family car stalls. It works.

The following excerpt from "Fragments" August 14, 1983, is a response to this column:

I slowed down. The car blocking the service road swayed back and forth, but went nowhere. It looked as though the gears were stuck. So I stopped, got out and tapped on the window of the stalled vehicle.

The lady behind the wheel rolled the window down. "Need some help?" I asked. She measured me up and down, first with recognition and then with growing frustration. "I read your column in *The Times*," she said, "and you can't fix anything mechanical."

I admitted to that, and she sent me off to a nearby service station to find somebody who could fix something.

Ah, fame.

One Wrong Turn
and I Was Lost

March 1, 1981

Ellen had carefully clipped the story out of *The Times.* "There is hope for you," she said. The article read:

"DETROIT (UPI)—Are you the type of driver who gets lost because he has trouble reading maps and road signs?

"Help may be on the way, according to RCA scientist Dr. James Vollner, who forecasts that cars may one day be equipped with electronic position indicators in much the same way that ships and planes are now. . . ."

As Ellen knows, if anybody has trouble reading maps and road signs, it's me. In fact, I have trouble on directions, period. I once took a wrong turn in Jonesboro and was totally lost for a half-hour. Nobody has ever been lost in Jackson Parish before.

That only starts it. Late one night, returning from graduate school at LSU in Baton Rouge, I somehow missed a turn and—in the wee hours—found myself exploring downtown Opelousas instead of rolling toward Ruston. Magellan I'm not.

Is Hilburn safe on Interstate 20 between Shreveport and Ruston? Nope. Headed home from a meeting at *The Times* I approached the extremely well-lighted underpass at Arcadia—and there I was, all of a sudden, taking an unscheduled tour of Mt. Lebanon and other Bienville Parish historical sites.

Invited to address the Louisiana Press Women in Baton Rouge, I crossed the Mississippi River just fine, but something went haywire and then I was re-crossing that bridge—unwillingly headed home again.

How that happened I will never know; especially since I stopped at a filling station right across the bridge for directions. I got turned around again and made it to the motel in time to talk to the Press Women, but just barely. There was nobody named

ONE WRONG TURN AND I WAS LOST

Hilburn on the Lewis and Clark expedition; that's for sure. I can't even get across the Mississippi River.

If Jackson Parish and the Mississippi River constitute uncharted territory for me, it's not difficult to imagine the trouble I have reaching any destination in New Orleans. New Orleans, in fact, remains as much of a mystery to me—after countless visits—as the back alleys of Beirut, Lebanon. I would need a bulldozer to break into the French Quarter.

The fact that I was born without a compass in my head is not lost on my friends—or my boss. Whenever Tech President F. Jay Taylor asks me to accompany him on a trip, I know he wants my company—not my driving ability. He rejects all my offers to pilot with a matter-of-fact "You'll get us lost."

Dr. Taylor has reason for this cynicism. On a trip to that same New Orleans, he once asked me to drive. He had, in fact, driven all the way from the Tech campus to New Orleans; we were safely within the city limits when he pulled over to gas up.

"Can you drive for just a couple of blocks?" he asked, getting back into the car. "I just want to take a quick look at this speech." He told me the number of an exit to take three blocks down the avenue.

I took off. "Hey," said Taylor two minutes later, looking up from his speech notes. "You are on the wrong road!" Yeah, I took the wrong exit. Actually, Dr. Taylor was only twenty minutes late for his address. I guess he took it pretty well. Now he never lets me drive.

In fact, I thought it was a little out-of-line when Taylor and Vice President George Byrnside recently waved me (I was headed for a Louisiana Press Association meeting in Alexandria) off the road on their way to a Board of Regents meeting in Baton Rouge. Grinning, they wanted to know if I was going to Shreveport.

Very funny. And the fact that I took the wrong turn on the Alexandria traffic circle on the way back from my meeting wasn't my fault. Well, it WAS raining.

VDTs Are Here, But I'll Go Down with My Typewriter

May 3, 1981

Newspapers, in case anybody out there cares, have gone electronic. After centuries of recording progress with essentially the same printing process that gave us the Gutenburg Bible, the profession has surrendered, finally and abruptly, to technology.

Even in the basement dungeons of Keeny Hall at Louisiana Tech, where generations of journalism students have pecked out their first comma-faults on ancient Underwoods, there stands a marvel of newspaper technology: a VDT.

A VDT, for those who have yet to master the robot rhetoric of technology, is a Video Display Terminal. It looks like a television set mounted on a typewriter. Don't ask me, please, to further explain—or to operate—this creature of computer science.

The creature was installed in the Tech journalism department only because a majority of U.S. editors think journalism graduates need to be "VDT-trained" (more computer corruption of the English language). Also the journalism faculty at Tech, which is completely out of control, has imposed the present and the future on me.

Still, I have a physical hatred for that lone VDT in *The Tech Talk* newsroom. The original Luddite, I smiled inwardly when it was accidentally plugged into the wrong outlet and blew its electronic brain. "A little shock treatment never hurt a VDT," I mused bitterly to myself.

Even when the Tech VDT was working, I gave it a wide berth. This amuses my students, most of whom quickly mastered the terminal—or, I prefer to think, vice-versa. "Hilburn can't even

VDTs ARE HERE, BUT I'LL GO DOWN WITH MY TYPEWRITER

scroll up and down," snickered Associate *Tech Talk* Editor Jimmy Brown.

No. I can't. When the Gannett technological van came to Tech, I was obliged to pay a ceremonial visit to the electronic Castle Frankenstein. I didn't understand anything that was said, and escaped with a migraine headache.

All this is due, of course, to my own total technical incompetence. As readers of this column know (all three of you), I have trouble unlocking doors (dead-bolts scare me) and changing lightbulbs. The electric can opener in the kitchen mocks me.

Maybe it was this incompetence that led me to the newspaper field where, twenty years ago, a literal iron-age culture prevailed. As a working reporter, the best professional time of my life, the world consisted of a Smith-Corona portable, a paste pot, a Linotype, a web press and plenty of number two pencils, preferably yellow and very sharp.

The Smith-Corona, now a quarter-century old, still has a tough, hard, *human* touch. How anybody could create a feature story on the blinking and impersonal face of a television screen, much less edit it, remains a mystery to me.

Of course, I do live in the past. I drive a 1971 Karmann Ghia. My grades for journalism classes are averaged in longhand; pocket computers, in my mind, are untrustworthy and refuse to calculate intangibles like attitude. My favorite thing in the house is an eight-day clock that I can wind. True, twice I have wound it too tightly and Ellen's daddy had to fix it.

Not that I'm waxing nostalgic or doubting the staying power of the newspaper technological revolution. Newspapers are cloning VDTs. A generation of young reporters have never heard of hot type. And my working newspaper friends tell me that computers and cold type have made things easier, quieter, quicker and cheaper. That litany makes me think, somehow, of that movie: *Invasion of the Body-Snatchers.*

The pod-people of modern journalism have prevailed, but sometimes the same editors who praise the system will, in whispers, criticize the computers when the VDT isn't listening. The computer can forget whole stories sometimes—casting them forever into the great black void of technology. Years ago, the only time we ever lost a story was when the managing editor threw it into the waste basket.

Again, the good old days of hot type were not that good. The old web press at the Ruston *Daily Leader* swallowed printers whole, we typed out stories on the back of Holsum Bread wrappers at the old Monroe *Morning World*, and the late William Bronson, publisher of *The Times*, personally ordered me to quit marking editorials to be set on the paper's last Linotype, the old "Blue Goose."

Yes, it's all for the best—this wave of newspaper technology—and I admit it. *Times* Editorial Page Editor Jim Montgomery can call up the whole world for me on his VDT. And other innovations are looming. Ron White, my associate in Tech journalism, speaks glowingly about something called "pagination." I don't listen; even the word "pagination" is a perversion of the English language. Who let the engineers into the newsroom anyway?

I do wonder, though, where the gadgetry revolution will stop. A University of Tennessee journalism professor (oh, how one likes to hear his own prejudices confirmed) told a press association meeting that many publishers and editors are investing more time and more money in electronic computer systems than they spend on reporters. Another voice crying in the wilderness of reaction; we should all do something profitable, like joining the British League of Empire Loyalists.

Meanwhile, no need to hurry that VDT with the blown brain back to *The Tech Talk* newsroom, fellows—or to rush delivery of the two pods (pardon, VDTs) on order. (Even when I pass by the University newsroom at night the VDT-creature is blinking green and white in the darkness.)

Just pass the number two pencils and the paper clips. And talk to me, Smith-Corona. Keep me awake. We're all alone now.

The Bruised (Me) Legend of the First Lick

June 21, 1981

Why it happened I'll never know.

It started with an early-morning flat tire. There was no time to fix it and still get to *The Times* building at 9:00 A.M. So I called the service station located only two blocks from where we lived then in Shreveport.

The idea was for somebody at the station to fix the tire right there at home. I would take Ellen's car to work and pick up the repaired tire on the way home.

That whole idea, simple as it was, turned out to be a crucial mistake. But the day at the office, a series of frustrations, didn't help. The galley proofs were slow coming up. The late Don Ewing, associate editor and my boss, wondered again why I couldn't spell.

A reader called in with an obvious factual error in my editorial castigating college anti-war demonstrators. William Bronson, then publisher, observed after reading my editorial on state finances that *The Times* would be happy to pay for me to sign up for a course in basic economics at Centenary College. Raymond McDaniel, city editor at the time, wondered not for the first time why I didn't write more local editorials.

So the fuse of frustration began to burn, leading to the explosion that was to blow the day apart. But it was the Legend of the First Lick, inculcated in me by a father who was an all-state football player, that caused the detonation. More about the First Lick later.

Finished at *The Times*, tired, I stopped by the station as planned to pick up the tire and pay for the work. The assistant manager had the place all alone that late afternoon; the manager, a pleasant fellow, was gone for the day.

Quite honestly, I can't summon up even a blurred memory of that assistant manager. In the years since that day, though, my mind has created a picture of how I would *like* for him to look: a huge fellow, naturally, wearing a T-shirt with a pack of cigarettes rolled up in the sleeve. Camels, of course.

In that fantasy, the assistant manager keeps at the station a chrome-blinding pickup truck with a gun-rack in the cab. He talks only about LSU football—"Tigers gonna win the national championship this year"—and keeps his eyes sheathed in silver sunglasses.

That may be the New Journalism, adding details that sharpen the story, but the truth is—again—that I can't remember the assistant manager at the service station. He might have been a Baptist Student Union missionary with a summer job for all I know; he may have weighed 110 pounds.

What happened next at the station, though, is written in my head in seventy-two point banner type. The assistant manager totaled up my bill for fixing the tire. All I remember is the figure seemed 'way too high. I reminded the assistant manager that we lived only two blocks from the station and I traded regularly with him.

How he answered my complaint, offered civilly, is also clear to the word: "Take your business elsewhere then," he said, his voice flat and casual. Then, ringing up the money I gave him, the assistant manager walked out the door.

"Anytime those tires hit the pavement," he tossed back over his shoulder, pointing at his pickup, "it's . . ." and he said whatever the price was. He did, you see, have one of those high-legged pickups but the details of it don't come to mind.

What followed does come to mind. In that same seventy-two point type detail, too. I tracked the assistant manager toward the gas pumps. Maybe it was the frustrations of the day exploding.

THE BRUISED (ME) LEGEND OF THE FIRST LICK

More likely, it was advice heard in childhood that set me off. "Get in that first lick . . ."

Now, the strategy of the First Lick is not new. And it may work for an all-state football player or the Israeli Air Force. I'm not a football player—Barney Fife has my exact build—and I'm not Moshe Dayan. This logic, however, did not prevail; the Legend of the First Lick, based on the premise that a surprise first blow can win all, did.

So I called the assistant manager's name, which now escapes me. And when he turned around, I hit him. It was a good shot, if I do say so myself. I hammered him flush on the side of the cheek. The shock of the blow tingled all the way into my shoulder. It felt good.

He fell back, almost in slow motion it seemed, sending a case of empty Coke bottles shattering all over the concrete. I saw his eyes then. Their color eludes me yet. But I do remember that those eyes were filled not with fear but with pure, galloping astonishment.

What happened after that is also clear. The assistant manager got up from the concrete and, pardon the expression, beat the hell out of me. Actually, that first lick was the only one I landed. This fellow, whoever he was, had quick hands. My swing would go wild and he would pop me three, four times. Bap. Bap. Bap.

I didn't even know what was happening—all that bapping didn't seem to hurt at the time—until a guy wearing a Pak-a-Sak hat pulled us apart. "Hey," he whispered in my ear, "this man is killin' you."

Yep. My face, on examination, was a bloody mess. Half my shirt was gone, too. I was glad, when reason returned, to take the Strategy of the First Lick and retreat. The assistant manager, unmarked, looked at me like I was a certified nut.

Ellen met me at the door. "What happened to you?" she said. Feeling totally stupid, wondering the first of many times what had possessed me, I answered: "Well, I got into a fight at the filling station." Greg, then five or six, was thrilled.

He disappeared but turned up shortly with a big stick. "Take this to the station with you next time, Dad," he said, knowing his father had lost the fight.

That was nice of Greg. As a reward for his help—I kept that stick under the bed for a long time—he has never heard about the Legend of the First Lick from his father.

And if the assistant manager of the service station is reading this—maybe he's president of Gulf Oil or a missionary to Nigeria or still driving that pickup—well, all I can say is that it was a long day and you did charge too much for fixing that tire.

What? An Eraser in His Ear?

July 12, 1981

It happened, evidently, while I was reading George Massie's new book, *Peter the Great*. Mention is made of the book only because it shows what trivial, dumb things happen to me even in the company of historical giants like Tsar Peter—company once removed, of course, from the Lincoln Parish Library.

Anyway, a glance at the new Dixon Oriole number two pencil I was using to take some notes for a *Times* editorial review of *Peter the Great* (okay, students mine, so I can't walk without a number two in my hand) told me that the eraser on the end of the pencil was missing. Gone, baby.

At the same time, rather alarmingly, it occurred to me that my left ear itched during the Battle of Poltava, a soaring and climactic part of Massie's book that absorbed me. Maybe I absentmindedly scratched that itch with the eraser tip, and it came off in my ear?

WHAT? AN ERASER IN HIS EAR?

Naw. *Naw.* I couldn't be that dumb. Besides, I couldn't feel any foreign object in my ear, which didn't hurt at all. I tested my hearing. "Hello, dummy . . . hello." I could hear myself clearly. Still, a close search of the couch where I had been reading *Peter the Great* didn't turn up the eraser.

Nah. It couldn't be in my ear. Maybe this pencil came without an eraser. That was it! A breakdown in quality control at Dixon Oriole. Another failure of American technology—a pencil without an eraser.

So I forgot the eraser for a solid two hours. Then, during a telephone conversation, the doorbell rang, and I turned my head a certain way. *Bonk.* No doubt. That bonk came from the depths of my ear. There *was* an eraser in my ear.

Pretty soon Ellen came home. I put it off for a while and then decided to break the news. "Ah, honey, I've got an eraser in my ear." At first Ellen registered blank disbelief. Then she considered the source of this announcement—me—and believed it.

"You'd better call Larry," she said, resignedly. Dr. Larry Neal is an ear, nose and throat specialist who belongs to our church. Well, I wasn't sure about calling Larry. The whole thing was embarrassing, and the eraser—if it was in there—had only bonked me one time. People survive for years with bullets in their bodies. Surely I could live with an eraser in my ear.

But after three more bonks I decided to call Dr. Neal at home. "Larry, please don't laugh," I started the conversation. Larry promised not to laugh. "Well," I told him, "I think I have an eraser in my ear." Dr. Neal laughed. He sort of chuckled, anyway. "Come in first thing in the morning," Larry told me, a ripple in his voice, "and I'll take a look."

Greg, a curious sort who is properly majoring in journalism at Tech, was of course, eavesdropping on my purposely quiet conversation with Dr. Neal. "Daddy's got an eraser in his ear," he yelled and then collapsed into hysterical laughter. Fun-ny.

By morning I had convinced myself that there was no eraser in my ear. A little thing like an eraser could be lost forever in the

WHAT? AN ERASER IN HIS EAR?

cracks and crevices of a couch. In any event, Larry's nurse met me first thing as promised. A smile pulled at the corners of her mouth. "Are you Mr. Hilburn? . . . You have an, uh, eraser in your ear?" My gruff answer was, "Probably not."

Enter Dr. Neal. He stuck a light in my ear. "You have an eraser in your ear!" he cried, astonished. "It's a big one," Larry said, suddenly interested in this particular case. He wanted to know if I needed a shot or something. "I'm going to have to hook that thing out . . . it's deep."

I turned down the pain killer. I deserved a little pain. It didn't hurt much anyway, and soon Larry handed me a three-quarter-inch-long Dixon Oriole number two eraser wrapped in gauze. It was an eraser, no denying it, and he had hooked it out of my ear.

At that point I made one last desperate effort to rationalize the situation. "I guess this happens a pretty good bit," I said casually to Dr. Neal, putting the still new-looking eraser in my shirt pocket.

"Yes," he answered, also casually, "to three- and four-year-old children."

So much for the rationalization.

When I got home, Greg, who doesn't like to be mentioned in this column, had a question: "Gonna put this in the paper, Dad, that you had an eraser in your ear?" Done, Greg.

Incidentally, I never did finish *Peter the Great*. I just want to erase the whole episode from my mind.

Oliver. Frog. Fish. Bootsie. *Lance.*

February 14, 1982

A name can literally drive you crazy, says a language expert in an interview with the Associated Press. "You will have a higher chance of being in an asylum or jail if you have an unusual name," warns Dr. Leonard R. N. Ashley of Brooklyn College, past president of the American Name Society.

That's probably true, but the fact is that even so-called ordinary names can be a burden. Because from the schoolyard to the graveyard names are inevitably associated with behavior or looks. Fairly or unfairly, names—yes, even ordinary names—imply something about their owners.

I knew an Oliver, for example, in high school; just like everybody named Oliver he was pale, bookish and withdrawn. And what would you expect from a Woodrow? A Woodrow would be a shy and unassuming fellow, of course. Susan is a yearbook beauty. Harriet heads up the firm.

Butch is always the schoolyard bully. Or maybe a Bubba gets that role. It surprised me when Bubba Henry, now state Commissioner of Administration, turned out to be a pleasant interview. Bubbas are usually bad. A kid named Guy Ludlum beat me up in high school. As anybody can tell, Guy Ludlum is a mean, muscular name.

So Dr. Ashley is right when he contends "the way you perceive people depends on their name." And, to hammer home the point, he asks rhetorically, "Have you ever heard of an Episcopal priest named Buck?" Certainly not. I agree with Ashley, too, when he says that a really weird or unusual name can have a terrible effect on a person's life.

However, overcoming the stigma of an unusual name can strengthen a person, the doctor maintains. He cites examples to

OLIVER. FROG. FISH. BOOTSIE. *LANCE.*

prove it. The late Ima Hogg, daughter of Texas Gov. James Hogg, became a big Houston socialite and philanthropist. Hubert Humphrey, clobbered with a name that would get mugged on the playground, became vice president. Somebody named Jaime Sin is archbishop of Manila.

But let's get back to ordinary names. Like Wiley. I think Wiley is a fairly ordinary if not all that common first name and I don't know what it implies. But—excuse me, parents mine—I've never felt entirely comfortable with it. New teachers, for instance, always started off calling me "Willie."

People still do that. "Good to meet you, Willie." Wiley is hard to spell, too. The Ruston Department of Water and Light sends its bill to Wylie Hilburn. My dean at Tech, Dr. Paul Pennington, wrote me a nice note the other day. "Dear Wyly," it started. A person with a ringing, alliterative name like Paul Pennington—he was sure to make dean—is inclined to take liberties with less powerful names.

Initials in or for a name can be rough, too. Or, initials can be used to hide a disaster of a name. E. S. Foster, vice president for Student Affairs at Tech, is named Elijah. Elijah is a Biblical name, I know, but students awaiting disciplinary action might tend to snicker at Elijah while E. S. can and does command respect.

Sometimes people want to know what my middle initial—it's Wiley W.—stands for. "Wilson," I say, explaining defensively that my grandmother admired Woodrow Wilson and so my folks stuck a Wilson in there. For some reason people smirk when they hear "Wiley Wilson."

Burdened with Wiley Wilson, I gave myself a new name when the roll call sheet was passed out in Ruston High School's fifth hour study hall. "Lance Corbett," I wrote down on the paper and answered to that name until the teacher caught on. *Lance Corbett.* Now that's a heck of a name. With a name like Lance Corbett, I could have made the RHS football team. That's why Billy Cannon was such a star on LSU's national championship team; how could he miss with a football name like Billy Cannon?

OLIVER. FROG. FISH. BOOTSIE. *LANCE.*

One kid I knew at Ruston High actually changed his name. Yep. Marion Tillery Meadows started writing "Bee" on all his papers and "Bee" it came to be, although I'm not sure Mrs. Meadows appreciated the arbitrary change. However, if Bee had not changed his name I'm sure he would never have become first-string quarterback on the winning Bearcat team of 1955. Ever heard of a quarterback named Marion Tillery?

If names can be a problem, nicknames are often cruel. Really cruel. My first cousin Charlie Barham, now one of Louisiana's most distinguished and senior state senators, had to overcome the nickname "Frog." That's right. *Frog Barham.* And the nickname fit, if you know what I mean.

I haven't been spared nickname abuse, either. Being called "Fishface" can do something to a seventh-grade ego. That stinking Fish was mercifully buried by high school but my folks—bless their hearts—stuck me with a pet name that has a half-life of a million years. It's Bootsie. They said I loved cowboy boots as a baby or something. I didn't mind Bootsie—didn't even think about it—until college when non-Ruston students sort of grinned when they heard it. *Bootsie?*

Ellen still calls me Bootsie as do a ton of other people in Ruston. Actually, Ellen does say "Wiley"—it always sounds forced—when my students or newspaper people are around. Every year some nosy journalism student asks with a taunting smile: "Is your name really Bootsie?"

In all fairness, though, I've heard worse nicknames than Bootsie or Frog or even Fish. Try *Waterhead* on for size and consider that this poor guy literally had a case of the big head. Like I said, cruel. At A. E. Phillips School in Ruston we called that fat fellow in class "Cuddles."

Finally, on the same subject, Dr. Ashley offered some guidelines for parents naming children:

—Don't choose a famous name that is too faddish. "If you name your kid Farrah, twenty-five years from now everybody will know her age because the Farrah (Fawcett) phase was quick," says the doctor.

—Watch those initials. Ashley says that when Arthur S. Sullivan grows up and gets a briefcase with his initials on it, he's going to be furious.

—Pay attention to double meanings. "I once had a student," Dr. Ashley said, "named Warren Peace. He signed his name W. Peace because he was embarrassed."

—Pick names that offer a lot of nicknames, he advises. Such as Margaret, which yields Maggie, Peggy or Margie. The child has an option then.

—Bury "family heirloom" names. If the name is ugly, just give the the kid an extra name or two," concludes the language expert.

"Major Credit Card, Please"

May 2, 1982

NEW ORLEANS—"Major credit card, please," routinely intoned the lady at the registration desk, not taking her eyes off the blinking computer terminal which, presumably, was confirming that I was expected at the Royal Sonesta.

"Uh, I don't have a credit card," I answered, feeling somehow guilty and naked at this terrible admission. It was an admission, in any event, that finally got the attention of the desk clerk. "No major credit card?" I detected a note of disbelief and even suspicion in her voice.

Feeling really ashamed now, wondering what the impatient crowd around me was thinking of a person guilty of not having a major credit card, I fished desperately in my billfold. Finally, much relieved, I deposited my blue, orange and white Gulfcard on the desk.

"MAJOR CREDIT CARD, PLEASE"

Well, Mr. Jimmy Lee, chairman of the board of Gulf Oil Corporation, Honored Louisiana Tech Engineering Graduate, that lady at the Royal Sonesta looked at your Gulfcard like it was a cow chip. *Like it was a cow chip, Jimmy, I swear.* "That is not a *Major Credit Card*," she pronounced.

I hastily removed the offending GulfCard from the desk and inventoried my billfold. All that remained—besides the cash to fund the trip—was my Lincoln Parish Library card, driver's license, and pictures of Ellen and the kids. *The Times* hasn't even given me a press card.

It was humiliating to stand in the ornate lobby of the Royal Sonesta without a major credit card. I know people who can open their wallet and send a cascade of plastic popping down to the floor—from the utilitarian-looking blue, gold and white Visa to the plain but ultimately classy Gold Executive American Express card. I have a friend who loves his Libby card and likes to use it even when he doesn't need the money. It's a sin not to have a Major Credit Card; I admit it.

However, I finally managed to point out to the Royal Sonesta clerk that the square indicating cash payment had been checked. The clerk was looking at the computer terminal again; I imagined that its electronic sentence had been rendered. No major credit card, it was blinking. "You'll have to see the cashier, sir," the clerk said, her head in the terminal.

Now I really felt guilty. The "You'll have to see the cashier" sentence was pronounced in the same magisterial tone invoked by my geometry teacher at Ruston High School. "You will have to see the principal, Mr. Hilburn." Or when I lost at monopoly on Bill Upchurch's front porch. *Go to jail*.

Go to the cashier. So I crawled to the cashier. He took enough cash—dirty old green bills just do not stand up to a nice, clean major credit card—to secure our room on the fourth floor for the whole stay. "I'd like a receipt for that," I said sternly, trying to recover my dignity.

I finally got back to the car with the huge brass key provided by the Royal Sonesta. Ellen was wondering how I would manage to screw up reservations so carefully arranged by my associate in the Tech journalism department, Ron White.

I told her. No major credit card.

Convicted.

The "Compliments" He Gets

December 18, 1983

I saw Dr. Wallace Herbert coming toward our table at the Huddle House. Dr. Herbert, a distinguished retired mathematics professor, reads this column. So I knew a compliment was most likely on its way—and I was especially glad because all the coffee-drinking buddies who poke fun at my writing would have to hear it.

Sure enough, Dr. Herbert wanted to talk about "Fragments." "You know I read you," he began. I nodded, grinning at the guys around the table, all of whom immediately assumed an air of bored resignation. Meanwhile, Dr. Herbert was struggling for the words to describe how much he liked my work.

Like in the classroom, he looked thoughtful and put a contemplative finger to his cheek. I waited, still grinning, for the praise; I knew the professor was a reader. "Yeah," he said, "*I think I like your column because it requires so little thought.*"

When my 5:00 P.M. coffee friends heard that, they about fell out of the booth laughing. Their hooting and the sudden disappearance of my grin told Dr. Herbert that he had not exactly made my day with that "compliment."

Of course, Dr. Herbert then said that wasn't what he meant at all, but gave up in the gale of laughter sweeping the table. It's okay, Dr. Herbert. I'm glad you read me, for whatever reason. Anyway, one good thing came out of it. George Kilgore was so tickled he paid for the coffee.

Biting Through Red Hair

June 17, 1984

Chaperoning the recent junior-senior prom at Ruston High School took me back to my first formal at the same RHS thirty years ago. It was, quite literally, a hairy experience for me—one that would foreshadow a future of similar mishaps for one Wiley Hilburn.

As usual, this particular misadventure started nicely enough. It was the Kit-Kat formal, as I recall, and a redheaded freshman who shall remain anonymous—Ellen says don't embarrass the poor girl at this late date—was kind enough to invite me.

I remember purchasing a yellow dress shirt at Glasgow's Men's Store for the occasion. We had all learned the two-step, more or less, in Mrs. Hobgood's dance school the year before. So I was ready for the dance, which was held at the old Montgomery's Steak House on the Farmerville Road.

As an uncoordinated 119-pounder who had already flunked spring football in 1954, I was still somewhat nervous about the first waltz of the evening—despite Mrs. Hobgood's best efforts. So I stuffed in a whole package of Spearmint gum.

Thus fortified, I twirled my redhead to a recorded rendition of "Secret Love." The two-step served me well. I even dipped a couple of times to Doris Day. Finally relaxed, it only gradually dawned on me that something had gone desperately wrong.

BITING THROUGH RED HAIR

My redhead, you see, was very short. So I rested my chin on the top of her head while we waltzed. A ballad will make you do things like that. It was all okay, except that somehow my enormous wad of gum had gotten entangled in her red hair.

After a moment of shock, I settled down to two options: I could give a mighty yank, risking a major scalp wound for my unsuspecting date, or use my teeth to saw through the strands of red hair before "Secret Love" concluded.

I took the second option, and started to grind away—hoping to separate gum from hair and boy from girl—while two-stepping around the crowded dance floor as if nothing was amiss. Thinking back, I realize the other dancers must have wondered if I were glued to the top of my date's head.

Soon, however, Doris Day began to wind down: "And my secret love's no secret anymore." My own gummy secret was soon to be unmasked as well. I had severed ropes of red hair, it seems, but the gum held like rubber cement. Unless I wanted to return to our table attached to my date's head, the second, radical remedy loomed.

So, I gave a great yank. "Yikes!" yelled my date. People looked at us briefly, but I didn't care. I was disengaged, even if a heck of a hairball had to be digested. Oddly enough, the redhead didn't say anything; she was probably afraid. Here was weirdo biting her hair, after all.

Nothing so disastrous happened to my daughter thirty years later at another Ruston High dance, and I'm glad. Dancing has never been very much fun for me since that first formal on the Farmerville Road when I literally gummed up the works.

Another Failure for Hilburn

October 7, 1984

Since everybody in Ruston knows it already, it's time to tell the world: I flunked the Louisiana written driver's test. Flunked it flat. In fact, I watched the lady at the license bureau grade it. A "52" is what I saw her write at the top of the paper.

That's an "F" in anybody's grade book, and the lowest score I've gotten on a test since the "40" I scored on a Math 109 final at Tech more than twenty-five years ago. That long-ago blow was softened when my first cousin, Robert Barham, made a "7" under the same teacher.

But even Barham has never failed a driver's test. In my defense, however, it must be said that this new exam isn't one of those what-does-it-mean-when-the-light-turns-green crips. I was wrecked with questions about acceleration lanes, the "two-second rule" and how many feet it takes to stop at fifty-five mph.

I think the guy in front of me in the line failed too. And he looked like Mario Andretti. Pass this new test and you're licensed to fly the Columbia space shuttle. Well, that's not entirely fair to the Office of Motor Vehicles either.

Everybody knows I'm not exactly the king of the road, and rules and regulations have always escaped me (I got so many parking infractions at LSU-Baton Rouge they parked me on a penalty lot in Baker). And, to be truthful, I only had to take the test because, well, I lost my driver's license. And not only that, to be perfectly honest.

When the lady at the bureau called my lost license up on the computer (another reason for me to hate terminals), it turned out to be more than two years expired. Both of us were very surprised.

Actually, I should have had an inkling that a renewal was in order several months ago when I looked at the picture on my license (to provide Social Security identification for *The Times*) and mused to myself, "Damn, Hilburn, you look young." But it didn't register.

So I *had* to take the test or face the prospect of establishing a Tech-Angola academic branch. The lady administering the exam looked at me with a certain amount of sympathy after marking all the crosses and allowed that "a few" other people had failed it. "It's *new*," she said.

That didn't make me feel any better. It amounted to another mechanical failure for a guy whose wife had to fix a blowout last fall. And Ellen, my employer and a person employed by me all deepened the humiliation as follows:

—After explaining to Ellen that this was a new, tougher exam, she inconveniently recalled that I had also failed the old driver's test in 1971.

—When I entered a one-way street at Tech—the wrong way—while driving President F. Jay Taylor back to his office after a reception, he uncharitably cracked, "You'll never pass that driver's test . . . I'll have to get you a tutor."

—Sallie Rose Hollis, on *my* journalism faculty at Tech insubordinately noted that she had "missed only one" on the same test.

I'll conclude on two more positive notes:

1. I passed the test the second time after a weekend studying the *Louisiana Driver's Guide*. In fact, I haven't studied so much since facing one of Dr. Robert Holtman's Russian history tests at LSU.

2. I now know that at fifty-five miles an hour it takes 228 feet to stop the car, that bike riders have to share their lane and that "you must drive only in the direction indicated by the white arrow."

Of BB Guns and Blooper Balls

February 2, 1986

The subject at the Ruston Huddle House was BB guns. Men in their thirties and forties were going crazy talking about the great BB gun wars of the 1950s.

Part of the discussion was inspired by a good HBO movie, set in the 1940s, which dwelled on a kid's dream of owning a Red Ryder BB gun and his mother's fearful admonition that "you're going to shoot your eye out."

We all went through that, it seems. The ownership of a Daisy Red Ryder air rifle was a rite of passage in a North Louisiana boyhood, along with that same mother's warning—issued in the movie—that "you're going to shoot your eye out."

Your dad always broke down and bought one, and suddenly you were armed and daring and dangerous—ready to take on the entire Sioux nation.

My first cousin Bob Barham, whose rusty arsenal of BB guns thrown around his Goode Street yard would have armed Nicaragua, remembers that you had to jiggle the air rifle up and down before it would fire.

I remember the wonderful martial feeling of feeding 1,000 golden BBs into the magazine and the confident rattle that came out of a full rifle.

Of course, you graduated from a Daisy air rifle to a Benjamin Pump. Legend had it that, pumped up twenty-four times—a feat that Steve Reeves would have envied—this gun actually had the velocity of a .22 rifle.

Myth had it that somebody in Dubach pumped a Benjamin sixty-four times and blew a gaping hole in the Tech smokestack. In 1954, in Lincoln Parish, a Benjamin Pump was a howitzer.

Actually, the Benjamins varied in velocity and ammunition.

OF BB GUNS AND BLOOPER BALLS

Some of them fired BBs; some pellets; some both. The kid who had a Benjamin Pump that fired pellets was the Rambo of his day.

Joe Thomas, comptroller at Louisiana Tech and one of the Huddle House gang, claims he had a Benjamin Pump that fired feathered darts. Joe doesn't lie, but nobody could believe that.

Barham swears that four BBs could be crammed into the chamber of a Benjamin. The result, he said, was to transform this air rifle into a mighty shotgun.

Many a squirrel went down in a fiery pattern of steel from Barham's Benjamin "shotgun." That's what he says, anyway, but I think the Benjamin shotgun fits into the category of Joe's feathered darts.

But back to BB guns. Bill Upchurch and I wouldn't make a woods patrol back of his house on Old Highway 80 East without our BB guns. But an argument between Bill and me once led to something that could have been as bad as that you'll-shoot-your-eye-out fear from mothers.

Bill and I were great friends, but we argued and fought a lot. I was two years older and I always won—until Bill went out for football at Ruston High and got muscles.

Anyway, before that, we got into an argument about the blooper ball. Bill's daddy had told him that a blooper ball, a pitch that arched high, was the best weapon in baseball.

I demurred, noting that the high arc of the ball would bring it down right on top of the plate. That couldn't be a strike, I said. We put our BB guns down and started arguing baseball.

Bill felt that a blooper ball could be a strike, and as usual the dispute led him to make a familiar and, to me, infuriatingly unfair accusation.

"Are you calling my daddy a liar?"

No, I wasn't calling Mr. Upchurch a liar, but a blooper ball couldn't be a strike.

Words led to words, and then to blows. We fought all the way into Mrs. Milam's yard and crashed through her privet hedge, fists flying. Then we stopped fighting and argued some more. That was when he accused me again.

"Are you calling my daddy a liar?"

It made me so mad I lost all control, picked up my BB gun and shot Bill. As it happened, he was standing on the other side of Mrs. Milam's hedge and the BB went through it and hit him in the chest.

It didn't even break the skin, but Bill—who normally wasn't afraid of anything—went down, howling, like he had been hit by an air-to-ground missile.

Of course, I didn't blame him for howling; it's scary to get shot. Even with a BB gun. So I ran across Old Highway 80 East home to Marbury Drive, leaving Bill writhing in Mrs. Milam's yard.

Now, Mrs. Upchurch, Bill's mother, was a wonderful woman—well-read, intelligent and tolerant. She gave me my first books from her library; she liked me. I liked her.

But this was the one time—the only time—she called my mother. They were talking when I got home. The conversation could be reconstructed something like this:

Mrs. Upchurch: "Marie (my mother), this time Bootsie (that was my nickname) has gone too far."

Bill's mother had this dry, penetrating voice, like her wit. I could hear that voice over the phone.

My mother: "What has he done now?"

Mrs. Upchurch: "He shot Bill."

My mother: "Oh, my God."

Me: "Well, I never called his daddy a liar . . ."

Eventually, it was all patched up and my confiscated BB gun was returned. Bill not only survived being shot in the chest but today heads corporate planning in New York City for Exxon.

Tech President F. Jay Taylor still has me confined to the basement of Keeny Hall at Louisiana Tech in Ruston.

Meanwhile, the great BB gun wars of our boyhood are over,

the woods have been cut down back of Bill's house, and we have all gone on to other things. Still, I'd like to fill up the magazine of a Daisy air rifle and hear the enormously satisfying rattle one more time.

PART FOUR

LAUGHING—
INSIDE AND OUT

Taylor and Turkey Creek

June 18, 1978

It was the weekend Louisiana Tech beat USL in football, but lost to Turkey Creek.

F. Jay Taylor, Tech's president, had topped the slight South Louisiana rise at what seemed a very moderate rate of speed. He hates speeding tickets and, even when somebody else is driving, is inclined to lean over and take unsubtle glances at the speedometer.

So it was with some surprise that we noted the elderly man waving at us, scarecrow-like, in the autumnal dusk. Dr. Taylor pulled over and soon stood in the flickering blue lights of the Turkey Creek constable. Even though we had been stopped, presumably for speeding, I was sure there would be no ticket.

I had every confidence in the persuasive skills of the Tech president, skills well-known to legislators, governors, education board members and even newsmen. Knowing Taylor, he would wind up with the key to Turkey Creek—if there was one.

My window was rolled up against the October chill, but I could see Dr. Taylor talking to the old lawman. There it goes, I thought. The president was gesturing and smiling. In the gathering gloom I even imagined Dr. Taylor in academic cap and gown, presenting the old constable with a certificate of appreciation (framed in Tech red and blue) or maybe even an honorary diploma.

The constable reached into his pocket. Taylor had probably talked him into making a contribution to the new Assembly Center, I thought. But, no, the constable had pulled out a pencil and that was a speeding ticket he was writing out.

It was the only time I ever saw Jay Taylor lose, and I rolled down the window and caught the end of the conversation. "And you ought to get a flare . . . I nearly ran over you out there," Dr. Taylor was saying in a voice he doesn't employ at commencement, putting the ticket in his pocket.

But he took the defeat gracefully enough once the battle was decided. "The man does need a flare," Jay Taylor said defensively, starting the car and heading for Lafayette. I didn't say a word. I wasn't driving. Thank goodness.

A Forearm, a Rural Mailbox, and . . . ARRRRRRAH!

July 8, 1979

He was a blockbuster tackle at Tallulah High School in another era. During the football season opponents just gave up running at his position. But in the summer, with nobody to tackle, the big fellow took his pent-up energy out on the rural mailboxes of northeast Louisiana.

A FOREARM, A RURAL MAILBOX, AND . . . ARRRRRRAH!

That's right. He would line up a few yards from the offending mailbox, hunker down into his three-point stance, get up some RPMs and—framed in the headlights of a car full of giggling teenagers—throw a savage forearm into the flimsy structure.

The whole thing would give way, and the footballer and his entourage left a trail of splintered mailboxes in the wake of their long July nights. Sometimes the big tackle would level the same mailbox three times in the course of the summer.

But it was one of those thrice-savaged boxes that turned the tables. The routine, which had become a kind of violent summer ceremony, started like always. In fact, the big tackle got a real bead on this familiar postal target and thundered down on it as if to destroy the whole Delhi football team.

The headlights were on him as he swept past the box at full speed and threw the splintering forearm like so many times before. Arrrrrrrrrrrrrrrah! And suddenly, this time, it was the big tackle leveled out on the ground, kicking, and holding his arm. The mailbox stood proud and tall and utterly undamaged. The football player got his broken right arm repaired at the nearest hospital emergency room.

Some northeast Louisiana farmer, it turned out, had gotten tired of seeing his mailbox smashed. So he sank a steel pole in concrete and then filled up his mailbox with the same unyielding stuff.

So far as we know the mailboxes of this whole region have been safe ever since that night in July.

A Thanksgiving Bet, 1932

November 18, 1979

It was 1932. And the livin' was not easy. Robert Pittard, a consummate salesman who was to parlay a peanut franchise (Tom's Toasted Peanuts) into a successful brokerage career, desperately needed a new Stein suit.

So he went to my dad. The two were inseparable. "Wiley," he said, "can Ruston beat Jonesboro?" It was Thanksgiving and nothing was bigger in North Central Louisiana than the annual Ruston High-Jonesboro game.

And Dad was the man to see about the game's prospects. He was left-half and captain of the Ruston Bearcats of '32. Probably not, was Daddy's answer to whether Ruston could win. Injuries and the flu bug had weakened the Bearcats. Jonesboro was favored.

Robert told his best friend about the suit then. "I'm going to bet ten dollars on Jonesboro," Bob said. He had saved up ten dollars already, and with the bet doubling that fund he could get a Stein suit and a pair of shoes. In fact, suits were advertised in a November 1932 issue of the Shreveport *Times* for $11.90 and shoes for $2.95.

Anyway, Daddy was so sure that Ruston couldn't win that he told Bob Pittard to put five dollars of his money on Jonesboro. All this represented a considerable investment for the time. President-elect Roosevelt was vacationing at Warm Springs, Ga., the November *Times* said, and preparing to do something about the Great Depression.

To put things into perspective, *The Times* was advertising hams (whole or half-pound) for fourteen cents a pound; pork chops were going for fifteen cents a pound. And if Daddy and Robert Pittard won their bets they could easily afford to dine Thanksgiv-

A THANKSGIVING BET, 1932

ing Day at the College Inn in Ruston where, said the local *Daily Leader*, you could get a turkey dinner with all the trimmings (including asparagus tips) for fifty cents.

They could also take in the current movie, starring John Wayne and "Duke, his Devil Horse" in *Ride Him, Cowboy*, for ten cents. So Robert Pittard's Thanksgiving bet of 1932 was no chicken-feed wager. A dollar would buy more pork chops then, sure, but there were not many dollars or pork chops.

Thanksgiving of 1932 dawned wet and cold. In fact, it had been raining all week in North Louisiana, breaking up a long dry spell. Centenary was playing the University of Arkansas that day in State Fair Stadium (the game was to end in a 0-0 tie), but people in Ruston and Jonesboro were more interested in their big game: the Bearcats and the Jackson Parish Tigers. Bob Pittard, of course, had a special interest in the game; he had bet the whole thing, and Daddy's five dollars, too—on Jonesboro, of course.

Oh, yeah. Ruston won the ball game 18-0. Wiley Hilburn, Sr. scored all three touchdowns for the winners. The next day Bob Pittard drove up in his peanut truck, without his Stein suit and his nestegg. "Wiley, you are crazy, son," Daddy remembers him saying.

And Bob Pittard, his voice rumbling over the long-distance line from his home in Minden, remembers that Thanksgiving bet of 1932 very well indeed. "Wiley didn't get hurt at all in that game, but afterwards I sure did want to hurt him," he told me the other day.

The Haunting of Clear Lake

February 3, 1980

Premonitions.

We all have them: the little warnings of danger, the moments of creepy anticipation, the strange and shapeless dreads of the deep night.

Then there is always the dream that was too real, and the nightmare that was so unreal, so terrible that the subconscious buried it forever out of sight and out of mind.

There are other odd things that happen to all of us. You know: the feeling that the red-light and the house on the right are so intimately familiar . . . and yet, you have never been near this street, this neighborhood before.

And what about those times when the wind did unsettling things to the trees and set the skin crawling with apprehension; something—something evil—was surely astir in those pines.

These are universal experiences. Yet, nothing remotely supernatural—beyond these run-of-the-mill goosebumps—has ever happened to me.

Except there was that one time, of course, at Clear Lake near Natchitoches. Clear Lake, it must be understood at once, will never he haunted for me. The three sloughs alive with bass, the beautiful mystery of Pecan Island, and Cap Barham's rickety old camp on the hill will always hold the best of memories.

For all of fifteen years, from grade school to college years, we—Robert Barham, Eddie Hood and I—grew up water-skiing the blue open expanse that gave the lake its name, hunting the wild pig-populated wilderness around it, and swimming buck-naked on top of the salt-water well.

But there was that one strange weekend. The caretaker, we learned on arrival at Cap's camp, had died a week earlier. The caretaker always reminded me of a *Tobacco Road* Santa Claus. He was a big man with white hair and a long white beard. Little rivers of tobacco juice ran from both corners of his mouth.

A quiet man, the caretaker never said much to me. Still, I always had the feeling he was on the edge of telling me something. But then he ended up loading the boat and pushing us off. We never talked. Then he died. And because the camp is isolated, it was a long time before they found him.

It wasn't at all unnatural that I would dream about the old caretaker—we had been talking about his death—and I did that very night. I dreamed he stood at the end of my bed. It was very real. I could see the little rivers of tobacco juice springing from the corners of his mouth.

Once again, it was like he wanted to tell me something, but at the last second decided against it. It was not a nightmare at all. He just stood there at the foot of my bed, wanting to say something, and then it was over. I was not frightened. Not then. It was just a dream.

The thing was, the cook could see into my room—the dining room where he slept had been added on and the windows completely exposed the bed where I slept. "Mr. Cap," the cook said, dishing out the scrambled eggs that weekend morning on the lake, "you scared me to death coming into Bootsie's room (my room) in the middle of the night."

"I didn't come into Bootsie's room last night," Cap said, looking up intently from his eggs.

"He couldn't have," I chimed in, icewater cascading down my spine. "I latched my door from the inside." I had carefully done exactly that before retiring for the night.

"Mr. Cap," the cook said, "if I had known that, I'd still be running to Ruston."

Ordinarily such an incident would have made me the butt of a lot of kidding. Cap, indeed, was a champion kidder. But Cap was uncharacteristically quiet after I told him about dreaming of the old caretaker. In fact, nobody said much. We left the lake several hours earlier than usual that weekend and the car was silent all the way back to Lincoln Parish.

The caretaker was in my mind all that time. And I can still see him now: a *Tobacco Road* Santa Claus standing at the foot of my bed. No, I'm not haunted by the Ghost of Clear Lake, but I haven't forgotten him.

He wanted to tell me something, either before or after the end; that I do know. What he wanted to tell me I will never know. I hope.

I Think He's Naked in the Tank

August 31, 1980

The names have been changed to protect the writer, and maybe the innocent, but nothing will be reported here that did not happen that summer afternoon twenty years ago out on the Farmerville Road.

Let's call them Richard and Sam for practical purposes, and see how—as I have told you before—Tom Sawyer and his friends never died. They just came to North Louisiana, and they never grew up.

In fact, the cliche "he never grew up" best describes Richard. Aw, you know somebody like him; somebody who is always and forever the kid.

For example, it was Richard (he was around forty years old at the time) who borrowed the deputy sheriff's car on a pretext and then tore all over Lincoln Parish in it, siren screaming and red-light blazing.

On that same wild ride Richard roared through somebody's

I THINK HE'S NAKED IN THE TANK

backyard and emerged on the main road trailing a day's wash and a clothesline and laughing like crazy.

The sheriff was not amused, but somehow Richard came out of the incident okay. Richard always seemed to come out of things okay, no matter how crazy the escapade. Maybe it was because he had a generous nature. People would say that if you were Richard's friend he would do anything for you.

Richard's friends laughed and called him a card. Of course, a lot of people said Richard was crazy, and they muttered dark things about him when he passed on the street. On the other hand, everybody said Richard's wife was a saint. That she had to be.

Meanwhile, Sam was thought to be at least as generous as Richard. When Sam left and paid for everybody's coffee, people would say, "That old Sam would give you the shirt off his back." And they were right.

Sam, if you caught him right, would move your whole family into a new house and paint the ceilings and never want a thing for doing it. Of course, some people thought Sam was a little crazy, too. Truth to tell, Sam did have a trigger-temper, and he could get loud in an argument. "Don't interrupt me," he would say. And Sam was impulsive, just like Richard.

Anyway, the two got together that early afternoon for coffee at Richard's little part-time business operation. It was August and the heat was rising off the Farmerville Road in greasy, rainbow-colored waves.

The two men talked for a minute, and then Richard gestured toward a little tank outside the building. "That old tank needs cleaning out, but I'm just too old to do it," Richard said resignedly. "Besides," Richard admitted, "I'm probably too fat to fit into that tank." Sam took the bait, even though he had roofed the preacher's house just the day before.

"I can clean that lil' ole tank in about a half-hour," Sam said. Richard gave the idea a token shake of his head, as if he had never considered such a thing, but Sam was already hollering out the door, bound for the tank.

The tank was about six feet high and a tight fit for Sam. In fact, Richard had to give Sam a boost. Inside, Sam found a mop and a bucket and about a foot of smelly chemicals and water. Sweat stung his eyes. It was hot in there.

Sam worked hard, but he made little progress. The sun seemed to be telescoping right into the tank. Sam's arms ached. Finally, he gave up and yelled for Richard. Sam didn't like to give up, but his clothes were already soaked with chemicals and sweat. It was too hot in that tank.

Richard's close-to-chuckling voice penetrated the tank like an echo. "You can handle this little job in a half-hour, that's what you said, boy. 'Sides that, who's gonna help you out of that tank." Then Richard laughed out loud.

That pulled Sam's trigger-temper. "I'm gettin' out of these stinkin'-wet clothes," he hollered over the top of the tank. "I'm burnin' up in here. You hear me?"

Richard was still laughing. "Take 'em off," he said.

That did it. Sam's shirt sailed over the rim of the tank. His pants followed. Then his underwear. That done, Sam leaned against the edge of the tank.

That was when something blue and swimming in the glass seams of the tank caught Sam's sweat-blurred eye. It was another eye, looking back at him, and it belonged—Sam could just make out—to a woman.

Sam somehow vaulted out of the tank, wearing the bucket and the mop. Richard was halfway to Farmerville in his old jeep, and once Sam had jumped into his chemical-stinking wet clothes he found out what had happened from the two startled strangers who had observed him in the tank.

Richard, it seemed, had flagged down the first car that came along after Sam's last article of clothing had cleared the tank. "There's a crazy man in my tank," Richard had told them. "I think he's naked. I'm going to get the police. You watch him." The woman was very apologetic to Sam.

That was it. Sam told me about it. And he tells me he and Richard are friends today. Richard is like that; as I said, he can get away with things. Still, there is a little flint in Sam's voice when he talks about being naked in the tank twenty years ago—or when he talks about Richard, period.

As for Richard, he is older now, but he's still the same guy when I see him. No, he'll never grow up, and people either love him or loathe him. And his wife is still a saint.

"I Did Quit... But *They* Blew Smoke in My Face"

May 24, 1981

My Uncle Fielder was pulling hard on the long Kent. "I thought you quit smoking," I told him.

"I did," he answered. "It was easy . . . no problem at all." He blew out a fogbank of smoke.

"But you are smoking right now," I persisted.

Fielder put his hand on my shoulder, taking me into his confidence. "I did quit smoking," he said, "but *they* blew smoke in my face." At the time it seemed to me that Fielder was either suffering from the mild paranoia that we all experience from time to time, or just rationalizing the resumption of a bad habit.

Now I'm not so sure. It's a smoky world out there for nonsmokers like me and for somebody trying to shake the habit among all those fumes—well, it must be like an alcoholic trying to stay on the wagon while driving a beer truck for a living.

"I DID QUIT . . . BUT *THEY* BLEW SMOKE IN MY FACE"

All this is brought to mind by a *Recent Editorial Research Reports* article by Richard L. Worsnop titled "Smoker's Guilt." "Deep down," he wrote, "every smoker feels guilty, and not just about the self-inflicted danger to his own health." Worsnop continued:

"In recent years, various studies have indicated that non-smokers also face significant health risks by coming into contact with smokers. Hence the continuing campaign for separate smoking and non-smoking sections in planes, trains, restaurants and other public places."

Hence, the emergence of "Smoker's Guilt." With all due respect, Mr. Worsnop is blowing smoke himself. It's true that the anti-smoking movement has gained a little momentum, but *my* smoking friends, at least, are not on a guilt trip. In fact, they still blow smoke in my face.

Yes, some of my best friends are smokers—and, in all fairness, they are not consciously (most of the time) laying siege to my lungs. It's just that the message that some people don't like smoke hasn't penetrated their smokescreen as yet. Why, you can ostentatiously try to fan away their fumes or even switch chairs to escape frontal suffocation—and still they just puff away.

It's just that smokers have owned their blue-haze world for so long; they like it. Billows of smoke. Banks of it. Layers of it. Smokers float on a Cloud Nine of nicotine. It rarely occurs to them—even now—that entirely apart from health considerations, non-smokers find their exhaust not only noxious but obnoxious as well.

For once, let's drop the customary veneer of Southern courtesy and express the feeling of many, many non-smokers: smokers, you are inconsiderate, irritating, and downright arrogant. And, yes, we mind if you smoke—if you bother to ask.

And what we mind most is the smoker who, not satisfied with polluting restaurants, cars and other public places, insists on bringing the habit right into the home of the non-smoker—fill-

"I DID QUIT . . . BUT *THEY* BLEW SMOKE IN MY FACE"

ing up the air-conditioning vents with a sour, ashy breath that persists for days. That's the worse offense.

To be fair, some smokers find ways of venting their smoke. Others, like a long-time friend of mine, fire smoke grenades at all who venture near. Still others exhale great explosions of smoke that quickly overcome every cubic inch of air in a room—or a football stadium.

It's an annoyance, to be sure—except that smoke is also a health hazard to non-smokers. A fourteen year study in Japan showed that non-smoking wives exposed to their husbands cigarette fumes developed lung cancer at rates up to 2.08 times higher than women whose husbands did not smoke.

These Japanese findings only confirm earlier surveys on the effects of cigarette smoke on non-smokers. The American Medical Association estimates that at least 34 million people in this country are vulnerable to smoke from cigarettes. They include people with emphysema, asthma, bronchitis, sinusitis, hay fever and heart disease.

Mr. Worsnop, in his article, sums up the problem as follows: "Whenever anyone lights a cigarette, cigar or pipe, tobacco smoke enters the atmosphere from two sources: 1. directly from the burning tobacco (sidestream smoke) and 2. from the smoke the smoker sucks (mainstream smoke) and then exhales. According to the American Lung Association, sidestream smoke contains twice as much tar and nicotine, five times as much carbon monoxide, and fifty times as much ammonia as mainstream smoke."

Smokers are more aware of the danger to themselves now. And the Surgeon General's office, which sounded the first real alarm on smoking in general in 1964, reports now that "today there can be no doubt that smoking is truly slow-motion suicide."

But the idea that smokers feel guilty about that self-inflicted damage to their own health—or about sidetracking such pollution into innocent lungs—is a puff of smoke.

"I DID QUIT . . . BUT *THEY* BLEW SMOKE IN MY FACE"

Fielder, you were right.
They did blow smoke in your face.

The Last Practical Joke at Tech

January 24, 1982

It all started with one of those pyramid games—this one based on a chain letter effect—that was winding its way through Keeny Hall on the Louisiana Tech campus. A couple of us had refused to participate, but only because we didn't have the ready cash at the time.

The leaders of the game finally took no for an answer, but the holdouts were harangued for being tighwads and kill-joys. And when a few of the pyramid players reaped some initial payoffs they let the non-participants hear about it—to the point of literally waving their winnings in our somewhat envious faces.

That's when I hit on the idea of countering the chain-letter gang with a practical joke. The joke took the form of a newspaper editor's letter to Tech President F. Jay Taylor. I made up the letter, of course, on official-looking newspaper stationery. It was a heck of a letter, if I do say so myself.

The letter "alleged" that the newspaper's "investigative reporters" (this was before Watergate too) had turned up a chain-letter operation that "while not technically illegal could possibly be construed as morally questionable." A story to that effect would appear shortly, the newspaper editor's letter to Taylor said, together with an appropriately scolding editorial on, of all days, Sunday.

Then I "borrowed" Dr. Taylor's seal and had the bogus letter stamped "received in the President's office." This way the communication carried all the authority and awe of an imprimatur of the Holy Roman Emperor. Again, Dr. Taylor didn't know about it. Until later.

After all that was done, Vice President George Byrnside, who was let in on the joke and embraced it without reservation, summoned the chain-letter conspirators to his office and handed them copies of the accusing letter, in which they were all individually named in dreadful looking capital letters.

Naturally, I never expected to be summoned to that final scene; Byrnside was to fill me in later. But this practical joke produced a bonus for the instigator. After digesting the editor's letter with a mixture of horror and disbelief, their eyes darting from the newspaper heading to the presidential seal, the chain-letter gang spoke as one: "Maybe Wiley Hilburn can help us . . . he knows these newspaper guys."

So I was called to Byrnside's office. It was too good to be true. I found the pyramid participants, important administrators all, deployed in a desperate semicircle around the vice-presidential desk. Byrnside looked very stern, I recall.

"This is going to be a scandal," one moaned.

"My parents live here . . . what will they think?" said another, his eyes gone all bloodshot.

"To think I just bought a house," said a third member of the accused.

Only one administrator spoke up for himself. "How dare this newspaper editor question my morals?" he wanted to know.

A fourth administrator, famed for his filibusters, actually could not speak. He sputtered and stuttered and finally grew quiet.

After that initial outburst, the pyramid players began to incriminate others, as if that was the solution. "Dr. Taylor's secretary signed one of those letters," proclaimed a participant, implicating the highest office of the university in the growing stain.

Another pyramid player seemed to have the problem solved.

THE LAST PRACTICAL JOKE AT TECH

"I know some people from Temple Baptist Church who participated," he said triumphantly in sudden inspiration.

It was enough. Those bloodshot eyes got to me. That, and the knowledge there was nothing wrong with the game—even if all but one of the participants now seemed convinced there was. "It was a joke, fellows," I confessed, more in contrition than pride.

There followed a moment of silence.

"I wrote the letter and everything," I explained. "You guys kidded us about not participating so I dreamed up this thing. It's just a joke."

More silence.

Then slightly hysterical laughter. Shortly after that the administrator who did not like having his morality questioned threatened to punch me out. I didn't blame him much.

Actually, the chain-letter gang took the joke pretty well in the end. I swore to myself that this would be the last such prank; they all swore revenge and retribution.

After that, a bunch of my university vouchers were looked upon with extreme suspicion. Then an ad in the Ruston *Daily Leader* invited everybody in Lincoln, Bienville, Union and Jackson parishes to dump their used Christmas trees in my yard. Luckily the publisher called me on that one and I got the ad reworded.

Unfortunately, I was *not* warned about the siren somebody wired to my car engine in Keeny Circle. Classes at Tech were disrupted and everybody in Greenwood Cemetery awakened when I tried to make it to Dr. Taylor's office. The president *was* in on that joke.

Despite such undeserved provocations, I've stuck to that oath—no more such pranks—for a dozen years while maintaining that the last, great practical joke at Louisiana Tech originated in the basement of Keeny Hall where the journalism department lives.

And remember, chain-letter gang. I could have used names in this column.

An Explosive Gun Safety Lesson

October 17, 1982

The young professor was reluctant to request the auditorium in the new Tech engineering building for the presentation. He taught in another college and even now, he says wryly: "You know how engineers are." Still, the teacher needed space to accommodate the forty odd students he was advising in an extracurricular activity.

Besides, the subject to be covered was gun safety. What could be safer, for the new auditorium and the students, than gun safety? So the group gathered in the auditorium and the professor remembers that the place, dark-paneled and deep in carpet, still smelled new. A lot of the kids he was advising turned up, and it looked like an instructive evening.

The speaker on gun safety looked impressive, too, what with all the patches plastered on his shirt advertising honors won for expertise in this field. Situated in a little recessed area of the auditorium, the expert surrounded himself with rifles, pistols and one old musket. Professor and students settled in for the lecture.

After the usual cautionary note that it's the unloaded gun that kills, the safety expert unlimbered the old musket for the first demonstration. As well as the professor can recall, he next poured in the gunpowder and rammed home the wadding. Then came the explosion—BLAM! The teacher recalls that the deafening report sounded like a "stick of TNT going off."

The gun safety expert, meanwhile, completely disappeared in a cloud of blue smoke. When that cloud lifted, the man and his musket were revealed again—along with a hole the size of a fifty cent piece blasted by the wadding into the new paneling.

Nobody was hurt because the gun had been pointed away

from the students and toward a wall. Everybody, of course, was stunned. All eyes looked to the teacher-adviser. He slid down into his seat and rolled his eyes. As for the expert, he continued the lecture almost without pause as if nothing had happened—and without further incident.

In fact, nobody said anything. Southerners are polite to a fault, even under fire, and quiet prevailed—except, the professor remembers, for an occasional cough. You see, that thundercloud of blue smoke clung to the ceiling and the new auditorium reeked acridly of gunpowder. But the speaker finished and departed and nothing was mentioned about the explosion. "We didn't want to hurt his feelings," said the teacher.

The professor obtained the cost of the paneling from a university vice president (my original source) and repaired the damage himself. That was ten years ago, and the teacher wasn't fired or anything. In fact, a piece of the wadding embedded in the paneling was framed by some of his students and now hangs in his campus office.

He hasn't spoken to the gun safety expert since and would prefer that a certain grinning vice president keep that explosive lecture in the engineering auditorium to himself. And the teacher, even a decade later, doesn't venture inside that auditorium unless it's absolutely necessary.

"I can still smell the gunpowder in there," he says.

"I Don't Mow," He Told Us

January 23, 1983

It wasn't that he was unwilling to work. Not exactly. In fact, we once made a list of jobs he had held—ranging from planting pine

"I DON'T MOW," HE TOLD US

trees to running a paper route—and stopped at fifty-six because everybody had to leave. That's a lot of jobs, yes, but he always had reasons for quitting.

He would quit because the boss had some unfathomable grudge against him. Or because the night shift was intolerable since he couldn't sleep in the daytime. Or because his car broke down and he couldn't get to work. Or because they gave him too much to do. Or because they gave him too little to do.

It was never his fault, and he always sincerely wanted to work again. So we would pitch in and help him look for something else. Every time. Even so he was pretty selective; not just anything would do. But he was a good old boy, a friend, so we looked. Every time.

And once there was the time Sonny Barnard, the Shipley's sage, found the "perfect job" for him and told me about it. I agreed. Though temporary, it was the perfect summer job. So we told our out-of-work friend to meet us at the cafe. We had this job for him. This perfect job.

"These people are leaving for the summer," Sonny told him over coffee. "All you have to do, really, is live there. It's called house-sitting, and I've told them about you." The jobless one nodded, and we had cleared the first hurdle. He was interested.

So Sonny continued while we drank the coffee. "All you have to do is check the freezers, bring in the papers, watch the mail, make sure things are locked up at night. Like I told you, just live there for three months." Our friend nodded again. We were encouraged. He liked the job.

"They'll pay you pretty good for this," Sonny went on, "and you can eat right out of their refrigerator and freezer . . . use their kitchen. Sleep there. Use the television anytime you want to . . . run the air-conditioner . . . everything." Our friend was smiling. It was the perfect summer. He liked it.

So far, so good. Sonny decided to wrap up the selling job. "That's about it," he told our unemployed pal. "Of course, they

"I DON'T MOW," HE TOLD US

said you might need to mow the yard once during the summer, but . . ."

"I don't mow," our friend interrupted, slamming down his coffee cup, the smile vanished, the job interview concluded. He was dead-serious, and repeated the rejection: "Sorry, I just don't mow."

For a moment after that everything went quiet at the table. Sonny looked at me. I looked at him. We looked at our jobless buddy. Then Sonny started to laugh, thunderous gales of laughter, and I joined in. Suddenly, our friend was laughing, too.

But he didn't take that summer house-sitting job.

"I don't mow," he said.

That same Sonny Barnard was talking about another job—a summer job he held, long ago, on a farm near Clay, La. He and another kid milked cows and did other odd jobs for five dollars a week. Sonny remembered easing a cow into the stall one day to milk her.

While Sonny did the milking another hired hand filled up the feeding trough or held the shovel. Sonny explained the shovel this way: they wanted to keep the stall clean and so they just held a shovel under the cow while she was milked. It seemed easier that way.

One day the bossman, a tough farmer who drove his tractor like a tank, came around the barn to supervise. He decided to hold the shovel while Sonny milked and the other guy fed the cow. When the cow suddenly held up her tail, the bossman steadied the shovel; he knew the routine. Sonny's friend poured out the feed, a dry and dusty mixture, that the cow—just as she raised her tail—coughed and choked on.

About that very time Sonny stopped milking to look at the farmer. "The shovel was clean," Sonny remembered, "but the farmer was covered from head to toe with a green-brown, wet mess." The explosive cough had done it. For a moment, Sonny recalled, the bossman just stood there, blinking his eyes, dripping, his mind blown.

Then Sonny and his helper had to take the shovel away before the man killed his own cow with it. A little while later the two kids could hear the farmer's wife yelling at him—up at the Big House: "Don't you dare come in here like that . . . hose yourself right down!"

Sonny and his friend fell down laughing in the barn.

In fact, Sonny is still laughing about it.

Every time I sit down in Dickie Thompson's barbershop in Ruston I think about it, and mentally flinch. I was eleven or twelve years old and getting a haircut in Patterson's Barbershop on East Mississippi in that same Ruston. The late Pat Patterson was clipping away and I relaxed, looking at a long bank of mirrors across from me and over to one side.

The back of somebody's head—or the side, I can't recall precisely—caught my eye. "Gosh, that poor kid has an awful bullet head," I distinctly remember thinking. Then I looked closer and the truth gradually, traumatically, dawned on me.

I was looking at my own head in the double mirrors. "Hey, don't jerk like that; I might nick you," Mr. Patterson said. He didn't know I had just seen my own bullet head for the first time.

I don't think Dickie has double mirrors in his shop.

It doesn't matter; I just read *Field and Stream* and don't look at any heads in the barbershop.

Country Pride at the Crossroads

August 28, 1983

It was stinging hot, and people were lined up to buy watermelons at the North Louisiana crossroads. The farmer was selling the good, green-striped kind out of the back of a cratered pickup. The rough, red-lettered cardboard sign said "A dollar up."

The farmer looked to be in his sixties, maybe, and his gray jumpsuit showed darkening sweatbands from neck to frazzled boot tops. His face was a deep red under the tan, the kind of permanent underburn that isn't obtained at the pool or golf course.

But the man was obviously enjoying his work. Every customer was given a patient survey of the melons in their straw bed in the back of the old pickup and those who wanted to thump for ripeness were encouraged to do so.

Once the selection was made, the farmer insisted on gently depositing the melon inside the car, making small talk about how yellow meat was actually better in the melon but allowing that, of course, red meat was what everybody wanted. He took a lot of time with every customer, even in the dusty heat.

It was my turn. The farmer mopped his face with a blue bandana while I pretended to make a learned assessment of the six remaining melons. "They're all guaranteed," he said. I made an eeny-meeny-miny-mo choice, and pointed to it.

The farmer nodded approvingly, as if I'd made an expert pick. "Give me a dollar and a half," he said, hoisting the melon. I didn't have any change and sweat sparkled on the farmer's face; it was burning up at the crossroads, and people were waiting.

So I offered two one-dollar bills. "Keep the change," I said. At that the farmer's face turned a shade redder; you could see it. He put the melon down. "I don't take no charity," he said, his voice steady but steel-edged.

I had made a mistake, and I knew it. "Hey, I didn't mean to hurt your feelings," I said. "I didn't think you had any change and it was hot and . . ." He cut me off. "I got change," he said, "I'm in business."

I took the two quarters in change and he insisted on putting the melon in my car. Thunk! It hit the floorboard hard. But our eyes met again. The heat went out of his face. We both grinned.

"It's just been a long, hot day," he said then. "I'm taking those last five watermelons and headin' home." I nodded. It was late in the afternoon. "But I do have change," he told me one last time.

That Buzzard Wasn't a Chicken

October 16, 1983

It was 1959. The Byrd-Fair Park end-of-school dance not only drew people from Shreveport. They came from all around. Representing Lincoln Parish were Larry Clinton and Skinny Jack Rockhold, both of Ruston High School. They had been looking forward to the dance for a long time.

Of course, they departed in Larry's remarkable turquoise and white 1956 Ford Victoria. He was proud of it—especially the twin glass-packed mufflers. "The kind that talk to you." Things were lined up in the big city.

Alvin Gore, Rockhold's cousin, was a Byrd student and a star fullback on the Yellow Jacket football team. A swimming party was scheduled for the afternoon at somebody's house on Fairfield Avenue. Larry still remembers that very well. "Country come to town" is the way he tells it even now, thinking about the song.

Anyway, they left Ruston early with the twin glass-packed mufflers erupting nicely in Larry's ears. It was bright June-cool, and they had the windows down. Skinny Jack saw the buzzards

THAT BUZZARD WASN'T A CHICKEN

first from 'way down Old 80 West, three of them, feasting on a shattered armadillo.

Two of the buzzards lifted off as the sparkling Victoria neared. Larry remembers they were somewhere between Dixie Inn and Princeton. The Old Arkansas Bar loomed up. So did the one buzzard that refused to take off.

"That old buzzard won't fly," observed Skinny Jack, not a bit bothered. "I'll *make* him fly," Larry said. He hit the accelerator. The twin glass-packed mufflers responded lyrically. So did the Victoria. 80—85—90 mph. Larry remembers seeing 95 mph on the speedometer. That Ford would fly.

But the lone buzzard didn't fly. Larry recalls a burst of air and a noise "like a freight train." He got control of the Victoria on the shoulder of the road and came to a spinning stop, sending up a plume of red dust.

The front window was gone and Skinny Jack's face covered with blood. At first, Larry thought Skinny Jack was dead. But he was okay—just covered up with buzzard's blood. The thing was, the buzzard was pretty much all right, too.

He blinked malignly and flapped a wing from the back seat of Larry's once-gleaming Victoria, which was now swimming in gore. The janitor at the Arkansas Bar came out and helped. Larry threw a burlap bag over the still-blinking buzzard and pitched him into a ditch.

A few miles down the road at a filling station, cleaning up the Victoria, Larry and Skinny Jack got really mad at the buzzard for not flying. They bought a supply of gas and decided to return to the Arkansas Bar and "cremate"—Larry's word—the bird.

The janitor at the Arkansas Bar came outside again when Larry braked the Victoria in, its twin mufflers still singing. But the buzzard was nowhere to be found. Larry remembers exactly what the janitor told them. "I last saw that old buzzard limping on one leg toward Shreveport."

It's true. The buzzard, Larry, Skinny Jack and Alvin Gore all survived. In fact, Rockhold and Clinton made it to the swimming party on Fairfield Avenue, even with the Victoria's windshield gone. And that trio (leaving out the buzzard) has done pretty well in the world every since.

And their names have been legend in Ruston ever since that afternoon when there was a little chicken game on Old 80 between Dixie Inn and Princeton and a certain buzzard turned out *not* to be the chicken.

C.L., and the Hot Breath of Hell

January 22, 1984

C.L.

Just mention those initials and even now, more than fifty years later, anybody who lived around Antioch and Trussell's Store and the Four Corners during that time will toss a quick, nervous look over his or her shoulder.

They will be just making sure, a half-century and more removed, that C.L. isn't around. C.L., you see, was the meanest bull in the history of Lincoln Parish. Old C.L. was as black as a thunderhead, and all hooves and horns and red-eyed hate.

C.L., named after his owner and my grandfather—Chester Leroy Trussell—even hated children. "Walking home from school we always looked for C.L.," my mother, Marie Trussell Hilburn, remembers. "If he was out, we'd hide in the woods or go to somebody's house until Daddy (Chester Trussell) could get him back in."

Yeah, C.L. was *that* mean. He came after people. Children. Dogs. Trucks. Outhouses. Anything or anybody. Compared to

"It was like the hot breath of hell on the back of my neck."

C.L., AND THE HOT BREATH OF HELL

C.L., the Schlitz malt liquor bull is a lamb. My mother can still see him "spraying dirt everywhere with those horrible hooves."

My Grandfather Chester tried to keep C.L. up, but he finally acknowledged that there "isn't any fence that old C.L. can't jump or break down." So C.L., loose a lot of the time, terrorized Louisiana 544 from the Antioch Methodist Church on down past Trussell's Store where the road went four different ways.

Still, if anybody around Antioch felt halfway safe from C.L., it was at night. Usually he had been somehow herded behind another fence by suppertime. It was on just such a spring night, smelling of honeysuckle, that my father came to visit his girl at Antioch—that same and then soon-to-be Marie Trussell Hilburn.

As usual on a warm night in Antioch, Marie and Wiley Sr. sat in the front porch swing. The porch on that tin-roofed house at the four corners was long and open, and the swing hung, exposed, at the east end of the opening.

Unknown to Marie and Wiley Sr., C.L. had escaped one more time. Quietly, for the bull was surprisingly light on his feet for all that battleship displacement, C.L. approached the east end of the porch and swing until his great snout was maybe a quarter of an inch from the short hairs on the back of Wiley's unsuspecting neck.

Then, at that very moment, C.L. bellowed. *Bellowed.* "It was like a sonic boom went off inside my eardrum," Wiley Sr. remembers, frowning even now. "But what was even worse," he recalls "was that hot, moist, stinking breath."

"It was," he says, "like the hot breath of hell on the back of my neck. And then he always adds: "And I thought the very devil had me." Wiley Sr., who had not long before set the 100-yard dash record at a tri-state track meet in Ruston, broke every speed mark that night.

"I flew off the other end of the porch," he says, "with my legs poking air, still running." Wiley Sr. finally did stop running that night and discovered that it was indeed a black devil—old C.L.—who nearly got him.

C.L. is long gone now, of course, and the old tin-roofed Trussell house and general store at the four-corners have been torn down. But ask people who lived in Antioch during that time about the legendary C.L., and that haunted, hunted look will sneak back into their eyes.

"I Came to Collect My 'A'"

September 9, 1984

He was a young college English instructor, teaching for the first time, and a little full of himself on the first day of class. "Don't cut my class, and don't think you can put anything over on me about cuts or absences," he told them at the end, "because I've done it all."

Then, right at the bell, feeling smug in his patched sleeves, he made the mistake. "In fact, if anybody thinks they have pulled something on me, and can prove it, well, you've got an automatic 'A' for the next semester." The class laughed obediently.

But when everybody filed out, one girl remained behind. "I may *have* to miss some of your classes," she said. The instructor felt his resolve about being tough on cuts recede. This student had melting brown eyes. She was pretty. She seemed sincere.

"What's the problem?" he asked, as sternly as possible. He had, after all, made his position on cuts very clear. "I get these terrible headaches," she said. "In fact, my head is killing me right now." The teacher imagined he could see a tear or two in those brown eyes.

"I CAME TO COLLECT MY 'A'"

"Try to get here," he said, all the gruffness gone out of his voice. She nodded. But then she didn't get to class much at all, and his resolve mounted as the term hit the halfway mark. There was no way the pretty girl with the headaches could pass. Sorry, but no deal.

Then he got the telephone call. It was from the father of the girl with the headaches, calling long-distance. He had a deep, commanding voice. "I know my daughter has missed a lot of classes because of those headaches," the father told the instructor.

"Yes, she told me about that, and I'd like to help, but you see everybody has to pass the mass examination, and she's just missed too much to have a chance on that," the teacher said, not wanting to sound unreasonable but at the same time planting his feet on the solid ground of academic integrity.

The father seemed to take it all in stride. "I understand," he said in that deep voice. "It's just that . . . well . . . I . . . oh, forget about it—and thanks for your time, professor." But now the teacher's curiosity was aroused. So he asked the question: "Just what is your daughter's problem, anyway?"

"She's dying," the father said, all in one breath. But he added quickly: "I understand . . . you can't do anything about that mass exam." The teacher, by now, was entirely taken aback. "Why don't you just withdraw her from all her classes?" he asked.

"We haven't told her," the father said. "We want the last days of her life, up to a certain point, of course, to be as normal as possible—school and everything." The father seemed ready to hang up at that, but the instructor was hung up on the conversation now.

"How long has she got?" the teacher asked, totally sympathetic. "Two, three months at most," the father said, his voice sad. "But except for those headaches she told you about, well, there's nothing to make her think she's dying."

"I'll ask my departmental chairman what to do about the mass exam," the teacher said, desperate for a humane solution. He could see the girl's pained brown eyes. "If you can, it would be appreciated, but don't do anything wrong," said the father, his deep voice resonant again.

"By the way, I will have our family doctor call you or your chairman to verify everything and provide the medical documentation," the father said. The instructor recoiled at such an idea; he had already been insensitive enough. "No, please, that won't be necessary," he said.

The next day the young teacher approached his chairman, an erudite but gentle philosopher steeped in humanity. The instructor knew what the answer would be, even before he explained the problem, and he wasn't disappointed. "If we err, let's err on the side of compassion," the chairman said. So the girl passed the course, even though she didn't even take the final.

It was a year later when the instructor saw the same girl with the headaches and the brown eyes on the front row of his class. "You're supposed to be dead," he cried out, not even able to think.

She smiled brightly. "That was my boyfriend who called you that day, not my father, and I came to collect my 'A'."

The story recounted above is true, but readers should know that the conversations are quoted from memory.

What's This? Dirty Movies in Ruston?

January 13, 1985

It was something I somehow, uh, failed to include in my part of a collaborative remembrance of Ruston's past, written for and

WHAT'S THIS? DIRTY MOVIES IN RUSTON?

duly delivered at the city's centennial program last year in the Thomas Assembly Center. I'm referring, of course, to Ruston's dirty movies.

That's right. As unlikely as it seems in a town where prohibition is still real, where Temple Baptist Church's Singing Christmas Tree remains the event of the year, and where people arrive late even for Lady Techster games when they are held on Wednesday prayer meeting nights, we had X-rated movies right here.

Finding a Lincoln Parish resident willing to admit he saw one of those movies is as difficult as locating somebody around here who will acknowledge voting for Edwin Edwards. Alas, I admit to voting for Edwin—and also to attending one of those dirty movies shown at the old Tech theater in the early 1970s.

I will admit to seeing an X-showing because my reputation, in Ruston, has been irredeemably established since I was apprehended at an early age for bombing East Mississippi Avenue with tiny torpedoes dropped from atop the James Building.

But most of our citizens were more reticent about showing themselves at the old Tech during its time as an X-house. It was part of the fun, in fact, to watch people pretend to be studying the shotguns in the side window of Ruston Hardware just across the street from the show—waiting for traffic on the two hundred block of West Mississippi Avenue to clear so they could rush, unobserved, for the ticket window.

The place was full-up the time I went, and the crowd included a lot of Tech professors, probably all doing work on research papers dealing with the redeeming social value of dirty movies. In fact, one of the guys I was with—he didn't mind being seen or *heard* there, either—spied a distinguished teacher of many years in the gloom of the very back row.

"Hey, Dr. ———————," my friend hollered, "can't ever tell who you'll see at a dirty movie, can you." That honored Ph.D. disappeared under his seat.

It wasn't long before I saw another one of my friends, not from

WHAT'S THIS? DIRTY MOVIES IN RUSTON?

the university, toward the front of the theater. He was deep into religion, and I had been the target of his revivalism. "What were you doing at that dirty movie?" I asked him a few days later.

"I didn't know it was going to be a dirty movie," he declared in an instantly hostile tone.

"But you stayed through the whole movie," I persisted.

"Well, the people on both sides of me just refused to let me out," he offered after some hesitation, finally vindicated as an innocent hostage.

Actually, the old X-house *did* claim at least one innocent victim. A university dean, entertaining an accreditation team, heard about a movie playing at the old Tech that seemed to fit in with higher education. It was called *The Dean's Wife*. Our dean honestly didn't know that the Tech had gone to X-films.

The whole accreditation group, led by a manifestly mortified dean, made a hasty exit before the first reel was finished. I don't know if the university's accreditation was adversely affected as a result, but since Tech now has all its major academic approvals in order, well, apparently no permanent damage was done. Right, dean?

The movie I saw was entitled *Tobacco Roody*. It did *not* have any redeeming social value, but we saw a lot of haystacks and what drive-in reviewer Joe Bob Briggs likes to call "nekkid" bodies. I can't offer much on the dialogue because somebody in front of us had asthma or something and made so much noise breathing we couldn't hear the talking.

The management at the old X-rated Tech was able to keep all that going for about a year, all told, by fanatically checking ID's and by *not* advertising anywhere—not even on the billboards outside the show. And when the churches began to protest, they would just close the place down—only to reopen it quietly a few days later.

People came from all over to see them. Only the locals would pause at the Ruston Hardware window. The rest walked right in. In fact, one couple drove from deepest Mississippi every weekend. But when Ruston-X was finally closed for good one Friday night they didn't get the message and found themselves watching a Walt Disney feature.

Well, the old X-house is long gone, all boarded up and abandoned now, but I wanted to include it among the remembrances of old Ruston—even if nobody from here (except, maybe, for a couple of those crazy Tech profs) ever even knew there was such a place, much less went there.

Atlanta, If You Change Coke Again, Don't Tell Us

August 18, 1985

The question is, why did I wait this long to write about Coke changing, and then making the Classic retreat—the victim of the first successful consumer revolution in American history? Why did I delay addressing the subject until it went as flat as the new (NEW!) Coke pretender in the silver sash with the Bill Cosby introduction?

Well, I was like the sports writer that night Billy Cannon ran 1,000 miles and made Mississippi weep. "I can't write it—it's too big for me," cried an overwhelmed writer. And he was there.

I was there when Coke blew its birthright, but I couldn't swallow the sweet news; it just wouldn't go down the well of the old Smith-Corona.

The Cannon run was too implausible, too glorious—at least from the Louisiana point of view—to be true that night in 1959. The Coke debacle of 1985 was too implausible, too dumb, to be true. Yet, I was eminently qualified to editorialize on the Coke biggie; I was on the scene.

Everybody was on the scene, of course, because just about everybody drinks Coke, but I was an insider on the issue. Ellen's daddy, you see, was manager of Ruston Coca Cola Bottling for fifty years. Hale Shadow, a family friend, is the local distributor and Mr. Coke in North Central Louisiana. His wedding gift to my son Greg was the first Cherry Coke to hit town, and that's a big deal in Lincoln Parish, even with the Saints here.

No, Mr. Shadow has never revealed the Coke syrup formula to me, but you can see how close I was—am—to the subject. So is Ellen. She doesn't take aspirin for a headache or dramamine for upset stomach. "I just need a sip of Coke," she says, and it makes her well. A case of Coke is a shipment from Lourdes at my house.

My middle son Kevin is a Cokeaholic. You hear the cap coming off a Coke before you see him enter the room.

As a matter of fact, all the Hilburns live out of the Bonner Street Coke plant. Ben Riser, my father-in-law, is retired as manager but he still brings Cokes over by the cases until the empties pyramid precariously, threatening the carport.

Me, well, I sneak a Pepsi now and then to secretly defy my father-in-law. But Pepsi wasn't my generation and it isn't my drink now. Cokes were it—the old Pause That Refreshed. Even when we were going to drink something else, we said we were going for Coke. Coke was the synonym for all soft drinks; it was that pervasive.

Some people drank Dr. Peppers because they were supposed to be tough. In the country stores of North Louisiana, there were strawberry Nehis but we didn't drink them much. In college, Seven-Up was a nice mixer, clear and sparkling, but you wouldn't order a Seven-Up to go with a Hood's hamburger. Serious eating required a Coke.

All right, a Coke wasn't always required. Fresh-roasted peanuts at the old Fraser baseball field in Ruston required a big Royal

ATLANTA, IF YOU CHANGE COKE AGAIN, DON'T TELL US

Crown Cola—the Big R.C. (on the other hand, a good, salty package of Fritos had to be washed down by a Coke; these things you just knew).

Something else, too. If I was really thirsty, like Sahara Desert-dying of thirst, I went for a Delaware Punch in the long, thin bottle. You could drain a Delaware Punch without stopping. But the old Coke didn't chug-a-lug; the old Coke, taken down whole, would bust your chest, boy.

But mostly, Coke was in, then and now. So when the word came out they were changing my drink, it was too big for me at first. It was like when I read they were taking "In The Garden" out of the hymnbook. Or when Louisiana Tech lost to NLU that time. I mean, it was inconceivable.

The change just struck me as being dumb. Why would anybody mess with a winner like Coke?

Had anybody in Atlanta Coke's corporate Fountainhead ever taken Marketing 101, where you learn that a tradition, even in taste, is something you can't buy for Brazil's foreign debt? Spending big bucks, you try to build a tradition with advertising—usually without abiding success—not tear it down with something "NEW!" even when a Cosby is doing the selling.

Had anybody in Atlanta shopped the Louisiana Purchase store in the cottonfields south of Shreveport and priced battered old Coke coolers selling for big bucks? An old Coke cooler shows the flag, boys, and that's why it sells. Matter of fact, Coke was at least a stripe in the flag.

All of this suggests who made the dumbest public relations move since the first major league baseball strike. It was Atlanta, as in Teheran. I remember Mr. Riser and Mr. Shadow complaining about revolutionary schemes hatched by Atlanta long before they tampered with the syrup.

Mr. Shadow, who knows people in North Louisiana are not wild about any kind of change, even fought the 16-ounce bottle as long as he could in his Ruston plant. Well, didn't you think Coke tasted better, colder, in that little bottle? I did.

ATLANTA, IF YOU CHANGE COKE AGAIN, DON'T TELL US

So that's it. The Mullahs in Atlanta took too many marketing courses. A master's degree in marketing can tear up your taste buds. That and Madison Avenue prevailed over Peachtree Street. Georgia surrendered to New York. The Yankees made them do it, after all.

The result was a sweet Coke, no bite at all, and a blessing from Bill Cosby. Coke, America's drink, ran up a red, white and silver flag with the word "NEW!" where the stars were supposed to go. It was the day they tore old Coke down, and it caused a rebellion, especially down here in Dixie.

Of course, Atlanta has since retreated, and now Coke is Six Flags Over the World with a taste for every generation. Still in all, the Contra Consumers won in the end—a Classic revolution—and so I can write about the whole thing at last.

It's also time for an admission: The Hilburns were drinking just as much of that silver stuff as the old Coke. Ask Mr. Riser. He delivers 'em.

And I'm not absolutely sure I could tell the difference between the old and new Coke in one of those dumb taste tests that Pepsi used to burn Atlanta one more time.

That much admitted, my last, late word to the Fountainhead in Atlanta is this: If you mess with the syrup again, don't tell us about it, dummy.

PART FIVE

ONE MAN'S FAMILY

At Pop's:
A Monkey
in the Bed

January 7, 1979

Peg and I had planned it from the start, but we let the night's routine unwind, anyway. It was a good routine. We had collard greens that Peg had bargained out of a horse-pulled vegetable wagon and pork soup for supper. It was my favorite meal.

Then we settled into big, upholstered chairs—the kind that sent up great motes of dust when you jumped on 'em—to listen to Gabriel Heatter, and the familiar voice boomed out of the cabinet set: "There's baaaaaaaad news tonight, friends."

After that, in the early part of twilight, we would sit on the front porch. Pop would whittle with a super sharp pocket knife and wonder if the cotton was getting too much rain. I made a game of counting the cars that passed by on Alabama and keeping up with what model was first, second, third and so forth.

The Chevys and Fords always battled for first place and Buicks (Pop had a black Buick) never failed to finish far back. Peg would

AT POP'S: A MONKEY IN THE BED

wonder when the "Templelites" (Temple Baptist Church was right across the street) were going to turn on their big lighted sign for the night. Peg was fearful of the night, and she always felt better when Temple brightened the street. It would be a long time before we pulled the trick, but I was already thinking about it.

After the "Templelites" turned on their light, we went inside—or at least Pop and Peg did. Peg unfailingly locked all the doors and made me check from the outside just to make sure. After that, we played dominoes. Peg and I would sneak dominoes into Pop's "woodpile."

At first he didn't notice, but then an expression of puzzlement and anger would come over his face. "Where did I get all these dominoes?" Peg would giggle about then and Pop usually blew up—sometimes sweeping all the dominoes off the sewing machine top we used for a table.

Of course, we had that other trick planned for Pop, but it wasn't time for that yet. After the aborted domino game, it was time for fruit. Pop took that gleaming knife and cut up some tart Jonathan apples while Peg and I peeled the oranges. Then Peg and I read from *The Christian Observer* and I presided over a devotional.

All that moved us pretty close to bedtime—and our trick on Pop. Bedtime preparation on Alabama Street at my grandparents' house was a great ritual of coughing, slamming doors, yawning and stretching and much swallowing of pills.

Peg, her run-over shoes beside the bed, took "Liver medicine"—huge, horrible-smelling capsules. Pop downed his alfalfa pills. His neck hurt him a lot—I rubbed it nearly every night—and he was sure the alfalfa pills (he had ordered them out of an agricultural magazine) helped ease the pain.

Trick time was approaching now. "It's time to fly up on the roost," Pop would say. He had changed into his longhandles and I could hear him gargling (he sounded like a tub draining) in the

AT POP'S: A MONKEY IN THE BED

bathroom. Peg gave me the signal. The thing is, I had won a toy monkey at the Lincoln Parish Fair that was amazingly lifelike.

While Pop was in the bathroom, I hopped out of my featherbed roost and secreted the furry thing at the very end of his bed—where his toes would barely brush it. I was back in bed before Pop completed his last tour of the hall, shut the icebox door one more time, coughed and switched off the bedroom lights.

Long and angular, he eased into the bed like always, his feet searching for the rails, yawning and grunting contentedly. I watched in the blue half-light that filtered into the room from the sign at Temple Baptist Church, my head half out of the covers.

Once fully extended in bed, a tentative, thoughtful look gradually suffused Pop's features—shortly to be replaced by bewilderment. I could see good from the featherbed. Gradually, very deliberately, completely perplexed now, he raised the toy monkey out of the loose bedcovers with his feet.

Finally, foot-pinned against the far bedrail, the creature was raised to full view. And, indeed, it looked very monkey-like in the poor light. It was just like that for what seemed an hour with Pop's face gradually, in slow-motion, collapsing into total disbelief.

Then Pop let it out like a thunderclap: "Roberta, there's a damned monkey in our bed!" I fell out of the bed, strangling with laughter, and Peg joined in. It was a few days, though, before Poppy would see any humor at all in our prank.

Growing Up, Goodbyes, Neighbors

January 14, 1979

The deep, sloping backyard is quiet. The crooked slats of wood leading up to the treehouse high in the big blackgum are rotting. The rope swing sways in the winter wind. In this cold silence, I think again of the Steinfeldts, the across-the-street neighbors who left. I miss them.

It wasn't that we ever socialized in the formal sense. We spared each other the sit-down dinners and month-ahead invitations. Neither family cared much for that sort of thing. Such events wiped out whole evenings and had to be planned and prepared.

We didn't have to plan and prepare our meetings. They were less than 100 yards away, so it was a long neighborhood communion of shared children's illnesses, rummage sales, borrowed butter, and brief, shouted greetings between errands and business.

But the Steinfeldts had a quiet strength, over there across the street, and just knowing they were there, ready to listen and to help, was somehow an enduring comfort, though like most busy people we didn't quite understand or appreciate it then.

Not that we didn't communicate. Oh, we all communicated, adults and children, as families, and one-on-one. Bev liked to bake and she would let Greg—who adored her—help in the kitchen. He would come out of her garage front literally trailing a cloud of flour.

And when Greg suffered a serious injury, she was along on the ride to the hospital, smiling, relentlessly cheerful, talking away the fear. Greg wanted her to come. I don't think he would have gone without her, as a matter of fact.

Like most good neighbors, we experienced the little tensions. Bev complained about the local schools and didn't like Ellen's new sofa and was sometimes so blunt it hurt. That didn't matter because we just said Bev was a Yankee (the fact that she was from Iowa didn't matter) and Yankees said things.

Lyle was the Lutheran minister in Ruston. His flock was small, and one afternoon, talking in the middle of our quiet dead-end Caddo Street, he complained that since nobody had died his pastoral experience didn't even include a funeral.

"Then you ought to advertise in the Ruston *Daily Leader*, 'Join the Lutheran Church and never die,'" I told him. "Then you would have more people than the Baptists." We both laughed at that.

The children of the two families, three on each side of the street (and two boys and a girl on each side) mingled, laughed, argued, fought, teased, wrestled, cried and made up. Together, with the help of the older Goertz kids, they built that exceptional treehouse in the blackgum and fashioned the rope swing.

It was Todd and Joey and Karl and Greg and Kevin and Anne Marie. And on down the short street, and just as close, were the Richardsons and the Goertzes and their boys. They called themselves the "Screaming Demons" and organized a club which served a timeless purpose—that is, to bar younger members periodically and send them home weeping.

The good thing was that home—a place where a one-sided tale of betrayal would be heard—was only a few steps away. Joey, in particular, could mount a pathetic picture of suffering while making his way home: Head down, shoulders slumped, feet shuffling, he trudged along, muttering dark incantations every sorrowful step. When Ellen feels depressed even now, she inevitably says: "I feel like Joey."

We had known they were leaving for months before it happened, but so long as they were there, right across the street, with the lights on and the shouts of the kids shrilling in the winter air, well, it was like they would never leave, not really. Nobody even thought about it; we put it out of our minds.

But the time came, and then their car broke down and so they had to leave in the night, in a black January rain. It was like a scene out of *The Grapes of Wrath*, with three children, a cat, a dog, potted plants and assorted luggage stuffed into a pitted, weary station wagon. Their journey was a long one, from North Louisiana to northern Illinois. The next morning's Shreveport *Times* told of a record midwestern snowfall.

The Steinfeldts have been gone three years now, and all our kids are growing up—ours in North Louisiana and theirs in the Midwest. Bev's letters are as relentlessly cheerful as she was, but sometimes I wonder. Because now I see the rope swing swaying in the backyard, and there are no children's cries to part the wind.

It's just that we have all grown up on Caddo Street, the Steinfeldts, the Goertzes, the Richardsons and the Hilburns, and some of us have gone. The rope swing blows in the wind, the backyard is mostly quiet, and a part of our life is gone with the Steinfeldts.

We all have to grow up, of course, and move on to other things. But somehow, this winter day, I want to see somebody—Greg or Kevin or Joey or John Richardson—swinging on the rope, and making noise in my backyard.

Of Parties and Pierced Ears

April 1, 1979

It was Anne Marie's first night party. The big invitation card said there would be dancing. The only concession to the fact that this was to be a twelfth birthday party was a subtle hint that everybody could bring a present.

OF PARTIES AND PIERCED EARS

The whole idea worried me, to be honest. Anne Marie still hugs me goodbye and hello several times a day. We say prayers together at night. I tease her a lot. It's a situation that I like and want to prolong as long as possible. The prospect of Anne Marie actually growing up unsettles me. This party, I thought darkly, would be a watershed in the growing-up process. The dancing part worried me, too.

As for Anne Marie, she worried for a solid week about what she would wear to the party and who she would know there. The afternoon of the party she was too preoccupied about it to converse properly with her grandmother. She said, for the record, that the whole thing would be a bore. That secretly pleased me, but two hours before the party she began to manifest a minute-to-minute interest in the time.

We left her at a big house on a hill and picked her up at 10:30 P.M., a very late hour I thought, and found out that she did have a good time after all. She had lost an earring and torn a hole in her new white jeans. Ellen said she would call the hostess and ask her to look for the earring.

"How did you manage to lose an earring?" I asked innocently on the way home and immediately detonated a family land mine. "I was embarrassed to let anybody know I lost it because it's a *magnetic* (Anne Marie's emphasis) earring, Dad," she said scathingly.

Anne Marie insists she is the only twelve-year-old in the Western Hemisphere with unpierced ears. I put pierced ears in the same category with night parties and dances: barbaric and dangerous, especially for pretty daughters. Ellen had said she could have the deed done when she turned twelve. I'm still holding out for twenty-one.

Still headed home, I got to the point and asked the fearful question: "How was the dancing?" When we drove up Anne Marie and another girl were jumping on the trampoline (that reassured me) and no boys or dancers were to be seen.

"Well," Anne Marie told me, "only two boys showed up so

there wasn't much dancing at all." My next question was what happened to the guys. "They were either scared or on vacation," Anne Marie said calmly.

That was when old Dad finally relaxed.

For the moment.

Life in America's Lourdes

May 13, 1979

HOUSTON—More and more this growing-out-of-control city is America's Lourdes. And in Medical Center, just off teeming South Main, all the shining surgeons mend as many as sixty literally broken hearts in a day.

But even if the already legendary Dr. Michael DeBakey is the doctor, life in the Intensive Care waiting room on the third floor of the Fondren-Brown Building is swiftly broken down into some brutal and elemental dimensions.

Those dimensions are fear, guilt, quivering stomachs, glazed stares, tears and, in this instant community of waiting and waiting for the physician's verdict on how the surgery went, compassion, confessions, shared caring, sudden friendships and even unexpected laughter.

This one room, the ICU waiting room, does shelter an instant community, and the relentless routine of the hospital is imposed on people—mostly women standing vigil for heart-stricken husbands—who have, for however long they are here, seen their worlds, priorities and dreams transformed. It's life and death, really, and this is the last dimension, the one that shuts out worries only hours ago regarded as paramount and shrinks them to nothing.

This waiting room, this community, even has its own language—again enforced by the regimen of Medical Center. "Going up" is the best phrase. It means the patient is doing well enough to be promoted out of ICU, where he lies in a tangle of fearsome tubes and wires, to the fourth floor and a more "normal" existence. The sixth floor is the last stop before home.

In this environment—disoriented, shocked people trying to get their bearings in the labyrinth of Methodist Hospital—amateur experts who can discuss coronary by-passes and mitral valves are created on the spot.

Social status doesn't matter in this room. Neither does race or nationality or occupation or language. The hospital is the enforcer, the equalizer, the leveler. We are all the same here, reduced to a single raw dimension, waiting to talk to the surgeon—that belly-flopping moment when the nurse calls out "The Hilburn Family," or later when a twenty minute visit is permitted in the swarming ICU ward.

It's a tight commonalty of fear and hope that binds us in this room, and out of that unlikely element grows a humanity usually unseen beyond hospital doors: "How is he doing?" we ask each other. We touch and talk and sympathize and comfort. Of course, there are the smiling, secret resentments: "Why did her husband 'go up' and why is mine still in the ICU?"

But mostly it is a shared struggle, and here are some of the people who helped me in the ICU world:

Priscilla: Ambushed by a lung infection after surgery, her husband had spent thirty days (when I left) in ICU. Priscilla spent her nights and her days in the waiting room—sleeping on an ICU couch. For twenty-five days she greeted the newcomers, telling them what to expect, preparing wives for the first traumatic visit to death-pale, zonked-out, wired-up husbands.

"I quit helping after the twenty-fifth day," she said. "I pouted. When the others finally went up, I was glad for them, but it cut me." But then Priscilla found another reservoir of courage and started talking to people again. "It helps me," she says.

Rena: Rena sleeps in the ICU waiting room, too. She and Priscilla have become best friends, sharing a table at the back of the room where nobody sits unless invited. Rena's husband came to the hospital facing amputation of both legs.

The doctor has decided that he can save one leg. But Rena comes back from a twenty minute ICU ward visit circle-eyed because her husband has bad pain—and because their insurance has only two more days to run. In the deepest part of the night, when depression overwhelms her, Rena visits the hospital chapel or calls an old friend long-distance from the ICU pay phone.

Fay: Fay lost her man in this very Medical Center a few years ago. She knows the waiting and the agony. Now she keeps vigil for a second husband. Like Priscilla and Rena, she never leaves the ICU waiting room except for coffee or a short walk. She tells me it will be all right, though, and we talk about our children.

Grandma: Grandma is in the neighborhood of ninety. But she, too, sleeps in the ICU waiting room—close to a daughter in Intensive Care. A young man has given her a rose, and she is sparkling with gratitude all day. One night, when there are only a half-dozen of us in the room, she tells us a love story. Her boy friend left for college, left her, and she nearly died from grief. He came back, later, to marry her. "But I had already kissed Mr. _____."

Then there was the woman whose seventeen year marriage failed. She experienced two more divorces. And then only six months before this day she looked up the first husband to introduce him to a son he had never known. They married again, after all that time, the same day as the first time, and now he was fighting for his life in the ICU. "He's costing me a lot of money," she tells me roughly. Then she shudders with tears.

We all had our stories. I told them how Daddy kept my spirits up the long, breathless night before surgery, laughing and cracking jokes; and I told them how he disappeared behind the gray elevator door to Surgery with a brave, boyish smile; and I told them, without embarrassment, how much I love him.

After Daddy had "gone up"—to the fourth floor and relative safety—I was gone, down South Main, to International Airport, and finally off to Shreveport and Ruston and home.

I left Priscilla and Rena and Fay and Grandma in that tight little ICU waiting room world, and I miss them even now, and wonder if their men have "gone up," and feel a strange and abiding tenderness for them all.

Time Is Measured by a Senior Ring

June 24, 1979

How is time measured?

For some people, time spans are divided by Sundays; a day calendared as the start of the week but regarded by most as a sort of official end to things. We say, not believing it, "It's Sunday again"—and so write off a segment of our lives.

Others measure time by the length of a construction project. A wedding, birthday or other anniversary can point to a passage, even when we don't want to acknowledge it. For kids, the six-week report card is an inescapable landmark.

However it's measured, most everybody past twenty-one years of age will agree on the verity of the old cliche: time flies. How often do we ask each other, in real wonder, "Where did the month go?" Even the seasons seem to blend indistinguishably.

For me, the flashing sign-posts of time read Column, Academic Quarter, Mid-term Grades and Senior Ring. Senior ring? How does a high school senior ring mark time for somebody past forty?

Easy. It happened the other night at the supper table when Greg, a sixteen-year-old junior, announced that he needed money for a Ruston High School senior ring.

In an instant, I was Greg's age, and sitting at my father's table on Marbury Drive, asking for money to buy a Ruston High School senior ring—the deluxe model with the sealed ruby-red stone.

"No," he told me from the end of the supper table, "you'll just give it to Ellen." It was the custom then, in the spring of 1955, to signify "going steady" by awarding your girl a senior ring.

Ellen and I were "going steady" and Daddy had guessed my exact intention. It wasn't that he didn't like Ellen, but at that stage in my life he wasn't about to encourage a high school romance. "You'll want to play the field," he said with an insular certainty that I always found infuriating.

But actually Daddy's reluctance to invest forty dollars in a senior ring with my initials engraved on the inside and "RHS, 56" on the outside was motivated more by his hard-headed business sense than any idea of discouraging an early-blooming courtship.

He understood the significance of a senior ring, he observed, eating his purplehull peas and porkchop, but why spend that much money on a ring I would never wear?

It took some persuading (and some crucial help from Mama), but Daddy finally relented and bought me the senior ring—on the condition that I would wear it for six months before turning it over to Ellen. Of course, Ellen had that ring dangling around her neck within twenty-four hours after it arrived.

That was twenty-four years ago, and as it turned out, Daddy didn't make a bad investment in that senior ring. I still have it—and Ellen, too.

All that flashed through my head when Greg asked for money

to buy his senior ring. But, I thought, it was only yesterday, surely, that I had posed the same question for my father.

But, no. Greg's senior ring (he rejected the idea of using mine) will read, "RHS, '80."

Time is a senior ring, and how it does fly.

"He's at Home in the Garden, Happy, . . ."

July 22, 1979

In a sense, Daddy was born out of sync with the times. A farmer by roots and unconscious inclination, I think, he turned to other pursuits because the red clay soil was growing pine trees instead of cotton. And so he finally raised his family out of a dry-cleaning plant built, in eighteen hour workdays, from the bottom up.

But the land was in his blood, all that time, and now in retirement it fills his hours and his dreams. The garden, though it is not very large, is almost an all-season job because he does it organically.

This year the garden, carved rather pre-emptively out of Mama's otherwise landscaped backyard, is even more special to all of us. Daddy had open-heart surgery in December, and the first thing he asked the doctor before and after the operation was if he could have the garden.

He was putting down the tomato holes (he dug only two a day in deference to the operation) in late February. And now, in the ripeness of mid-July, the garden fairly leaps green and strong against the buttermilk blue sky.

Oh, he has worked at it, shirtless and reddened by the sun,

stooping and sweating, and stopping now and then to sweep it all in, eyes proud, the farmboy spirit singing in his soul. His rows are clean and weedless, and they hum with life in the blaze of early afternoon.

It had showered late the day before, hard spears of rain borne on rending cracks of thunder, and now all the garden seems ashimmer, jumping and dancing in the dampness. One can almost see it growing, pushing up, and he walks me up and down it—glowing like a kid. "There is nothing as beautiful as a garden," he tells me every summer from his Lakeview plot, and he is so right.

In my own air-conditioned office, I can imagine him in the garden, standing tall in the corn and rows of beans, still a powerful man in his sixties, in his green element, a chew of Day's Work in his jaw, making the tough hill dirt grow things with all the skill and hard work born into him.

He's at home in the garden, happy, and I love him for it.

Magic Decoders and Ginsu Knives

September 2, 1979

Greg and Kevin cornered me in the den. "Did you really order that Ginsu knife?" I had to repeat that I did, calling in on one of the "once-in-a-lifetime" offers made almost hourly on Atlanta's Channel Seventeen.

The boys had to know why I wanted a Ginsu knife. Had the old man finally lost his mind altogether? I decided to tell them part of the truth. "I wanted to call that WATS line number to see if it really worked . . . I've always wanted to order something on the WATS line."

But the boys were still amazed. And suspicious. This was a real departure for the old man; ordering something from a television station. Greg, who likes to get people in trouble, was finally convinced that I had actually ordered the knife. "I'm going to tell Mama," he beamed triumphantly, storing away the incriminating information.

Actually, I had told them only part of the truth: it was fun using the WATS line and the excited announcer had made the Ginsu knife sound like a terrific bargain. But there was more to it than the Ginsu.

As a kid, I used to write for things that were advertised on the radio: "Order your Captain Marvel decoder now . . . Find out what will happen next week . . . And your decoder is made of bright red, sturdy, long-lasting material . . .!"

The mailman always brought me some flimsy plastic thing that broke within the day, but I never gave up. Surely the Ginsu knife, I thought, would be better than those sorry Captain Marvel decoders.

Finally Ellen arrived and the boys trapped her right inside the front door. From the den I could hear the little whispering informants: "Called on the WATS line . . . some crazy knife . . . he really did . . . cost $9.95."

Enter Ellen, with my two smiling sons formed up like a posse behind her. "What's this about a Ginsu knife?" Ellen is a Riser and very practical. She wanted to know why on earth, too, and I told her the same thing: I wanted to call the WATS line number and the Ginsu knife was a once-in-a-lifetime bargain. I did not mention the Captain Marvel decoder.

They all started in on me again at the supper table and I had to defend the Ginsu knife. "Well, we got a fifty-year-guarantee on it, and that's not all. (That's what the announcer kept saying: 'And that's not all!')"

I told them about the six steak knives with the genuine imitation mahogany handles; the carving fork, the six-in-one kitchen tool and the spiral slicer. "I thought you would love having a spiral slicer," I told Ellen defensively. She looked at me queerly.

"The whole package ('There's much, much more,' the announcer kept saying) only cost $9.95," I told the supper table jury. Ellen allowed that I sounded just like the man on television and that she could have gotten the knife cheaper at Wal-Mart. She didn't seem particularly excited about the spiral slicer, either.

We finally forgot all about it. But then, after what seemed like months, I heard the boys hollering at the front door. "Dad, your Ginsu knife is here!" They were really excited. I was calm after so many disappointments with magic decoders.

"Sign here for your genius knife," the delivery man said. "Uh, I think it's a Ginsu knife," I corrected politely. "Genius, pal," he answered briskly. I wrote "genius" on the check.

Greg and Kevin checked out the whole set: the sharp Ginsu that the television man had said would cut right through a beer can or a tomato, the carving fork (I could hear the announcer saying "and there's much, much more!"), the six-in-one kitchen tool, the six steak knives and spiral slicer.

The kids went absolutely crazy and savaged a bunch of tomatoes and carrots that we didn't need with the Ginsu. To be honest, once all the stuff was opened, I wasn't too interested. I have used the Ginsu knife once, cutting my finger and bleeding into the potato salad.

The Ginsu knife IS better than a Captain Marvel decoder, but the verdict is still out on the spiral slicer. The truth is that Ellen refuses to use it. Anyway, I got to use the WATS line.

They Gave a Revival and Nobody Came

September 16, 1979

I remember when the revival preacher came to Kate's house in Antioch. The sign he had nailed up on the post oak outside the store the week before told all about the special service. It was hand-written rather than printed, but the lettering was big and clear and bold.

Kate had helped the minister with the sign while I watched. I heard her invite him to take Sunday dinner with us (I was spending the week with her) before the revival the next week. He agreed that would be nice; it would give him some time to relax before the people started to gather for the preaching, he said.

My grandmother Kate Trussell never cooked much because, what with running the big general store at the crossroads all by herself, well, there just wasn't much time for it. But the day the preacher came we had salmon cold out of the store, sweet pickles, crackers and iced tea on the little kitchen table. The minister dug into the food, but he didn't say much. Mostly he rubbed a white Bible and asked what time it was.

The meeting was set for 1:00 P.M. in front of the old well across the road from the store. We finished our lunch well short of that time and sat in the living room, with the hot September sun pouring through the front door in dusty motes.

Nobody really started to worry until the black clock Kate had won by buying crates of Calumet Baking Powder for the store chimed the quarter hour before one. Nobody had showed. Cars occasionally rolled past the store, trailing clouds of red dust, but nobody stopped.

THEY GAVE A REVIVAL AND NOBODY CAME

When the clock hit 1:00 P.M. it was like the stroke of doom and Kate started to make excuses for the preacher. You couldn't really see the sign from the road, she said. And the Ruston *Daily Leader* had buried the revival notice down by the classifieds.

The tall, sandy-headed preacher just nodded and rubbed his white Bible. His black suit had a shine to it, but the creases were all knife-edged. He smiled and nodded and rubbed that Bible, but I saw his eyes darting all the time to the black Calumet clock on the mantel.

A green bottle fly buzzed all three of us. The preacher didn't move, even when I saw the fly disappear into his ear for what seemed like an hour before droning off in another direction. Kate got a flyswatter and blasted the thing with a terrible vengeance—making us all jump.

By the time the clock chimed two I had memorized the sheet music on the piano across the room. Kate got up with every passing car. The clock's ticks were thunder in my ears. My shirt-back was wet; my seat stung.

I just felt so sorry for the preacher. I prayed for somebody, one person, anybody to show up—even an hour late. I could see the sweat-rings even in his dark suit. His fingers worked the Bible. Kate finally sat rigid in her chair, making the still air move with a palmetto fan that had the name of a funeral home across it.

It was 3:00 P.M.; the Calumet clock nearly smashed its springs ringing that. Nobody had come.

At last the preacher rose and said his goodbyes and thanks for the lunch, not mentioning anything—he never had said anything, really—his voice steady and rumbling, like maybe he was giving a benediction. We watched him walk to his old car, parked in the shade of the post oak.

He hesitated and then very carefully took down the sign announcing the revival. Then he leaned on the oak and I saw his whole body shudder, just for one second. I looked at Kate.

She was wearing her green and white dress, she smelled like strong soap, and she put her arm around me there in the door.

"Don't worry about it," she said in that husky voice. "He'll be all right."

But there were tears in her eyes. I saw them.

The Day Pop Integrated the Parade

September 30, 1979

There was no way you could call Pop an integrationist. Of course, everybody was equal in the ginhouse and all of us, black and white, drank out of the same fruit jar of ice water on those hot, linty September afternoons when the wagonloads of cotton stretched out to South Trenton Street.

But that was long before the Supreme Court made its historic decision in 1954. Integration wasn't even a word, as we know it now. And Pop, though he paid equal wages and distributed responsibility on the basis of merit at the gin, wasn't ahead of the times in his racial attitudes.

Nevertheless, it fell Pop's lot to perform what might have been Lincoln Parish's first act of forced integration. Inadvertently, unconsciously, he made social history on South Alabama Street in Ruston and everybody, black and white, applauded. Literally applauded.

It all started with Pop's seething impatience, which has already been well documented in this space. During World War II he forced his way into an Army convoy that was negotiating Alabama Street and then only escaped the olive-drab line fifty miles down the road.

The thing was, Pop sort of thought he owned Alabama Street, or at least that section between his house and Temple Baptist

THE DAY POP INTEGRATED THE PARADE

Church. So any traffic that prevented him from backing the old black Buick into "his" street and heading for the Harris Hotel was hotly resented. In fact, he wouldn't tolerate any such interference.

So it was that one fall day Pop found himself blocked into his driveway by the Grambling College (now Grambling State University) band, which annually used to march down South Alabama in the school's homecoming parade.

It was a great band, and most of Ruston turned out to watch it parade at homecoming. But this time, as noted, the Grambling parade happened to coincide with the moment Pop wanted to get to his red-upholstered chair at the old Harris Hotel.

As with the Army convoy, Pop blew his horn and bluffed and fumed before finally whipping the old Buick into the middle of the high-stepping Grambling parade. Rather, he saw a gap between the floats and marchers and leaped into it.

The Grambling bandsmen, totally unruffled by this intrusion, simply closed up ranks and made Pop and his dusty car part of their parade. Except for the second or two when Pop forced the gap, they didn't miss a step.

Well, there were all sorts of folks lined up and down Alabama Street from Greenwood Cemetery right down into town and at first there were some puzzled looks as the parade, with Pop in tow, neared the center of Ruston. Pop, you see, was the only white man in a black parade.

But the Grambling band was obviously happy to have Pop as an extra float in their parade. They tied Grambling's black and gold streamers on his back bumper and radio aerial and pranced around and around the old Buick.

Now Pop was undeniably short-fused and impatient. But he was also incorruptibly good-natured. Pretty soon he got into the spirit of the thing and began to wave and smile at the crowd. The crowd waved and smiled back. Pop had forcibly integrated a parade, and everybody was clapping.

Given the circumstances, maybe it wasn't exactly social history Pop and the Grambling band made that day in North Louisiana, but it came close.

And, if anybody is wondering, Pop didn't learn a lesson about patience—or the lack of it—from that experience either. In fact, sometime later when Major L. J. Fox hesitated for what Pop thought was an interminable length of time after the red light changed on Alabama, he purposely crashed into the back of the surprised major's car. But that's another story.

Bob and the Great Soapbox Derby

November 25, 1979

When it came to determination and will-to-win, my Aunt Carice Barham had a blue-spark fervor about her that would have made Vince Lombardi look like a prone pacifist at an anti-war demonstration. So when Cousin Bob announced his intention to enter Ruston's soapbox derby that summer of our childhood, well, Aunt Carice decided that her son just had to win that race.

If it meant bending the rules to provide Bob with that little extra winning advantage—or more properly taking advantage of every rule—then Carice would be up to every challenge. But this is a story of how justice was served in Lincoln Parish and how the race went not to the swiftest but simply to the kid who stopped to get the prize.

Anyway, Carice ordered the wheels for Bob's derby racer from Shreveport. I think the design and blueprint came from New York City, but Bob denies that. Carice would have gone to Moscow for help on that racer; I know that. She did hire a woodcutter to carve out the floorboards. The frame was made from willow branches. And the cover material came off an airplane.

Joe Shick, a neighborhood pal of Bob's who could make anything, teamed up with a black man named A. T. Smith to put the racer together. So Bob's speedburner was born in the dark secrecy of the Barham's garage on Goode Street under the burning eyes of Carice Barham. Bob may have hit a nail or two, too.

The day finally came. The starting line was at the top of Graham's Hill on North Vienna Street. The judges stood down at the bottom of the hill at the finish. When Joe and A. T. unloaded Bob's racer out of the back of Cap Barham's pick-up truck (at any hint of recession or depression Cap invariably bought a pick-up truck and then sold it a few weeks later) a gasp went through the crowd.

And no wonder they gasped. Bob's racer looked as though it ought to be entered in the Indianapolis 500 rather than the Ruston derby. It was long and lean and graceful—like a greyhound. The July sun made its silver and red racing stripes gleam. Carice seemed entirely pleased, even when Bob had to be lifted by Joe and A. T. into his derby bomb.

There was some muttering among the other parents and children who were making final adjustments on their racers, which were all pretty much painted orange crates mounted on little red wagon wheels or even roller-skates. But this was a different time and people were inclined to take such things in stride.

It wasn't long before Mr. Duchesne blew his whistle and everybody's racer got a push. Bob, strapped into his willow-frame, New York-designed, Shreveport-wheeled bullet, took off as though he had been fired out of a thirty-aught-six rifle.

The race was strictly no contest. It was Bob, a silver and red blur, by a mile. But at the finish line at the bottom of Graham's Hill something strange happened. Bob was going so fast he couldn't stop. A couple of judges tried to get a grip on his racer as it flashed past, but that was like trying to stop an express train with bare hands.

Bob just kept flying, his eyes oddly glazed like those of a shot rabbit, until his silver-red racer disappeared, whoosh, down North Vienna toward the middle of town. Later we realized that his racer was going so fast that the hinge-and-spring brake burned up at the first pressure.

A puzzled police officer named Robinson finally flagged Bob down at a red-light in downtown Ruston. Otherwise I think he would have made it to Jonesboro. Carice and the pit crew (Joe, A. T., and me) did retrieve Bob and the racer. But as it turned out a kid in a converted orange crate had been awarded the ribbon when Bob never came back.

Nobody said anything, not even Carice, and like I said, even if the race had not gone to the swiftest, justice had been served in Ruston's Great Soapbox Derby. Except that Bob claims even today that he should have gotten the ribbon in absentia.

They Even Took My Razor

February 24, 1980

It was right after I started shaving that Daddy's Gillette razor with the red blades mysteriously disappeared. Of course, I had been using his razor, and when it turned up—obviously hidden from me behind some old sheets in the linen cabinet—it seemed like the old man was being downright selfish and unaccommodating.

The idea of not sharing your razor with a teenage son was lost on me then, but twenty-five years later I can certainly understand it—especially now that seventeen-year-old Greg has appropriated my Gillette injector for his first tentative experience with a razor.

And with fifteen-year-old Kevin beginning to look a little furry under the chin, I can expect a double assault on my injector. Seeking allies, I have tried to explain to Ellen and Anne Marie that there is something sacred about a man's razor; it just isn't to be shared, even with male offspring.

Using a man's razor is like invading a foreign embassy; it is a breach of sovereignty not to be sanctioned in the civilized Western World. Actually, I am suspicious that an even more barbarous offense has been committed—that perhaps the Hilburn women have used my razor. This, of course, would be unpardonable.

In all events, any time I mention the utter impossibility of sharing a razor, Ellen and Anne Marie give me a superior, sphinx-like smile and no support at all. It's obvious they do not appreciate the enormity of such an imposition.

But the hard truth is that I am being gradually stripped of all my possessions, and the girls are as guilty in this crime as the boys. For example, both Ellen and Anne Marie insist on sleeping in my T-shirts. It matters not at all to them that I am sent off to work at least once a week wearing an undershirt that smells of women's perfume.

It doesn't stop there. In the early morning I often hear Ellen telling one of the boys: "Well, here's one of your daddy's . . ." I know then that Greg or Kevin is headed to Ruston High in my socks.

Actually, there is a way to stop the sock-borrowing. The boys refuse to wear any of those long nylon jobs. So I'm loading up on these "old men" socks. Of course, Greg will still sneak off in my favorite suede jacket. And a Sunday or so back Kevin flopped around the First Presbyterian Church in my too-big Jarmans when his dress pair couldn't be found.

Speaking of Kevin, he borrowed my Gulf credit card six months ago. Now he owns Saudi Arabia. I did protest when

Greg confiscated my favorite tie to take to a Key Club convention. "It goes with his brown suit," Ellen said calmly, shutting Greg's suitcase with my tie inside.

After two wrecks, the boys have lately returned the family cars fairly intact, but filled with Icee cups, empty Skoal cans, tennis rackets, and Ronnie Milsap tapes. And I always find the car radio locked on the closest rock station and the gas tank dry.

If all this sharing was mutual, maybe I could bear it. But while what's mine is negotiable, what belongs to the boys is theirs—period. The other day I innocently tried on Greg's green, white and gold Oregon Fighting Ducks baseball cap. He was outraged. "You just don't wear somebody else's hat, Dad," he said very seriously.

The other night Kevin locked himself into his room with a sack of lovely fresh sugar-covered doughnuts he bought at the corner store with his money. No sharing. Greg wants to charge Anne Marie and me for using his Roffler's "Super thick and rich" shampoo—purchased with his money. I'm supposed to shampoo with the current Wal-Mart's special.

Dad, a quarter-century and three kids of my own later I understand why you hid that old Gillette razor and, believe me, it's okay.

"He's Graduating?"

May 25, 1980

Greg was graduated Tuesday night from the same Ruston High School that awarded me a diploma twenty-four years ago, and my father before that. He marched in under the no-smoking sign at the end of the gym. I felt this absolute surge of pride. "His graduation cap is on wrong," Ellen whispered to me. I shook hands with the fellow in front of me. We had graduated together. Dr. Gerald Cobb ("Skinny" to me) presided as principal. Skinny and I rode down pine trees after class at this same school. The only time Skinny frowned this Tuesday night was when the PA system momentarily rebelled. Mellie Jo Kelly led the choir. Gosh, Mellie Jo was soloist in the RHS choir when we were classmates. People coughed. Babies cried. I stared at Greg from my position between Ellen and Daddy. He's GRADUATING? And I wondered, like all the other parents and grandparents, where did all that time get to? At the end the band and choir joined in "America the Beautiful." And I was thinking, they are beautiful, these American kids of ours. All of them. Only, they don't know how fast it will all go, do they?

Frustration: Cars and Collisions

June 15, 1980

It was evident that my hypochondriac Monza was rejecting the transmission transplant—even though the operation had only just been completed. The grating, gasping sound told me that the appropriately lemon-colored car was still sick.

Automotive problems tend to focus the male mind on whatever has gone wrong, at work and everywhere else, for the past decade. It isn't so much the car, though with teen-agers driving, an automobile is economic hemophilia. It's just that car problems create a domino-like depression.

Anyway, that night I built a whole life-crisis on the oily hulk of a transmission implant that didn't take. I rose groggy and

FRUSTRATION: CARS AND COLLISIONS

grumpy the next morning, forced to catch a ride with the boys in their Mustang since my car refused to accept a used gear-system.

The three of us sardined into the front seat of the Mustang. There came a long, grinding sound when Greg hit the starter. No ignition. I could feel a Mount Saint Helens of a blood-pressure rise. "This car better start," I heard myself say, glaring at a blameless Greg. Desperately he turned the key and ground down on the accelerator.

The result was more grinding and two four-wheeled sickies in the carport. Mount Saint Helens erupted, and the boys were caught in a rain of hot volcanic ash—a genuine Hilburn temper tantrum. A basketball happened to be lying innocently in the driveway, very near the two crippled cars.

I put every ounce of frustration into kicking that basketball. No soccer star ever kicked one farther. The ball soared over the roof, lopped a limb off the top of an elm tree and hit the lake behind the house like a Japanese torpedo.

While the basketball was soaring, the boys were disappearing. How they got to Ruston High School that day I will never know. I don't know what restored my sanity: Ellen's soothing words while she drove me to Tech (in the only one of three cars still ambulatory) or kicking that basketball into the lake.

Bobby Willett, one of the Shipley's good ole boys, reports a similar collision of car and frustration. It seems that members of his family had been involved in a half dozen minor fender-benders within a few blocks of home.

Like most men, Bobby fumed and fussed and preached wide-awake responsibility behind the wheel, citing moon-shot insurance rates and how he never had a wreck. Every single wrecker in the Willett family knew his righteous wrath.

Then there was the day Bobby was in a big rush and didn't watch what he was doing. It happened right there in the Willett driveway. Bobby raked the side of his wife's Pinto and hence wrecked two family cars with one blow: a disaster that with to-

FRUSTRATION: CARS AND COLLISIONS

day's auto repair costs could be compared to the sinking of the *Titanic*.

"What did you do, Bobby?" I asked sympathetically, thinking of all of my teen-agers' mishaps.

Nobody lies at Shipley's on a Sunday morning and so Bobby Willett just told us the whole truth:

"I just sat down there on the grass and cried," he said.

Maybe my own father holds the record for car frustration. I was really small, but his old truck made a wheezing noise I could detect long before he pulled up the driveway on East California in Ruston.

I watched for him from my roost on the cedar chest in the dining room. Sometimes he had a Katzenjammer Kids comic book for me rolled up tight in his backpocket.

The wind was blowing that day when he stopped the truck and pushed the garage door to the side. There was nothing around to prop the door so he just swung it slam against the side of the garage and got back into the truck. I could tell from his stride that it had been a long day at the cotton gin.

The old truck gunned up and Daddy approached the garage. But the door swung around and shut just soon enough to block him.

He got out of the truck and shoved the door back again. This time his movements were rapid and determined and he backed up the battered red truck fast.

But there was that windblown door again, swinging back again just in time to confront the truck, which shuddered to a stop.

This time Daddy ran out to slam it against the garage and got a running start on the door and the wind.

There followed a crash and the old truck disappeared into the garage amid a great shower of splintering wood.

Nobody dared to say a word when he came into the house. I could see out the dining-room window. The old truck was parked in the garage. But the garage door no longer existed.

Vacation:
"Green ... It's Green"

July 27, 1980

The vacation was over.

We were headed back from Houston and the Astrodome. The kids were asleep in the backseat, sprawled out, arms and legs akimbo, mercifully quiet in a debris of comic books and orange Astro baseball caps.

As we passed the big pelican sign introducing Louisiana, in the deep night, I asked Ellen: "Did we have a good time?" The answer was a very long time coming. "Yes," was what she finally said.

I took her word for it.

Through the summers, you see, our family vacations have contained more than their share of misadventures. There was the time, for example, that I peered into the battleground of the backseat and noticed that Kevin was untypically quiet—and also extremely pale.

Crash-landing the car in a field of yellow wildflowers, I managed to get Kevin outside before he ruined the seatcovers. "What made him sick?" I asked Ellen while steering Kevin, whose color and voice were rapidly returning, back to the car.

Ellen was holding an empty Shipley's box. "The nearest I can make out," she said, "Kevin ate eighteen doughnuts between Ruston and Arcadia." It was, you have to admit, a valid explanation.

Compared to what happened on Interstate 20 East on the start of another vacation, Kevin's encounter with eighteen doughnuts was easy to resolve. As usual everybody, including Ellen, wanted to go to the bathroom before we cleared the Choudrant exit.

I pulled over into what passed for a roadside park, but there

VACATION: "GREEN . . . IT'S GREEN"

were no toilet facilities. So my family jumped a barbed-wire fence and made for the woods. I stayed in the car and waited for them. I am the only member of my family with normal kidneys.

"Did you pick some muscadines?" I asked cynically when they all clamored back into the car a full half-hour later. One mile down Interstate 20 we stopped again, all holding our noses and accusing each other.

My roadside inspection revealed that each member of the family, en route to nature's bathroom, had somehow tiptoed through fresh manure. "Green, it's green," I observed with bitter resignation.

Greg's shoes, beyond redemption, are still violating Environmental Protection Agency rules in a ditch somewhere east of Calhoun, La. "Well, I knew it was a good idea to bring extra shoes," Ellen said defensively as we approached Vicksburg, Miss., with all the windows down.

That was the same trip when it rained—THE WHOLE VACATION. It was clear when we left Ruston, but as we approached Biloxi, Miss., the skies turned dark and the scenic gulf highway was totally obliterated by a monsoon.

"I can't see the ocean, Daddy," Anne Marie said. "Shut up," I answered reasonably in the tone of parents who have seen their own vacation expectations upset. Established in an expensive motel right on the beach, we tuned in a television weather report. A huge storm front was hunkered right down on top of our motel. The station's weather radar clearly indicated our soaked position.

So for three angry days (I regularly threatened to picket the Biloxi Chamber of Commerce) the kids made periodic races for the beach when the rain slackened—only to be driven back inside by great cracks of thunder and more cloudbursts before they could reach the water. We finally gave up and retreated to New Orleans where the kids fought and swam for a day in a small pool at an Alamo Plaza motel.

It also rained on our family during one of those Houston vacations—inside the Astrodome. That's right. Now the Dome is an incredible structure, but in all those thousands of air conditioned cubic feet there was one tiny leak.

Well, naturally it was raining outside and naturally the Hilburns' seats were located right under that tiny leak and I experienced nine innings of Chinese water torture. On the way out, of course, Anne Marie got stuck on the escalator.

There she was, feet moving the wrong way in a no-progress dance with Ellen hanging on grimly and going in the opposite direction. Traffic was halted on the Dome's upper level (a tremendously loud announcement was actually made to that effect) while our smallest one was extricated. "Don't worry," I told a red-faced Ellen. "Nobody knows us here."

It was after that experience, headed home, that I asked Ellen if we had a good time. She did say yes, and while contemplating this summer's trip to Biloxi without the boys (at eighteen and sixteen years they laugh at the idea of traveling with us) I have to agree with her. We will miss the boys—and all those terrible summer family vacations.

The Night the Gin Burned Down

September 13, 1981

It was an early, chilled November morning in 1949. Daddy stared into the blue flames of the gas heater in the front bedroom on Marbury Drive in Ruston. "We're ruined," he said softly, over and over again. "Ruined . . . ruined."

There were charred, ragged holes in his overalls and denim shirt. He rocked gently in the chair, his eyes buried in the blue

"Fire . . . gin's on fire!"

THE NIGHT THE GIN BURNED DOWN

blaze of the heater. "We're ruined," he repeated, to nobody, though I sat near him.

It was the night the gin burned down.

It was also the night Pop, my grandfather, lost everything—he owned that gin and two others—and still hit the jackpot in Winnsboro. But that's getting ahead of the story.

Earlier the same night Daddy was asleep in a little house only a hundred yards from the West Carroll Parish ginhouse in Northeast Louisiana, many miles from Ruston, where he lived and worked during ginning season.

What woke him was a cry that he still remembers, to the exact, gut-wrenching words: "Fire . . . gin's on fire!" There was no fire department to call, once the cobwebs of sleep cleared out of his head.

This was a remote region of West Carroll Parish 'way down the Boeuf River. The nearest real civilization was the little town of Holly Ridge. It was twenty miles to the north—a world away under the circumstances.

So Daddy struggled into his overalls. "Fire . . . gin's on fire!" Then he could see the roseate reflection of the flames projected on the wall by his single window. What he saw outside moments later was a vision of hell: the whole wooden gin platform ablaze from end to end.

Also on fire were the fifty or sixty cotton bales up there on the platform. One of them, he noted then and never forgot, had the ties pulled off. "So it will burn better," he thought, even in the literal heat of the moment.

After that, he would always feel that the fire was an act of arson. "It would have only taken five dollars and a pint of whiskey to get somebody to do it," he says even now.

That November night in West Carroll Parish, though, he leaped onto the platform and started shoving bales off the side, away from the inferno. Half-crazy, clothes smoking, he pushed and shoved. The bales, he knew somewhere off in a corner of his consciousness, were not insured.

THE NIGHT THE GIN BURNED DOWN

Then, in a second that sucked the breath out of him, Daddy pushed too hard, too recklessly, and he went over the side of the platform with a bale. Five hundred pounds of cotton pinned both legs. With a strength called out of the supernatural, he worked one leg loose and kicked away from the burning bale.

After that, nothing could be saved. Not really. By the time Pop got there from Ruston his Holly Ridge gin was a smoking pile of tin. So Pop climbed up on a half-burned bale to tell the farmers, materializing out of the dark, that he would build a new gin on the spot.

That would not happen. Though he thought so that cold November morning, Daddy wasn't ruined. Young and strong, he would build another successful, different business. But Pop was never the same again after the fire.

His dream of leaving each of his three children a gin had gone up in smoke. Pop didn't believe much in insurance, and the fire was the beginning of the end for the Hilburn Gin Company in Holly Ridge and Wisner and Ruston.

Pop brooded about it. He made up lists of people who might have set the fire, but nothing was ever proved. Even to the very end of his life, 'though, Pop ginned cotton in his dreams. But the real dream burned up that November night in the fire.

Still, that was the same fiery night Pop hit the jackpot. They had stopped in Winnsboro to drown the shock of the fire in hot coffee. Pop, raging and restless, put a nickel in the slot machine at the cafe. It was the first time he had ever played a slot machine.

There came a great splattering of silver and Pop yanked off his hat to catch the bonanza. It amounted to $14.50. "Son," he told Daddy, "I'm awful lucky. I just lost a gin, maybe everything, and hit a nickel jackpot."

It was the night the gin burned down and Pop hit the jackpot. It was a night that changed all our lives.

Little League: Twelve "Don'ts" for Dads

May 9, 1982

I was driving Greg to the Little League game. It was a big one, and we were both nervous—especially since he was pitching. I decided to introduce a bit of perspective. "Listen, Greg," I said, "remember that it's just a game, and go out there and have fun and relax."

Greg gave me a grateful look. Then, compulsively, I blew it. "But for God's sake," I blurted, "remember to follow through when you throw and bear down right from the start . . . don't start walking people." The words gushed out. And now Greg gave me a disgusted look.

The result of that "big game" has long since been forgotten, such memories blur after twelve years of where's-my-glove, lawn chairs and Icees. I do recall the suffocating July night Kevin booted four straight grounders in another "big game"—and the time the other parents got mad when Greg, pitching, hit six straight batters.

That's all over for us, and—to tell the truth—I'm not sorry. Yes, for the first eight years or so Ellen and I did enjoy Little League. I was even an assistant to the assistant coach for a year. We rooted for the Piggly Wiggly team and constructed our vacations around a schedule Ellen kept pasted to the refrigerator door. Those last few years we didn't much mind the rainouts though. Anything can get old.

But Little League is as popular as ever with parents who have children playing, and already this spring I hear them discussing it with a fervor that wasn't even matched in Atlanta when the

LITTLE LEAGUE: TWELVE "DON'TS" FOR DADS

Braves won their first thirteen games. For these parents, from the perspective of twelve years with Little League, I'm offering twelve "don'ts" (mostly for dads) originally introduced in a *Times* editorial several years ago—rules that, yes, I routinely broke during my long summers of baseball bondage. Here they are:

1. Don't put yourself in your son's or daughter's place out there. The kid at third base isn't you, Dad. If he makes an error, it's his error; if his home run wins the game, it's his home run. Glory or grief, it's *his* ballgame. Whether you were an all-American Legion shortstop or—more likely—couldn't make the church team even if the preacher was your father, has nothing to do with your kid's performance. Yet, I once heard a parent tell a child who made a wild throw, "You embarrassed me."

2. Don't talk about the "big game" all day. Chances are the "big game" isn't as important to your center fielder as it is to you, and that's healthy. The youngster will usually keep the game in proper perspective—and keep pressure to a minimum—if only you will, Dad.

3. Don't criticize one of the other players even if the errant kid decides to read his library book in right field. That's not only unseemly; it's dangerous. Because chances are the offending player's mother is smoldering in the next lawn chair. She will scratch your eyes out.

4. Don't yell instructions to your player ("Get closer to the plate, son!") when it's his time to bat. That is the coach's job, and besides, the kid can pick your voice out of the tumult. It only makes him more nervous. Shout only general encouragement.

5. Don't start analyzing your child's performance right after the game. All the player wants is peace, quiet and a snowcone.

6. Don't criticize the coach, even if it's apparent that Billy Martin he isn't. Listen, this guy is going to some dusty, potholed elementary school field after work and on Saturdays to throw batting practice in a hot sun. Before you complain, think:

LITTLE LEAGUE: TWELVE "DON'TS" FOR DADS

"Am I ready to give up all my valuable time free to a bunch of pre-juveniles?" Then shut up.

7. Don't complain when the good coach plays everybody and even goes with different starters every game—right down to the child who has a pathological dread of fly balls and the bespectacled baby-face who hasn't swung at a pitch (I personally know that "please-Lord-let-him-walk-me" feeling) in three summers. This is Little League, folks, and every ten-year-old is entitled, literally, to his innings.

8. Don't abuse the umpire, Dad. Baiting the college kid who's calling the game for four bucks isn't calculated to inspire respect for authority demanded from your child at home and at school.

9. Don't decide your player has a future with the Los Angeles Dodgers because he's a strike-out ace in Little League. Likewise, don't write off that baby-face with the bat on his shoulder. Kids, I'm told, mature athletically at different paces. Some are better than they ever will be again in Little League. Some of the worst players will develop into varsity athletes with time.

10. Don't forget to praise your Little Leaguer for simply performing. Don't overpraise a hit or a good play, either. And, above all, don't ever dwell on an error or failure to deliver the "big" hit—especially not with scorn or anger. You are not Vince Lombardi, Pop, and your kid doesn't play for the Packers. Your child is twelve, at most, and—again—this is Little League.

11. Don't forget to praise all the players after the game, especially if they lost.

12. And please, Dad, (mothers aren't nearly as bad about these things) don't take it so seriously. Even the "big game" isn't the Falkland crisis, an answer to World Hunger or even the World Series.

Okay, Mom. Paste this column on the refrigerator door next to the schedule where Dad can see it and let's everybody enjoy another Little League summer.

The Little Girl
Is Growing Up

October 24, 1982

There was a time when Anne Marie's bulletin board, bed and dresser gave me comfort. With her away, I'd pile up in the iron bed, elbow aside the stuffed tigers and monkeys, and just look around—at the pictures of Anne Marie's church, big brothers, grandfather, collie dog and best friend.

I liked the bulletin board especially—maybe because it featured a news story and picture about me. I also studied the placid swimming styles of Anne Marie's two goldfish; she called them Fred and Nancy. The giant-sized poster of Shaun Cassidy that all but covered the door was a little jangling but over all it was a peaceful room. I liked it.

However, when Anne Marie turned eleven or twelve, I began to notice certain disturbing changes. The tiger and monkey still resided on the bed, but the personality of the room altered dramatically. In fact, it was as if an earthquake had swallowed up most of the familiar and comforting landmarks of the bulletin board.

Gone were all the pictures I described—including the news clipping and photo of old Dad. In their place, dominating the whole bulletin board, was a sports clipping detailing the accomplishments of a group of twelve-year-old boys. Prominently underlined, with one of my red Flair pens, was the name of one of the boys on the team.

It was, to be honest, pretty hard to take. I asked her about it, including a low-key (I thought) reference to the disappearance of my picture. Of course, it was terribly wrong to say anything, but I blundered on anyway. "You're just trying to make me feel guilty, Dad," she answered brightly and rightly.

Well, all that transpired some time ago and, as this is written,

THE LITTLE GIRL IS GROWING UP

Anne Marie is fifteen years old. And now I must report, regrettably, that the *whole* landscape of the room has disappeared. The pictures show her smiling and obviously having fun with different girls *and* boys. The more formal prom pictures are there, too.

A rather faded corsage hangs on one side of the dresser; a huge red button screaming "Bearcats look good" anchors the other end. Ticket stubs from a Rick Springfield concert are tacked on the bulletin board. The bedside table holds a vial of perfume actually purchased in Paris by Anne Marie's friend Libby Woodard, and cassettes featuring (I never heard of 'em) the Chicago 16 and the Foreigner 4. I'd welcome Shaun Cassidy back now.

It's a foreign land, that room, but all is not lost. Like always, Anne Marie sometimes notices that I'm tired and that concern is appreciated. And the other night, dressed for the homecoming dance in a high-necked tuxedo blouse with a maroon bow, she looked so beautiful my eyes blurred.

Still, like fathers the world over, I'm gradually learning, to my bittersweet sorrow, that even little girls grow up. You want them to do just that, of course, and yet it kind of hurts. Where did the stuffed monkey go, I wonder (it wasn't under the bed; I looked) and what happened to the goldfish?

It just happened *so fast,* you see. It seems like it was only yesterday—actually, it's been years—when I bundled my daughter up in her pajamas for a night visit to offices in Louisiana Tech's Keeny Hall.

The student editors made a fuss over her and later Anne Marie wrote me a note: "My Daddy is boss of the *Teck* (her spelling) *Talk* and he wants students to do good. . . ." I kept that note in my billfold until it came apart at the folded seams.

Yes, they have to grow up—even talcum-smelling little girls (though Libby's Paris perfume may be too much) and that's only right and proper and natural. Still and again, it hurts some.

You see, I liked being on that bulletin board, and somehow it just never occurred to me, until now, that Anne Marie's room would ever change.

Batman, Where Have You Gone?

April 24, 1983

It is a murmur of voices that is now only just within my consciousness because our children are growing up. Still, I catch snatches of conversation about ear infections, nursery school pickups, chickenpox, pinned-on notes to teachers, chauffering endless screaming mobs on after-school missions and, a bit later, animated news of all those dusty twilights spent at the Little League ballpark.

All that's past us now, and the knowledge that childhood is only an eyeblink of time, a flashbulb exploding on a Christmas morning, really hit home the other day when nineteen-year-old Kevin—back in his room for a college vacation break—dug out a Little League team picture. I looked at it for a very long time.

Kevin was kneeling with the bottom row of Piggly Wiggly players, an unconquerable tangle of yellow curls escaping the confines of his cap, wearing the look of serene confidence I admire so much. Ordinarily a reliable second-baseman, Kevin booted three straight grounders in a big game that year and the Pigs lost, but back then an Icee could put anything right.

I showed the picture to Ellen. Her eyes took in that lineup, then grew distant with olive-green memories. "Remember when he wore the Batman outfit and cape all the time?" she said. Of course I remembered Batman leaping and jumping all over Cypress Springs, with only the same curls emerging undaunted from behind the hood to suggest that maybe this wasn't exactly the Masked Marvel after all.

"He really thinks he's Batman," Ellen said at the time, worried. "He might fly off the roof of something," she said. "No," I demurred, Kevin is Batman. Batman can't fly. You're thinking about Superman. Superman can fly." Unconvinced, Ellen gave me a familiar look that questions why she ever entered into a permanent relationship with a Hilburn.

Kevin never jumped off the roof (so far as I know), but he was Batman during those Caddo Street days. Substituting a towel for a cape when the Batman suit was being washed, he fell out of tall trees, nearly drowned in Clear Lake, and variously skateboarded and bicycled his way into the emergency room at Lincoln General Hospital.

"Why couldn't this have happened during school?" he wondered aloud once from the operating table after a mishap. "It would have gotten me out for two full days at least." "You are going to read a book while you're in bed," I said. Batman wasn't listening, though. "I was supposed to bat cleanup tonight," he was saying wistfully.

Ellen carefully packed away the Little League team picture.

And I was wondering whatever happened to the Batman suit. An eye had blinked, and a whole childhood was gone.

Barbados: A Glad Hour in the Sun

July 24, 1983

Ellen's face was buried in her hands. "This is a disaster," she said. I tried to be cheerful, but the word "disaster" did seem to describe what we both had hoped would be the dream vacation she had planned and plotted down to the last detail.

We had landed in Barbados all right, the Caribbean jewel Ellen had carefully selected from the necklace of islands strung from the Bahamas to this former outpost of the British Empire—"the eastern-most of the Caribees," said a guide—which actually looked closer to Venezuela on the map than any place else.

But we landed in the deep hours of the inky West Indies night, well behind schedule, and feeling very far from North Louisiana. The gruff, one-word answers of our cab driver (where were those friendly Bahans Mr. Fodor wrote about in his travel guides?) didn't help matters as he spun us down the winding, narrow coast road in a blur of blinding headlights.

We survived the Central American grand prix, but then blinked in disbelief at our destination—the Southern Palms. In the darkness, we could just make out a dimly lit (everything in Barbados is dimly lit) open breezeway and a registration desk (we didn't know yet that everything in Barbados is also out in the open).

Across the street from the hotel, sheltered under a gnarled oak (well, it looked like an oak) which reminded me of the tree that almost ate the boy in the movie *Poltergeist*, was something called the Oasis bar. Unfortunately, it did not have the least appearance of a tourist trap.

Our spirits sank even further after being led up to our "suite." The rooms smelled like the bottom of your grandmother's hope chest. *Musty*. An ancient window-unit air conditioner, of indeterminate origin, wheezed asthmatically and hopelessly against the tropical heat. We pretended not to notice strange, scurrying sounds. Our reservations had called for beachside; we could hear the surf, but this was not beachside. A damp and dismal night was passed in those confines.

A quick reconnaissance the next morning revealed the vacation beach of our dreams—clean sand, and sea layered up from white, surfable breakers to aquamarine to midnight blue. Beautiful. And, on daylight inspection, the Southern Palms was also very nice, even quaint; a network of archways, gates and courtyards linked up a broken line of pink stucco cottages. We liked it immediately, except for our sauna on the far side of the action.

On that issue, we confronted the Southern Palms management. I diplomatically explained the problem—we had reserved a beachside room—while Ellen repeated over and over again, "We do *not* like our room." The desk people ignored my diplomacy, but somebody pointed at Ellen ("we do not like our room") and it was agreed that we would be shown "number eight." "You will like number eight," we were told.

And did we ever like number eight. At once, and then it grew on us, and finally charmed us out of our minds. Here was a balcony suite, all but suspended over the Caribbean, cleanly painted in bright yellows and whites, high-ceilinged, and very cool. "I feel like a queen up here," Ellen said. It was, in a word, perfect. A Bahan dove even laid two eggs in its nest on our air conditioner, and various birds flew in and out of the suite, as if they were used to it. We didn't mind.

After that, everything went exactly right, and the dream vacation became a reality. We breakfasted on papayas and mangos on our balcony, took a cruise on the ship *Jolly Roger* (Ellen and others cooled off by riding a rope swing off the vessel into the green Caribbean), visited with the Bahans (who turned out to be just as friendly in their rainbow of colors as Mr. Fodor wrote), shopped the mini-market down the coast road for cheese, French bread and dill pickles, and in the evening dined on flying fish. Our favorite meal was at a little outdoor place called Boomer's where we feasted on a great native delicacy: hamburgers, shoestring potatoes and Cokes.

Just lying in the sun was the best recreation, though Ellen all but destroyed the delicate ecosystem of the beach by telling several vendors (Bahans who patrol the area in numbers, but always politely and unobtrusively) that she wanted a coral bracelet. We soon found ourselves beholden for every bracelet in the

Caribbean and Ellen wound up checking a coral reef into customs.

British accents were everywhere on this beach, but our nearest neighbors (just below us) were a bunch of French Canadians—the Lucien Mallett family from Montreal. A Swiss couple joined us, the Pierre Droccos, and remained neutral while Lucien and his sister-in-law, who was fond of breaking into cries of "Viva Quebec Libre," argued the merits and demerits of Canadian separatism. Lucien, who spoke English, translated. But his lively wife communicated even better with body English. We all parted fast friends.

We all watched when a girl from the adjoining South Winds hotel took to the water with her dog, bikini bottom, and nothing else. That was against the posted rules (though nobody in our group called to report it), but a couple of enterprising Bahan women solved the problem anyway. They designed, demonstrated and clothed the girl with a native top on the spot.

We didn't stay on the beach all the time, of course. Bridgetown, the capital of Barbados, is a steamy, swarming (no traffic lights) town of forty thousand with all the merchandise you ever wanted—in 1958. The island itself is afire with *flamboyants*, a tall-masted tree with red-orange blossoms. Poverty is evident in close-packed dwellings slam against the road and broken-up, forgotten piles of concrete, but the Bahans are a proud, erect and, yes, eminently civil people of many races. There is very little crime here, and everybody walks at night without fear.

That's a stereotyping, of course, but nonetheless true—just as it's true that these people insist on a siesta. We found the lady who sold us the papayas every day sound asleep, surrounded by her fruit. The lifeguard dozed on the beach. And even our digital clock slept three hours a day—slowed down by the leisurely Bahan current.

Back on the balcony, and on the beach, we buried our cares in the sand, rediscovered each other, laughed with the Bahans and our new friends from Europe, forgot there are such things as television, telephones and teenagers and gradually became children again ourselves. It was a golden, glad hour in the sun, and when it was over—so very soon—we were sad. But that is the best recommendation for a vacation, after all. And Barbados, Ellen, *was* the dream vacation.

"Was That Mule Drinking, Son?"

January 1, 1984

The whole North Louisiana landscape was a rippling lake of moonlight. That's why my father, forty-eight years later, still can't understand why he didn't see the mule in time. He was returning from a visit to Antioch and a date with the girl who was to become Marie Trussell Hilburn.

Of course, old Highway 122 between Ruston and Antioch is a rollercoaster of a hill road, diving down pine-shadowed curves and heaving up out of creek bottoms. In 1936, it was all gravel from Ruston to Trussell's Store and Antioch's four corners.

Anyway, the next thing Dad knew a mule's head came through the front window of the 1934 Ford V-8 with a shattering crash. Dad, car and mule rolled. He came to his senses covered with blood and broken glass. It was an awful feeling.

Leaping out of the ruined Ford, Dad tore off his blood-soaked white shirt, looking for mortal wounds. But there were no wounds. All the blood belonged to the mule, sprawled dead alongside the car. Breathing a great sigh of relief, Dad left mule and car in the silver sheen of that moonlit night and caught a ride back to Ruston.

Safely home on West Alabama Street, the next thing Dad had

"WAS THAT MULE DRINKING, SON?"

to do was inform E. W. Hilburn that the family car was wrecked. "The car is wrecked, Daddy," he remembers telling his father, who would later be Pop to me. Pop had been roused out of a deep featherbed sleep.

"It was my fault. The car is wrecked, but I couldn't help it. I was coming back from Marie's at Antioch and this mule just plain jumped in the car with me," Dad told his father. "I couldn't help it . . . it was that old mule's fault."

Pop finally raised up out of the covers, showing his familiar long-handled pajamas. "I've got just one question for you," he told my father who nodded, waiting.

"Was that mule drinking, son?" Pop wanted to know.

He Was Gone . . . But Not Gently

July 1, 1984

Pop didn't give up after we took him to the nursing home. Of course, he saw it all through his one angry eye: the empty stares, the bed sores, the woman who killed flies all day; the man who did not speak for years and then, suddenly, with a great smile, began to curse clearly and violently.

Pop saw it all, but he didn't give up. Naw, Pop found a girlfriend instead. "She is seventy-nine, but she doesn't look a day over seventy," Pop told me proudly. He was ninety-three. They found what privacy they could in those stark corridors. They liked to just sit silently and look at one another.

Once I found them, their wheelchairs locked in what small solitude that could be had in a foyer at the end of the hall. They

HE WAS GONE . . . BUT NOT GENTLY

were holding hands, talking urgently and sharing a Dixie cup of smuggled-in Mogen David wine.

"She's a good woman," Pop would tell me. "Not like your grandmother," he would hasten to say, reassuring me, "but she is a good woman." I was happy for him. For them. For the rest of the nursing home people who liked to gossip about that romance.

She was there, after all, when he nearly died, but somehow—against all odds—rallied and woke up and wanted a milkshake. Sometimes he was depressed, though, and I could see the light in his face recede. "I don't dream about cotton gins anymore," he told me once.

That nearly broke my heart. His whole working life had been taken up in ginning cotton, you see, and in the farmers who brought it to him. When the gin burned down, that time, he went broke making it up to the farmers.

He could still get mad, even during those nursing home days. He got into an argument at dinner and belted a man with his walking stick. Sometimes he berated us, in sharp and scornful words, for not coming to see him often enough. His one eye would burn.

I couldn't stand that. He had always been so good to me. I could bang loudly on his glass front door on West Alabama Street in the depths of the night, waking him out of a sound sleep, and he would still be glad to see me. Just glad to see me. I could tell. I loved him.

We played dominoes in that house. He let me cheat on him. We listened to Gabriel Heatter announce his radio newscast, "friends, there's goooood news tonight . . ." He peeled me oranges and bought all my papers when I had the town route and told me, over and over, "your word is your bond, son." Yeah, I loved him.

Once, while in the nursing home, Pop decided to sell that house on West Alabama where it all happened. Dad tried gently to persuade him not to do it. "Mama told you never to sell the house," Dad told Pop. Pop didn't say a word to that, but he walked right off. He was furious.

Later, though, Pop brought it up again. This time Dad laid it on the line. "I'll sign if you tell me to," he said, "it's your house, not mine." Relief flooded Pop's face. He relaxed. "I'll think about it then," he said.

"Son," he told Dad a week later, "I went back to my house the other day. I sat down under the big oak in the front yard and got myself a nap. A really good nap. When I woke up the birds were singing in the tree." Pop paused at that, and then he said it. "I'm not selling the house, son."

Sometimes he would make me take him back to that old house on West Alabama Street. It always made me nervous because Pop had rented the house, but he always insisted on walking right in, without knocking or asking permission.

"It's my house, son," he would tell me, and poke at the beds and gas stove with his walking stick. He tapped his way through the house. Such visits did not depress him at all; he just wanted to make sure everything was still in order.

He had his girlfriend right up to the end, wore his clean and pressed blue suit, combed his full white hair and took his exercises in bed when he couldn't get out.

Three weeks before he died I asked him what he was thinking about. "Women," he said. Then he reassured me again about how much he loved my grandmother.

A coma finally took Pop out for good. He was deep into it, the sleep that is final, and the doctors said it wouldn't be long.

Dad said we ought to get the blue suit ready. "He might hear you," I cautioned. But the doctor said no; Pop was too far gone. His chest was barely moving at all.

But I went over to his bed and said, deep into his ear, "Poppy, if you can hear me, squeeze my hand." I felt the pressure. I swear to God I did. I felt it. A few hours later, Pop was gone, slept away, but not gently.

No, not gently.

I loved him.
I still do.

The Cubs Were a Family Affair

September 30, 1984

When the Cubs clinched their divisional pennant last Monday night, Greg and I opened a bottle of German wine given to us by neighbor-friend Charles Tannehill and celebrated with the thousands of fans taking Chicago's Rush and Division streets apart.

At our house, the Cubbies had become a family project. Greg and I barely missed an inning and even Ellen, caught up in the Cubbie current against her will, called home from Shreveport where she was visiting her sister to get the score.

This is probably Greg's last full summer at home, in any event, and the unlikely champions of the windy city brought us even closer together during this period. We waited for each other to get home and shared the action with broadcaster Harry Caray on Chicago's cable giant, WGN.

When Tech got cranked up again this fall, I had to miss an afternoon game or two and Greg properly scolded me. "You don't *really* care about the Cubbies, Dad," he told me. I knew an engagement ring was in the works when—albeit reluctantly—he deserted the Cubbies in an extra-inning tie for a date with Tania.

The people at the Ruston *Daily Leader*, where Greg works, learned he could be found at home when the Cubbies were on television. John Hays, publisher of Ruston's *Morning Paper*,

THE CUBS WERE A FAMILY AFFAIR

would call me in mid-afternoon to say, "Wiley, when the Cubs are over, I need to talk to you about a Tech matter."

And let me say that Greg and I are not fair-weather Cub fans. We started watching the Cubs two years ago when they were still champion losers and liked them almost as much then. I've always had an affection for legendary losers, anyway—the Italian army of 1942, the Tulane teams that lost by 62-0 scores to LSU, Barney Fife and Dave Treen.

The Cubs didn't only fit into that great loser category, their last pennant coming in 1945. They don't even have lights at Wrigley Field, which pleases me. I'm old-fashioned. Night baseball, computer terminals, the robotic Dallas Cowboys and instant hamburgers at McDonald's are foreign to me. I liked the ivy-covered walls at Wrigley, even when the Cubs lost.

I also liked Harry Caray, even when the Cubs were losing. In fact, I liked Harry when my baseball team was the St. Louis Cardinals and he piped 'em to Ruston, static and all, over KMOX's long-reaching clear-channel radio in the 1950s.

No, Harry doesn't look like Frank Gifford or sound like Vin Scully, and he thinks he's still on the radio. He alternately roots for and roasts the Cubbies, depending on the circumstances and the score. In short, Harry is a fan. Just like us.

And boy, oh, boy did Greg and I root for the Cubbies when things started, remarkably, to go right for them—and roast 'em when things went wrong. On an inning-by-inning basis, we mostly got on people—Cub players who made outs or errors. That was the most fun.

Left-fielder Gary Matthews was our first target. The abuse we heaped on that poor man. Vicious. We even made fun of the way he ran, in kind of a broken shamble. Greg said that he'd rather have Mamaw Marie (his grandmother) in left field than Matthews, who seemed to approach every fly ball hit in his direction with abject fear. I suggested that Lindy Ellington, my nine-year-old niece in Shreveport (who played on a girls team), would make a better outfielder than Matthews. Of course, during the

THE CUBS WERE A FAMILY AFFAIR

last six weeks of the season it was the blazing bat of Matthews that actually carried the Cubs to the pennant. Now Greg and I call Matthews "Sarge" and speak fondly and respectfully of him. So does Harry Caray.

We also attacked third baseman Ron Cey. Unmercifully. Greg and I were not convinced even when Cey, the ex-Los Angeles Dodger, began to accumulate a lot of runs batted in. "He's never had a hit or an RBI when it counted," Greg growled. I agreed.

And when Cey did hit a home run, early in the season, we would say, yeah, sure he hits homers—when the Cubs are ahead by nine or behind by nine. We murdered Ron Cey. But now he has driven in around one hundred runs, they all counted and we say, hey, that Ron Cey delivers in the cluch. So does Harry.

Our last victim was Larry Bowa, the Cub captain and shortstop. We hated Bowa, Greg and I. Hated him. We said that he was old, that he lacked fielding range and that he made errors within that range—about one cubic inch.

Greg called Bowa "Auto"—for automatic out. It seemed like he popped up to the catcher every time. I said that Bowa hadn't delivered a hit in three years. But in the stretch, Bowa played good defense. So we shut up about him. So did Harry.

To tell the truth, Greg and I even got on Harry a little. We got tired of Harry relentlessly promoting the Cubs Cruise in November, spelling the players' names backwards and dousing every observation with a reference to Budweiser. You know what the pressure of a pennant race will do to you, Harry. We ask to be forgiven.

But that's the way it is with family; you get irritated with small failings and frustrations but when somebody is successful, well, that makes everything worthwhile. For a whole summer, the Cubbies—those small and toothless bears of sunshine—were not only family, but unexpectedly and enormously successful family members.

It was like the lovable uncle who had a good garden but never made the mortgages suddenly cornering the world market on tomatoes. It was like Anne Marie aceing a geometry test. It was like me learning to operate a computer terminal. It was like Uncle Sam kicking behinds in Grenada.

It was wonderfully improbable, but the Cubs did it. And when that last out was made Monday night, Greg ran all over the house beating on the walls and yelling, "Cubs win! Cubs win!" I started hollering too, and we drank some of that German wine out of Ellen's best crystal and stayed glued to WGN until the last hurrah.

In Praise (?) of Poor Grades

April 13, 1986

When the kid comes home with poor grades, how should parents react? If you believe Dr. Sanford Dornbusch, a sociologist at Stanford University, the position to take is a "low-key, positive response—offering praise for the positive aspects of the child's performance . . ."

Screaming at the child only makes matters worse, says Dornbusch, quoted in a recent New York *Times* "Relationships" column. Of course, the man has a survey of 10 million to make his point, and a title at Stanford that commands attention: Reed Hodgson professor of human biology, sociology and education. Wow!

But with all due respect, Dr. Dornbusch, bad grades were never *discussed*, much less *praised*, in my generation and in my part of North Louisiana. When your parents finally found the grades you had intercepted from the mailman or imperfectly altered with liquid paper, they yelled and screamed for at least

IN PRAISE (?) OF POOR GRADES

forty-eight hours. Your role was not that of a panelist in a discussion, Dr. Dornbusch; your role was to keep quiet and roll with the punch.

No, there was no discussion about bad grades, Professor Dornbusch. Our parents fired broadsides of death threats and denunciations at us, and we stood silently against the nearest wall, as if facing a firing squad. Maybe your mother offered a blindfold for the execution or relieved your father of his belt after a sufficient number of welts—not points of debate, Dr. Dornbusch—were raised.

What's more, you knew in your heart this punishment was deserved. Making bad grades was a sin against God—worse than climbing the Tech water tower or getting the third speeding ticket or making three straight errors in the championship baseball game. In 1959, making bad grades was *evil*.

All your parents wanted you to do in 1959 was write an occasional theme on good citizenship, read *The Good Earth* for English, learn the names and dates of the presidents and not get kicked out of fifth-hour study hall.

Your folks were working their tails off for you. They told you that every day. "Look, I'm working my butt off . . ." In return for their sweat and slavery, all *you* had to do was pass something called sociology, for God's sake. "Your mother and I are killing ourselves for you, and all we expect is a decent grade in geometry. Is that too much to ask?"

In 1959, we *knew* that wasn't too much to ask. So if we screwed up in school, well, we didn't expect something called *dialogue*, a tutor for freshman algebra and that's-all-right-son-just-try-to-do-better-next-time. No, Dr. D., we expected and got deprival, denunciation and—if the report card was a three-car wreck—a certain amount of physical abuse. In 1959, the result of this kind of reaction to bad grades was usually positive, to use Dr. Dornbusch's favorite word. Memorizing a Robert Frost poem was infinitely preferable to being mugged.

When I came home with bad grades, Dr. D., my dad got right

IN PRAISE (?) OF POOR GRADES

in my face and hollered at me for forty-eight minutes without stopping. I timed three such tongue-lashings. This kind of verbal abuse continued on into college.

In fact, as a journalism major at Tech I practiced my future profession by writing up my father's bad-grade diatribes. It was sort of like LABI getting after Edwin Edwards. One such story read as follows:

> RUSTON (AP)—In a bitter 48-minute lecture, Wiley Hilburn, Sr. formally disowned and disinherited his nineteen-year-old son, Wiley Jr., at their Marbury Drive residence last night.
>
> "You are lazy, no-good, worthless and you will never amount to anything," the elder Hilburn said, adding that Wiley Jr.'s transportation and his allowance would be suspended until further notice.
>
> In a prepared statement released to the Ruston *Daily Leader*, Hilburn, Sr. said that all he ever asked from his son was "an honest C" in "an easy civics course" in return for "free meals, room, board, car, car insurance, clothes, a college education and spending money."
>
> "With me working my butt off for him, the least he can do is make decent grades—the only thing he has to do," Hilburn Sr. said.
>
> Reporters failed to contact the younger Hilburn, who was rumored to be under house arrest. Neighbors reported shouts from the Hilburn home, but told newsmen that such disturbances were common about every six weeks . . .

In truth, bad grades did not get me locked in my room. Instead, my father locked me in the kitchen and piled my books all around me on the table. Sometimes, in an act of defiance, I would make the following statement:

"You can make me sit in this kitchen with these books, but you can't make me study."

Invariably he replied that "Well, at least you will be exposed

IN PRAISE (?) OF POOR GRADES

to them (the books)." Apparently Daddy felt that knowledge, like radiation, could be absorbed from a certain proximity. Anyway, my grades generally improved after such "positive" punishment. That kitchen was a frightening place on a Friday night.

My first cousins, the Barhams of Ruston, also got none of Dr. Dornbusch's praise and encouragement for bad grades. Cap Barham rose to lieutenant governor in a democratic society, loosely defined in Louisiana, but he didn't take votes at home. Cap Barham was more like Anastasio Somoza than Dr. Spock—or even Dr. Dornbusch.

As it happened, Cap's son Robert had an "F" in Dr. F. O. Adam's Tech Spanish class at mid-term. They gave pink slips in those days. So when Bob came home for lunch that mid-term noon, his customary purplehull peas, fried chicken and rice and gravy were missing. Bob's plate was empty. Except for that pink slip in Spanish.

The message from Cap Barham was plain, and Bob understood it. His food supply depended on a passing grade in Spanish. Learn Spanish or eat pink slips. Dr. Dornbusch might be interested to know that Cap's message had a positive effect on Bob. He didn't starve; he passed Spanish instead.

No, Cap Barham would not have understood the Dornbusch survey. If you don't believe Robert, ask Charlie Barham—Cap's elder son, and now North Louisiana's senior state senator. Charlie was subjected to the same pass-or-perish rule.

In fact, Cap expected better than just passing grades in some subjects—like ROTC at Tech. I arrived at the Barham's Goode Street residence just as Cap was hollering at Charlie for making a "C" in ROTC. Not wishing to be singed by the blast, I broke for the back door.

But I did hear Cap yelling that "Any (expletive deleted) fool can march."

Readers may wonder how I, as a parent, have approached discipline on grades. Dr. Dornbusch would be appalled, of course, but I have found that an old Louisiana political practice bears academic fruit at our house: bribery.

IN PRAISE (?) OF POOR GRADES

Good grades have been known to produce everything from money to new baseball gloves to a recent promise of a trip to Tech-Rome. When bribery fails, I holler, heaving up well-remembered selections from the abuse Daddy once heaped on me.

When bribery and verbal condemnation failed, our kids would find their cars up on blocks—the wheels removed. If that didn't work, we resorted to capital punishment: we turned off the TV.

Okay, equal time for Dr. Dornbusch. "In focusing on bad grades parents can say things like, 'I know you can do better if you just put out a little more effort.'" That would be the extent of the Dornbusch diatribe; the very *worst* thing he would say.

Now, I'm not saying anything bad about Dr. D. or his survey of 7,836 students in six San Francisco Bay area high schools. Who are we in Louisiana to be criticizing anybody on the subject of education and how to improve it?

Still, I know exactly what Wiley Hilburn, Sr. would say about Dr. Dornbusch's "low-key, positive response" to poor grades, and I would love to hear the late Cap Barham tell this learned educator precisely where to march with this theory.

PART SIX

A PLACE IN TIME

Storming Down Interstate-20

June 4, 1978

The authentic North Louisiana thunderstorm starts with a feeling, really, and nothing else; a not unpleasant sensation of tension, of expectation; a sharpened awareness of a yet shapeless something in the atmosphere, the mood and the mind. It is only a feeling, and it comes well before the first tangible signal that something is doing in the weather.

The old collie knows something is brewing out there, too. Restless, she bumps a gray-tawny muzzle against the front door, trying to push it open. The collie can sense a storm when the sky is whole blue and nothing seems astir. But then, after the dog has found her corner refuge, comes the first audible signal that she was right again: a little thump of thunder, away off, like the first note in a great symphony.

With that distant drumroll the tension, felt in a certain closeness, thickens perceptibly. And soon after that it can be seen at last: a huge hump of cloud, still white with a sparkle of sunlight at the top, but, at bottom, sits a mass of purple, pitchforked by lightning.

The storm, I know now, is real, and building; it is tracking east toward me down I-20 in long, splashing strides. Shreveport has taken its rainy licks, the deluge has subsided and the city's gutters and drains are choking on the flood. Taylor and Gibsland are under the hammer. Lincoln Parish, though still dry, is nevertheless under seige.

The tension feels good, like a safe scare in an Alfred Hitchcock movie. Ultimately, with the cloud mushrooming up over the Western horizon, comes the wind—flowing up out of the pasture like a fresh ocean current entering a stagnant lagoon, making old chimes sing somewhere, rattling sycamore leaves. It is a cool balm, this interlude, and it only lasts for a single moment. I have waited for it. I love it.

But the calm can't last; I know that. The rain smell, a vigorous compound of fresh-plowed soil and cottonseed, is everywhere. The storm has seized the sky now, nearly all of it. Everything is close, close, the moisture, unfallen yet, presses down like a soaking mattress. Then the lightning makes a ripping, tearing path through the tension, spearing across the top of the sky, and the pressure disintegrates, dissolves under that blow.

The crashes fall one on the other, salvos of thunder, and build to a crescendo. It's the last movement of the *1812* Overture out there, and the cannons are all firing. The split sky literally opens. And the rain drives down like a million cold, silver javelins. The tension torn to shreds by the storm, is washed away in a chaos of water; the thunder, muted now, is retreating to the east. The rain slows, too.

At the end the land and the spirit, purged by the storm, are at peace. There is only a dripping solitude in the aftermath of the violence, and a last, filtered light, the color of strawberries.

For Christmas: An Old Barn

December 24, 1978

What I want for Christmas is one of North Louisiana's old barns, preferably seated haphazardly on a slight incline, peering down from the shade of a gnarled hardwood into a low pasture. Granted, that wish isn't likely to turn up in my stocking in the morning, but it doesn't hurt to dream.

Actually, I have been dreaming about old barns, and poking unbidden into their cobwebby innards for years, trespassing on somebody else's forty acres. The raw gash of Interstate 20 in the 1950s exposed dozens of these structures, leaving them caught in the open, dilapidated and deserted, like so many old ladies surprised in curlers and ragged bathrobes.

Yet, like the old ladies that I know and love, there is a dignity and a beauty in their untended decay. Abandoned and unused they are, these leaning and groaning old barns, but even on a gray December afternoon there is the life and smell of memories—memories of vanished, vibrant early farm mornings—within the splintery walls.

This day, dodging bullets of cold rain, we invade just such a place off the Farmerville Road in Lincoln Parish. Inside, there is a musty hay-animal aroma, a not unpleasant odor, and sagging steps leading up to a big loft from a floor of dirt and cow chips.

An old wagon, tongue protruding, loaded with dusty lumber, is forever parked in the past here. Upstairs are empty fifty-pound sacks of range cubes and calf-pellets, old bedsprings, and a roll of barbed wire.

The loft shudders slightly in the brittle winter wind, but the tin roof shelters us from the thunderous downpour. It is secure and serene up here and this barn, though dying, can still shield us from the weather. It was built with pride and—almost falling down from exhaustion now—it still stands against the elements, and against time.

Outside is a covered well, and under a tough honey locust tree (they made fence posts out of those things) we discover the rusting remains of plows and harrows, an old blacksmith forge, and a set of wheels from an old cotton gin wagon. Again, time stops, and we take a last look before speeding away, toward the present.

It was not our barn, of course, and the sign said "For Sale: 183 Acres." The old barn, we tell each other, can buck the winter wind and rain, but not the bulldozer. And this old lady is perilously close to town.

All the old barns, I fear, are doomed: dinosaurs caught in a shrinking time warp; beautiful old women living out their last days. And if I can't have one for Christmas, then I will look again at Albino Hinojosa's acrylic-on-masonite rendering of two old barns, their tin roofs going red, which hangs on my den wall.

The only thing is, the artist calls his picture "Retired," and that is the sad part of it.

North Louisiana's old barns.

Retired.

That's why I want one, to keep, this Christmas—before it's too late and they are all gone.

A Sanctuary for the New Year

December 31, 1978

The First Presbyterian Church of Ruston is solid against the leaf-swirling winter wind of North Louisiana, rising up out of the

A SANCTUARY FOR THE NEW YEAR

early darkness in weathered bricks and great ropes of ivy, its steeple a silhouette against the cold stars.

It sits there serenely, cracked and cobwebbed in places, but somehow proud. Outside the guard is mounted by huge, broken-limbed oak trees. The stained glass windows flicker red and gold, offering a warm invitation to enter.

Once inside, seven tapered candles in each window make a buttery glow that gently defeats the darkness, but lets in long, soft brown shadows that shade the eyes and ease the mind. It is comfortable, even in the solid, hard pine pews.

The roof is high, soaring high, and crisscrossed with massive pine beams. Here is timber, clean-lined and unlaminated and hard, that could—I think—hold up the world. There is strength here, and endurance.

The consciousness drifts in the cadence of the first hymn. I sat here, in this very place, beside my grandfather, holding his gold railroad watch, timing the preacher. I used to kick the bottom of the pew in front, waiting until somebody soundlessly framed an "uh-uh" with their mouth and stopped me with a slight headshake.

I've dropped many a yellow number two pencil, and heard it roll down the slightly inclined polished hardwood floor, until it sounded—in my ears—like an avalanche. I remember spilling the communion wine in the little church kitchen and getting the black Bible with my name embossed on it in gold.

There was the time, in the high school class, when Bob Barham was innocently giving the opening prayer and I busted him in a tender spot with the red hymnbook. There was also the time when Peg, my grandmother, caught us disrupting a Sunday School class and scolded us all. I still burn with shame at the thought of that.

There was Mr. Davis, magisterial in his black robes; Dr. Thompson, gentle and sincere, who drew Ellen and me, then just dating, to his Sunday night services.

Now there is also my son Greg, and I can hear his voice mingling with my father's when we say the Lord's Prayer. It is a good sound. And there is Kevin, ushering in his new suit, and Anne Marie receiving an award for reciting the Catechism.

This night the congregation is, as usual, rather small. The people here know each other, though, and there is no need to make a fuss—except for a pat on the shoulder, a wink, a handshake behind the pew. The hymns, familiar ones, are sung reverently, with an unhurried grace.

Somebody is playing a fiddle now, and its sharp, clear sounds are enfolded in the deeper, more subtle tones of a new organ in this old church. The air seems fresh, and I detect fresh pine and cedar here and there.

There is an uplifting sense of generations here, a rhythm of time and timelessness, that unites young and old in the candlelight and stained glass and burnished brass, a feeling of continuity and conquered fear.

Here is a sanctuary in the true sense. A place of peace, of rest and renewal, of quiet calm. Outside the winter wind is blowing, and the noise of the New Year—a firecracker and a gunned car engine—intrudes on the Silent Prayer. But the New Year, for all its uncertain hours, can be faced now.

February, and Forever, in Boeuf Prairie

February 4, 1979

It was about this time last year—and it seemed that winter would never end. I was headed for a place called Boeuf Prairie to attend

FEBRUARY, AND FOREVER, IN BOEUF PRAIRIE

the funeral of the mother of a close friend. Boeuf Prairie? The map didn't list the name, and I stayed on the interstate as long as possible, listening to radio reports of snow and carefully following directions.

In the end, Boeuf Prairie found me this icy winter day, and the result was an editorial in *The Times* "North Louisiana" series. And when that editorial appeared, it turned out that little unmapped Boeuf Prairie had touched a lot of people from the composing room of this newspaper to Washington, D.C.

Blanche Williams of Fort Necessity wrote me an eloquent letter, and she summed up the feelings about Boeuf Prairie and the surrounding Northeast Louisiana region, where she was born and later taught school. "It was the proudest school in the world," she wrote.

The proud people of "The Fort" and Boeuf Prairie remain in my mind, too. A Mr. Ross who shook my hand outside the old church—and then the Daileys, the Buies, the Bonners, the Wooldridges, the Deshas, the Turners, the Masons, the Kincaids, the Pecks and the Moores, and others, they all brought a stranger home.

It's February again, and a good time to revisit Boeuf Prairie as *The Times* North Louisiana series saw it a year ago:

The February snowflakes were big and wet, and they disappeared without a trace into the grainy, gray soil turned fresh out of the gravesite. She had lived out almost a century in this part of Northeast Louisiana, in Franklin Parish, and had not seen a lot change in all that time.

The eulogy was that she had abided deep in the faith, was a strong woman of unadjusted principles, and had raised her children well; children and grandchildren now spread, in their unfolding lives, from Winnsboro to Washington; and, of course, children who had stayed at home, and tended the land.

This day they had all come home, at least in spirit. The priest was not long from Ireland, and his soft lilt lay easy and comforting, like a balm, on the consciousness. After the mass in Winnsboro, the road led directly home—to Fort Necessity.

There followed, almost within sight of her small house and thirty acres, that unforced and unspoken mingling of the faiths for which North Louisiana receives no credit in the great interdenominational church councils, but which is real enough—and common enough—in these parts where neighbors count more than doctrines.

The priest and the Protestant minister said the last words, near a storm-blasted hardwood with the cottonfields as a backdrop, and the final bittersweet parting—because she had given and received a full measure of life—was concluded.

A stranger among the friends and the faithful, we were led to the final ceremony by a Mr. Ross, who in the way of such people made us welcome with the grip of his hand. As we walked, braced against the cold air, he pointed to the clean, white building looming to our right.

"That's my church," he said, in a voice that measured pride on every syllable, and took us to the roots of this whole region. This was Boeuf Prairie, somebody told us then, and we thought of the Boeuf River which flows nearby. And the Methodist Church, we learned then, was raised on this spot before the Civil War.

Tall oaks stood around the church, trailing gray moss. And the churchyard ran right into the cemetery without a gate or a fence to separate them. Here, one saw life and death merge without embarrassment or formality.

It was snowing as we left the church and Fort Necessity—people here call it "The Fort"—and turned up Highway 15 toward Winnsboro and Baskin and Mangham and Alto, headed for Monroe and the interstate, and, ultimately, home.

The cotton left from the autumnal picking hung in limp and sodden shreds in the fields. It was blue-gray outside, and a little snow was beginning to accumulate in the empty fields. But no matter. We kept thinking of the woman who had lived her faith and of the man who said, with utter pride, "That's my church."

Boeuf Prairie was home all the time.

What I saw, that February day in 1978, was the enduring pride of North Louisiana. And North Louisiana, I think as this winter tightens its own grip, is Boeuf Prairie, and Boeuf Prairie is forever.

The Free Ferry at Duty

July 8, 1979

It was Steve Lawson who told me about the free ferry at Duty. He had read one of *The Times* North Louisiana editorials and suggested that the Duty ferry might provide some good material.

Ellen, Aunt Marie, Kevin, Amy Ringheim and I took off on Steve's directions early one Sunday afternoon, and we made good time. The delta roads on both sides of the Ouachita River in Northeast Louisiana are straight and swift, swooping into places like Grayson and Holum and Rosefield on the west and Liddieville and Jigger and Holly Grove on the east.

But Louisiana 559 leaps off the ponderous bow of Route 165 at Columbia like a dusty green arrow. It flies past the McKeithen Plantation, parallels the Ouachita right up to its edge, and knifes through fresh-plowed soybean fields en route to its target and our destination: the ferry at Duty.

And, just as Steve told me, it's a free ferry, right where the arrow of 559 splashes into the river, and it's the only way

THE FREE FERRY AT DUTY

across—a time warp, an almost literal gap in the river of history, a Ouachita ride on the waters of days forever gone.

The *W. Prescott Foster*, an ancient gray-and-white river tug that once plied the Mississippi out of Baton Rouge, hauled us, our car, and several pick-up trucks across the Ouachita. The old tug heaved and struggled at the ramp, panting black smoke in the strain.

But once in deeper waters the tug moved us all with breast-stroking ease. And we could look into the depths of the Ouachita, an obscure, bottom-of-the-bottle green this cool May Sabbath. I let the river passage float me back as we cross—back to cotton instead of soybeans, to old flags and blue bonnets.

It only lasts a moment, that ferry passage, but there is in the mind a sense of history, of something gone and recovered only briefly and lost again, in the crossing—a feeling Amy and Anne Marie and Kevin, caught up in the wonder of the ride, seemed to miss entirely.

The Duty ferry done, we glided through Enterprise and on to Harrisonburg. Just outside this place we climbed out of the flatlands into a high stand of pine trees—the air freshened—and falling away sharply below is Harrisonburg.

There it sits quietly, a church steeple and the columned Catahoula Parish Courthouse, in the embrace of the Ouachita—which, flanked by soybean fields and fringed by willows, meanders on toward Jonesville.

We stopped for cold drinks and conversation at a small Harrisonburg filling station. A snow-haired observer tapped his cane on a bench outside. Then the road was reversed because the children were tired and not looking outside anymore; and because I wanted to ride the Duty ferry one more time.

The kids were reading comic books as the *W. Prescott Foster* pulled us across the river a second time this afternoon. Soon we would ride the 559 arrow toward Interstate 20 and home.

But the gentle current at the Duty ferry had somehow taken me back home, across a great river, one more time. And that passage at Duty, even though Anne Marie and Amy and Kevin don't know it now, is ever so brief.

Yes, It Is November in North Louisiana

November 11, 1979

The summer is only just gone, surely. And September . . . doggone it, September, we hardly knew you. Where are the watermelons and butterbeans? School only just started, it seems; and with the books it was football, and October . . . was there an October?

It was all a blur; a sudden chill-edged morning, a dead battery, a shotgun shell in the woods, a red leaf in the wind, an end to twilight. Yet, the hummingbirds are gone south and the sky—well, the sky is all at once a very intense blue. Blinding almost.

Is it, then, November in North Louisiana? No, it's not November. It could not be November. Yes, face it, before it's too late. November it is; almost two weeks into the eleventh month of the year, at that. Here we are walking the last rickety bridge between autumn and winter. November, as unexpectedly as it arrived, seems old, somehow.

Thanksgiving is almost upon us, for gosh sakes; it's a bare week and a half distant. And those two holidays, Thanksgiving and Christmas, so different in mood and method, are actually jammed one on top of the other. Christmas? Don't even think about it; somebody might string the lights across Main Street, and rob us of yet another passage.

YES, IT IS NOVEMBER IN NORTH LOUISIANA

So keep quiet about Christmas. It's still fall, anyway; even if November sneaked up on us and whispered, all soft wind in our ear, "you are missing a whole season." And late fall is the time of collard greens sealed by first frost; the time when collards smell the loudest and taste the best. Mrs. Hilman's wild pear tree is a remarkable red now; before this month is gone its leaves will burn like an oil fire, dark and violent.

Here and there, too, there are glimpses of falling gold, and those thoughts of growing old. From the summit of a hill shown to us by Sonny Barnard we can look far down. It is quiet, and leaves spiral down slowly, rhythmically, not afraid, like children drifting off to sleep.

And in the cool solitude of the woods below, down the cluttered slope to the creek, there are leaves on the water. Viking ships they are in what remains of the child's mind; or, in the adult consciousness, Chinese sampans, floating serenely in the slow but inevitable current. There they go, these ship-leaves, twisting, spinning, turning out of sight toward an unknown destination on the dark, autumnal flow.

They are the last glorious fleet of all, these leaves on the water. They are riding out on sails of amber, orange and lemon, and they are bright and bold. But they are the last ships of the season, these leaves, and soon they will disappear around the bend of the creek on that slow current. Gone.

Maybe we are so slow to notice November because it is the dying season in North Louisiana. But up the bank of the creek, in the mulch of the leaf, is the dormant stuff of life. For under the debris, in a graveyard of bramble, microscopic yet monumental forces are at work.

They are, our neighbor-zoologist John Goertz has told us, forest floor invertebrates; the earthworm, the millipede, the springtail and the familiar rolypoly. This is their world, this rot and ruin, and in the great leaf-fall of November, they eat.

These organisms, unseen and unappreciated, do their crucial work in nature's redemptive cycle; their eating is the breaking-down of material, of mold, so that minerals are returned to the earth. So it is once again that in death, the death of a season, there is life.

Yes, it is November in North Louisiana, and the leaves are on the water. For the leaf-ships of autumn, brilliant in their moment, the final destination is beyond December and January and February; beyond winter even. It is spring, really, that lies around the bend of the creek, sleeping under a quilt of clutter.

It's November all right, and the leaves are on the water.

But that is only the beginning of it all.

Milkworms and Magic and Morgan's Pond

July 13, 1980

"One cannot help but be amused by the armament these fishermen have raised against the wily bass," wrote James Seay in his excellent essay, "The Southern Outdoors: Bass Boats and Bear Hunts," for the book, *The American South*.

That observation took me back a few years to a magical pond just off Highway 80 East outside of Ruston where, armed with milkworms dug out of a pecan orchard and splintery cane poles, Bill Upchurch and I challenged all records for numbers of bluegill, white perch, goggle-eye and bass caught in the course of two childhoods.

This place was called Morgan's Pond, and it was more than a mere fishing hole; it was a way of life for Bill and me. Those July mornings we literally raced separately for the pond; me through a tropical growth that extended from the edge of Marbury Drive

"We always caught something at Morgan's Pond."

MILKWORMS AND MAGIC AND MORGAN'S POND

to the water's edge and Bill from up and across then-roaring Highway 80 to Monroe.

Once we were established on the dam (where our fishing day always started), the world receded from that piney sanctuary into oblivion; Morgan's Pond was our world, even into the first years of high school when most young lives became automated and thus forever altered. Our friends honked at us from the highway; we distractedly waved them away and checked our tiny blue bream hooks.

We always caught something at Morgan's Pond. The mystery was what species would be dragged out of the water. Dug in 1900, there were actually two ponds separated by a pinestraw-carpeted dam. What we called "the little pond" was scarcely more than a mudhole; it was jammed slam against the highway and sat there still and red like a bowl of Campbell's tomato soup with a little milk added for good measure.

However, even that placid bowl of soup next to the highway held a special prize—incredibly large, red-chested chinquapin bream. Positioning the cork just outside the shade line cast by two enormous pines on the dam guaranteed at least a couple of these fighting, flounder-sized creatures.

But the little pond was only a sideshow. The big pond, a teardrop shaped lagoon of black-green water, dominated our minds. It was a fish cafeteria; decide where to fish and hence what to catch.

The Western bank, a tangle of pine and sweetgum, was designated for speckled perch. We fished the dam for battling, handsized bluegill. The eastern shore was reserved for goggle-eye that fought like banshees, making our light line scream for mercy. The slough, at the tail of the teardrop, raged with largemouth bass.

Bets could be laid on what would be caught out of those particular holes, but part of the fun was that, no, we couldn't be sure, ever, of what was tearing up the water. This was because the ponds were fed by a big underground stream that tunneled under the highway. The underground spring surfaced in a branch on the other side of Old 80 that, in turn, ran into Choudrant Creek.

So, besides the resident bass, bluegill, chinquapin and goggle-eye, Bill and I occasionally landed what we called a sunfish—a creature painted in the hues of broken rainbows, so beautiful we always threw it back.

The appetite of the fish in those ponds, established for well over a half-century when we discovered them, is not a childhood dream. When Bill and I ran out of milkworms—or exhausted the red wrigglers we shoveled out of the Upchurch dogyard—the bluegill went nuts over Holsum bread filched from our mothers' pantries.

Gradually, Bill and I moved up from the cane poles to rods and reels. Bill's dad was an expert angler and his tacklebox bulged with more than three hundred lures. We learned casting on the dam at Morgan's Pond, snagging Hawaiian Wrigglers on the overhanging twin pines.

The first largemouth bass I ever caught blasted a white jitterbug tossed into the far end of the slough, sending up a plume of spray and showing me a green gatemouth that flooded my fourteen-year-old consciousness with awe and amazement.

Bill and I had a series of those arrogant bass snap our lines, including one outraged Moby Dick that surfaced all over the big pond for a full half-hour, trying to spit out an offending Tiny Torpedo.

But my best memories of the rod-and-reel time on Morgan's Pond are focused on a lone stob in the smackdab middle of the big water. Drop a black River Runt an inch to the left or right of that enchanted stob and the result was always the same: reeling in a pound-and-a-half "speck."

It was like pulling in a log, not much of a fight, but the fun was not diminished; it took pinpoint casting to crease the Great Stob. It also took a hard and long throw from the dam to reach that bull's-eye.

MILKWORMS AND MAGIC AND MORGAN'S POND

Bill's dad introduced him to a Pflueger Supreme reel. On the Upchurchs' good advice, I saved up for a whisper-quiet, green Shakespeare with silk gears. Some of the specks the Shakespeare produced were so large I ran home with them to show my parents.

Before we discovered the rod and reel, Bill and I had already run into trouble in the paradise of Morgan's Pond. It started when we made the mistake of dragging a washtub slick with bluegill through the backyard of one of the owners of the pond—who had spent a week on Black Lake near Natchitoches without achieving half our catch.

The pond was forbidden to me after that, but the ban only added another dimension of attraction to the place. We sneaked down to the dam just as much, and caught almost as many goggle-eye. Daddy added his injunction to the ban on Morgan's Pond, but after Bill and I caught him cleverly camouflaged on the west bank, fishing for those magnificent specks with triple-pronged hooks and minnows, his edict lost all moral force. Mrs. Morgan would sometimes yell us away from her brick house on the hill overlooking the pond, but we always came back.

What finally took me away from Morgan's Pond was a 1957 Chevy, a blonde named Ellen and the deadlines of the Ruston *Daily Leader*. My seven-years-younger brother Chet Hilburn inherited my Shakespeare reel (he ruined it) and Morgan's Pond. He regaled me with stories of shark-sized specks when I came home from the graduate school of journalism at LSU. Morgan's Pond slowly receded into a golden childhood and I have never really fished seriously since then.

But, in an era when great impoundments like Toledo Bend and D'Arbonne lakes have turned bassin' into a televised science, I still think longingly of the magic and milkworms of Morgan's Pond where Bill Upchurch and I grew up.

A Crazy-Quilt for Thanksgiving

November 23, 1980

There is a good, high perspective near Gibsland in Bienville Parish. From this summit, in these last autumn hours before Thanksgiving, North Central Louisiana looks like one of Grandmother Kate Trussell's crazy-quilts: haphazard, unsymmetrical patches of amber, red, green, lemon and orange.

It's a perspective that I pull over me like one of those old quilts on Kate's big bed at Antioch from vanished childhood autumns. The quilt was light, but it warmed me—and there was the clean-musty smell of security in those rough covers.

Indeed, there is something secure about the whole Thanksgiving season. A lot of scattered, random, small blessings weave into something solid and warm that, in another season, would go unnoticed and unappreciated.

Around this time of the year, though, I do begin to notice a few little things: like the Air Force-ROTC cadets sounding taps as they carefully pull down the American flag right outside my Keeny Hall office window at Tech. The sound is at once proud, sad, hopeful.

Then, just the other day, a young construction worker on campus caught me at the door of the Karmann Ghia, hogtied by a typewriter, twenty-two folders and four number two yellow pencils. "Let me get that door for you," he says. I notice that cheerful kindness; it's Thanksgiving season after all.

Suddenly, there is more to notice: six different hues of turning sweetgums counted in an hour between Ruston and Shreveport; the smell of my mother-in-law's collard greens; the golden shower of hickory leaves in the backyard. And there is Daddy in his backyard, strong as ever, grinding up compost for his spring garden. Thanksgiving.

There is the moon coming to life on one side of Black Lake near Natchitoches and the sun dying beyond the other bank. And there is the tough kid from Grant Parish who wrote, "Hey, Hilburn, I'm a closet reader of 'Fragments.' " Thanksgiving.

Ellen is gone for a night, and I miss her. Kevin is on the honor roll at Ruston High School; Greg brings a girl named Cindy home. Anne Marie tells me she will be playing Mary in the eighth-grade Christmas play. "All I have to do is look tranquil all the time," she says, grinning. Thanksgiving.

The ninety-sixth anniversary of Ruston's First Presbyterian Church is celebrated—home-fried chicken, deviled eggs and squash casserole on the grounds—and I talk to a lot of people who raised me in the church. It's Thanksgiving.

Best of all, maybe, the hill country roads are still open to me these cool last hours of November. They are free roads, fair roads and friendly, and blowing with the leaves of the season. It is on such a road near Gibsland, a rising road, that I notice the crazy-quilt perspective of North Louisiana. This is where I remember Kate.

This is where I find Thanksgiving.

" 'Way up Saline, a Dog Died"

February 21, 1981

They were 'way up Saline Bayou—past Salsbury Bridge and Sand Point and deep into the still rank-smelling cypress wilderness. The few who come this far don't like to talk about it, for fear that others may start coming in numbers that will rip and tear the heart out of the place.

"'WAY UP SALINE, A DOG DIED"

That's where they first saw the little dog last spring—'way up in the wilderness of the National Forest run of the bayou—wearing a flea collar and gnawing on the last bony remains of an alligator.

The high water had isolated a stretch of ground where the bayou made a big turn. It was a small male dog, evidently very young, with short black hair. Shy and scared, it ran quickly into the brush and disappeared when they called and whistled.

Back at their Saline Lake Camp, the couple speculated that the pup had come in with some other, older dogs and somehow gotten itself stranded on the creek turn. It could easily swim out and find its way back home—or maybe somebody would come looking. The flea collar proved that somebody owned the dog.

The next weekend the pair fished the same wild stretch, and there—stretched out beside the skeleton of the gator—was the same black dog. This time they beached the boat; the dog was obviously lost—lost and trapped.

But, again, the small pup retreated quietly and swiftly into the willows. The dog never barked once, but it moved quickly when they approached. A long search failed to locate him. Wood ducks broke for cover, but the black dog was not to be found.

The third weekend, they had to admit, was reserved not for fishing, but for rescuing the dog—though he assured her that this time the animal would be gone. Surely. They didn't fish at all; it was just a matter of measuring the distance between an abandoned stove, the last sign of civilization, and that turn in the creek.

Guiding the boat past the pipeline, he thought about how much she had worried about this little dog all week. She owned three dogs, loved them, and also specialized in nursing broken-winged birds back to health. Things like this hurt her. Surely, he thought, the dog would be gone this weekend. He hoped so.

They made the turn on Saline, and there was the dog—again lying close to the alligator bones. They raced for the spot, gunned the motor, but again the dog disappeared. This time, though, she noticed that the pup ran very slowly when they approached. Very slowly. "He's starving," she said, tears in her eyes. But another search, pushed nearly to dark, failed to turn up the dog.

The fourth weekend she came prepared with five pounds of dogfood. The trip was the same, with green herons scattering in their hurried wake. She was anxious. And there, in the same place, loomed the turn, the alligator skeleton and—she was elated—the dog. Her partner landed the boat, ramming it up on the bank.

This time, however, the dog did not run. The spring breeze ruffled its black fur, but that special and utter stillness—that unutterable stillness—told the story before they got there. The dog was dead, starved to death, beside the alligator skeleton.

It wasn't a big deal, not a big tragedy, he told her. A dog had died up Saline. She just sat up in the front of the boat, holding five pounds of dogfood. He couldn't see her face. But her shoulders shook all the way back to Saline Lake.

Kate's House: The Last Moonrise

July 26, 1981

It was, I thought at the time, an illusion.

Robert Barham and I were recently parked in the rutted driveway of my Grandmother Kate Trussell's old house at Antioch's four corners, talking quietly and listening to a screech owl over in the pine thicket.

That's when I saw the moonrise, a bright lantern of a moonrise, right through the tin roof of Kate's house. I didn't even tell

KATE'S HOUSE: THE LAST MOONRISE

Bob about it; he thinks I'm crazy, anyway. We left soon on the ten-mile ride back to Ruston, but the moon stayed in my mind.

An illusion.

But then I walked into Shipley's cafe the other morning and Eddie Hood, who was raised in Antioch and knows every red-clay sweetgum and gas well in that whole rock-spined territory, told me they were tearing down Kate's old house.

It was a blow, although I tried to hide the disappointment. The moonrise wasn't an illusion, after all. I just saw it through a skeleton of rafters. Kate's house, after all that time, was coming down. And it hurt because I've often stopped there at the four corners.

I don't know why, exactly. Kate has been gone for a long time, and, for years the old house has been a rotting eyesore. It belongs to somebody else. It's just that I could pull up there, near Kate's house, and sift my thoughts and somehow feel better. Consoled.

Crazy, Bob would say—crazy sentimentalism—and he's right. Now, though, I'm not sure where to resolve those restless hours. I used to stop at my other grandparents' old house on West Alabama Street in Ruston before it was torn down, too.

The land sits there at Antioch, of course, and some of it is still in the family. Somehow, though, it won't be the same without the old tin-roofed country house. Maybe I'll go back, after the tearing down is done, but I doubt it.

There was something final about that last moonrise at Kate's house.

The sign says Salem United Methodist Church, and it's a landmark set square against the flying feet of time in the shadowed green hills of North Central Louisiana. The church itself, which stands quietly among a half-dozen regal oak trees at a junction of Louisiana Highway 151 out of Dubach, is made out of native iron ore rock.

In fact, it was about this time in 1939, in the heat of July, when the men of Salem community began to haul the stones out of their fields and woods and to raise them, one by one, with their own hands.

That hard work was completed in September when the first service was held in the ironstone sanctuary. Actually, that new rock building was erected on the same property the Salem Church purchased when it was organized in 1859—the third building, most probably, in all that time. The first Salem Church was a cabin with a split-log floor.

The stones for this last structure were transported to the site in mule-drawn wagons. Then, led by a rock mason from Gibsland named Jones, the Nobles, the Dyes, the Henrys, the Mitchells, the McCrarys—with others, the names of north central Louisiana—labored it up that summer of thirty-nine, rock by rock, sweating, until it was all done by September.

So it stands today, enduring, a cool, cobwebby sanctuary of stone. Inside the ornaments of worship are few, but they are—I notice—made of sturdy wood that will survive. It's small, this church, really small. There is no great organ to sound—no grand cathedral this—but the old hymns will be sung proudly here.

Outside again, within the brown shadow of the church, the light summer wind makes only a small stirring in the old oaks. The dirtdauber nests stuck to the crevices of the rocks are undisturbed. They belong, too.

There is an aura of peace and permanence all about, and Salem United Methodist Church seems to speak to the character of rural North Louisiana: plain and unpretentious, but with a spine of solid iron ore rock that stands against time and the river.

Vienna's Syrup Bucket Mystery

February 28, 1982

Times were hard around Vienna, La. in the early 1930s; times were hard everywhere. The railroad had long since bypassed this North Central Louisiana community for Ruston, and the Depression didn't help matters either. But these were proud hill-country folks—farmers, mostly—and if anybody did go hungry, well, it wasn't something you talked about.

Of course, none of the kids at the Vienna schoolhouse seemed hungry those days; money was non-existent but people had always raised enough food to eat. Or said they did. The school children, in any event, were happily and loudly swapping sandwiches by recess.

The fact that T.C. and his sister wouldn't participate, ever, in the swapping was the start of the problem. Instead of eating with the group, T.C. and his sister unfailingly slipped away from the hilltop school to open the syrup bucket which contained their lunch. They ate alone. Every lunch period. Every day.

It was only natural that the other kids got curious about what T.C. and his sister had in their syrup bucket. T.C. wouldn't answer questions about it and his sister stood shy and silent behind him. But every high noon that rose over Vienna the brother and sister eased off down the hill, past the outhouses to a tangle of pine and sweetgum to eat their lunch. In private.

The mystery of why T.C. and his sister wanted to eat by themselves eventually turned from kidding to open irritation. Spying didn't work and T.C. kept the syrup bucket close to him with the lid on tight. Most of the Vienna kids had plain, spartan fare and speculation grew that T.C. and his sister were eating high on the hog; that maybe there was even fancy store-bought candy

VIENNA'S SYRUP BUCKET MYSTERY

in their syrup bucket. It was contrary, even downright mean of old T.C. and his silly kid sister not to share or to swap. That was everybody's feeling, anyway.

Irritation continued to mount and finally a couple of kids tried to take T.C.'s syrup bucket by main force. Well, T.C. fought like somebody possessed, kicking and screaming and biting. He won the fight and hung on to the syrup bucket. And later that day T.C. and his sister slipped down the hill under the barrage of catcalls where, once again, they ate their lunch alone.

What finally happened was inevitable. One of the big, brash kids swiped T.C.'s syrup bucket early in the morning before school started and, with a great yell, pried the lid off while everybody gathered around to see what unsharable goodies were hidden inside.

Then everybody got quiet.

Real quiet.

That surprised, open-mouthed kind of quiet.

Because there was nothing, not a crumb—*nothing*—in T.C's bucket.

He lashed out at everybody within reach, cried himself redeyed down behind the outhouses, and wouldn't come to school until the teacher escorted him in by the ear an hour later. But T.C., even after all that, wouldn't answer any questions and his sister, like always, stood right behind him. Silent.

None of T.C.'s classmates understood it, but a couple of boys went to see their grandmother—one of those great mamaws who knew about everything and everybody. Of course, Mamaw already knew all about T.C., his sister and the empty syrup bucket. She had known all along.

"Boys," Mamaw told them, not unkindly but with a flake or two of flint in her low voice, "every morning when T.C. and his sister left home that syrup bucket was full up to the top. *With pride.*" Mamaw let those last two words, *with pride*, come out like hollow-point bullets. They hit home.

"But you and your schoolmates," she finished, "have taken T.C.'s pride away."

The boys understood then, and the mystery of the empty syrup bucket was settled at Vienna school. In fact, nobody ever spoke of it again. Yes, the kids did sort of make a little room for T.C. and his little sister after that—until the circle closed and both of them were just Vienna school kids again. Pride and all.

Was this story of the empty syrup bucket at Vienna made up? Maybe, but it was told to me by Jewette Farley, Lincoln Parish's tax assessor who is a native and still a resident of Vienna, La. The subject came up after my recent column on the depression and the answers to it from area readers.

Jewette, you should know, is Ruston's answer to Will Rogers—full of folk wisdom and tales about the hill-country and proud of his red-clay ancestry. But Jewette swears this is a true story—about T.C. and his empty syrup bucket—and I believe him.

After all, Jewette's grandmother told him the story for the gospel truth, and his grandmother—as everybody in Vienna knows—didn't lie. It doesn't matter anyway. Given the abiding character of North Louisiana, I imagine there were a lot of T.C.'s and empty syrup buckets around these parts during the depression. A lot of pride, too.

Let Us Look, Please, Before Winter Comes

October 30, 1983

'Slow me down, Lord'
—Richard Cardinal Cushing

From the end of the dam to the other the little lake reflects the colors of North Louisiana in November; an opaque rendering of reds and russets and lemons that fall out twenty feet from the tree-lined banks.

In the late afternoon, when a rosy flush lights up the landscape, the whole pond is literally a watercolor painting of autumn in mid-course. Of course, winter lies just beyond the horizon; the reflection will dim and disappear with the black limbs and dark torrents of that approaching season.

But for now the colors of fall have dyed the waters. The result is a mirror held to the face of November, a reflection of time and a season—a thing of beauty of which poets speak. Yet, so few of us stop to look.

Slow us down, Lord, and make us look—before winter comes and finally darkens the lights in the water that reflect autumn in North Louisiana.

Legend has it that Davy Crockett stopped at Cloud's Crossing en route to the Alamo; legend also has it that A. V. Tait Jr., our guide for this late October foray into Northwest Louisiana, "heard a whippoorwill sing on Saline, and knew what Hank Williams meant."

Saline Bayou does come singing through Cloud's Crossing, running hard and swift over cypress stumps, dividing Winn and Natchitoches parishes. The crossing stands tall in gum and hick-

LET US LOOK, PLEASE, BEFORE WINTER COMES

ory, its cool floor scattered with hay from trail rides, and Mr. Tait tells us we missed the great autumnal color-turn by a week.

No matter. It's easy to see why Crockett may have camped at this crossing; or why, as also rumored, the James and Dalton gangs rested their horses here. Or why the Taits, and others from as far away as Oregon, light the crossing with their campfires these soft fall weekends.

Cut just into the national forest, Cloud's Crossing has a wildness about it; a deer is almost sure to break across Louisiana 1233. Yet, there is a sheltered look about this place—maybe it's the tall trees—and a good measure of seclusion too. And, as we said, Saline Bayou fairly sings through here.

Mr. Tait has taken us the long way to Cloud's Crossing, he said, because it's nicer. We headed out of Jonesboro on 167 South, took the first right past the Red Barn on Louisiana 126. From there we crossed the Dugdemona River, passed Brewton's mill, and turned left on 1233 into the national forest—and there was Cloud's Crossing.

From Cloud's Crossing, it was straight on to Black Lake, which we crossed with moonrise on one side and sunset on the other. We finally stopped for a supper of catfish and green tomato pickles at Lakewood Inn. The whole tour is recommended—by us and Davy Crockett and Jesse James and A. V. Tait of Jonesboro.

We left Northcentral Louisiana in a spatter of rain last week, under skies the tint and texture of out-of-style gray flannel pants, with the temperature at seventy-eight degrees, and the car air conditioner running.

The calendar said October, but the season was summer, and humidly so. Fall seemed far down the road this soggy early afternoon, despite the number of hunters in their fluorescent caps and green jackets patrolling the woods' rim in Claiborne and Union parishes.

Yet, when we got out of the car not far across the Arkansas line and just a few miles up Highway 167 to shake hands with

LET US LOOK, PLEASE, BEFORE WINTER COMES

the Craig Durretts, recently added to *The Times* family and themselves headed for El Dorado, it was—in a rush of north wind and a swirl of sycamore leaves—unmistakably autumn.

Everything was finally altered at that chance meeting the other side of Junction City, and suddenly we were shivering in the short-sleeved shirts that, a season and a half-hour before in Lincoln Parish, had seemed so appropriate. Now headed north for a meeting with the Arkansas Press Women, we changed clothes, moods and climates. It was fall at last.

And crossing the Ouachita at Calion, we ran into signs that confirmed that changing of the seasons. For in southeastern Arkansas, the gums are turning—turning to lemon and russet, and even to deep and burning orange.

The cool wind sharpened our senses, it seemed, and we observed a low-built barn with a moss roof, hay square-baled in the fields, seas of black-eyed susans, and a swaying pick-up truck which advertised: "When you cuss a farmer, don't talk with your mouth full."

We saw the skies clearing, showing an eggshell blue over Hampton's (population 1,601) green water tower and Corner Cafe. Some of the Hamptonites had put on their winter coats and the neighborly talk in this town, even as we zipped through, seemed alert and animated and free of summer.

Of course, the front had pushed the cold air and the season into North Louisiana by the time we got back home, but for us the fall of 1978 was born oh so miraculously, so very swiftly, just across the state line, somewhere between Junction City and El Dorado, Ark.

A Book About Us, a Century Ago

May 27, 1984

In the violent Reconstruction times of North Louisiana, it wasn't the Hatfields against the McCoys but the Grahams against the Greenes. It was a lethal time, when armed bands from Lincoln, Claiborne, Union, Jackson and Bienville parishes hunkered down at night in D'Arbonne bottom—braced for an attack from Federal calvary.

E. M. Graham, a Confederate officer in the Civil War, led what was nothing less than a guerrilla war against the forces of Radical Republicanism, headed by former Union loyalist Allen Greene. The battleground, again, was Northcentral Louisiana, and the issue was not completely decided until a Washington political deal ended Reconstruction in 1876.

This dramatic hill country duel is the focal point of Dr. William Y. Thompson's new book, *E. M. Graham: North Louisianian* (Center for Louisiana Studies, University of Southwestern Louisiana, Lafayette, La.). But the full-length view mirrors North Louisiana a century ago as seen through the life of one of this region's most prominent citizens—the same E. M. Graham.

Van Graham, as he was known, rose to prominence as a Confederate colonel, lawyer, judge and political, civic and church leader from the 1860s to the early part of the twentieth century. He lived in Downsville, Vienna, Vernon and Ruston, where he died in 1908—the very epitome of pillar-of-the-community cliche. Graham's Hill is still a Ruston landmark. So is the old First Presbyterian Church, where Graham and his family worshipped.

But, as Thompson points out, it was Graham's "implacable" bid to wrest this region from Radical Republican control, whatever that took, which made his name. He was, writes Thompson, "ever the sober-sided God-fearing and proper man, a stereotyped Victorian who found himself in the pine hills of North Louisiana."

Yet, as Thompson says, the cold and Cromwellian Graham was also a rebel "in the two most important segments of his life, the Civil War and the Reconstruction." In both instances, the unromantic but utterly unafraid Graham was prepared to lay down his life "outside the law."

He was wounded while leading Confederate troops into the flaming mouths of Union cannons at the historically bloody Battle of Franklin, Tenn. Then, ten years later, there was Graham "lying with his friends in D'Arbonne Swamp anticipating an attack by Federal troops."

Graham's archfoe in that last war against Reconstruction was Greene, regarded at the time as a scalawag legislator who had nevertheless brought Lincoln Parish into political being. Thompson, in a balanced judgment, obviously finds Greene the more human of the pair—more gentle and more generous.

In that desperate and often dangerous combat between two so different men—both of whom remained armed even in their homes—Thompson wisely decides against choosing a hero. "Allen Greene . . . was a man ahead of his time, the tolerant, farsighted village sage who sought to heal the wounds of war and welcome the new freedmen into public life, and yet a man whose political self-aggrandizement would call into question . . . his motives."

Graham, on the other side of the schism, is seen as "the man more in keeping with his time . . . his people, who led the struggle against the excesses and sometimes bad government of Reconstruction, and yet a man willing to resort to force and violence to thwart changes . . . that were anathema to him." Graham was respected, even by his enemies, but not loved.

In the end, Thompson finds Graham the "proper rebel, similar to so many of his generation in North Louisiana. . . ." He never doubted, not once, the rectitude of his Presbyterian God nor his political cause. "Of such stuff romantics are not made," acknowledges the author.

"But Graham never pretended to be one (a romantic) and would have been most uncomfortable with such an image," writes Thompson. "He (Graham) may not always have been right. But it is extremely doubtful if he could have been persuaded that he was not. Such was Evander McNair Graham. And so were hundreds of North Louisianians a century ago."

That last line sums up what Thompson has done in his book: That is, to portray upland North Louisiana as it was one hundred years ago, and to hold that mirror up to this very generation. The author would say that Van Graham's life made for that exciting tale, but Thompson is a skillful storyteller, an accomplished *writer* as well as historian who has already produced two other well-received books.

So on that score, he advised: This is *not* yet another local book praising unstinted another local if obscure hero, to be dutifully reviewed by a colleague who has engraved a similar tombstone of a volume. No, Thompson writes the way he teaches as chairman of Tech's history department. He is dramatic in an appropriately low key, possessed of a dark wit and sense of humor, and yet ever the researching scholar.

For example, Thompson fondly dwells on the black sheep of the Graham family. This is a certain Uncle Henry who breaks sober-sided tradition to "drink copiously" and declare that he "did not love his wife as he used to and intended to get a divorce."

As Thompson tells it, the wayward Uncle Henry was finally collared by his Presbyterian clan at a camp rally "up on Hatchet Creek" where he signed an oath promising never to imbibe again. Uncle Henry's "poor wife on hearing it rejoiced aloud" but Thompson recalls that this rebellious Graham soon rebelled again.

This is, then, a well-written and readable book by any measure—one that provides perhaps the first serious historical measure of our own North Louisiana—and it's available in area bookstores. It is, in the end, a book about us, one hundred years ago. I enjoyed it.

Maybe Some Things Are Forever

November 25, 1984

In the eye of the poet, "the mighty oak" has ever loomed large and tall, taking on human dimensions of greatness, fortitude, stability and endurance. Nobody will argue those noble personifications.

But as November runs its leafy, sun-blinking course to the far corners of fall, I'm thinking of a pair of big beech trees discovered a half dozen years ago off the Old Vernon Road in Jackson Parish. I wonder now if those beech twins, the subject of an editorial written at the time, are still standing.

Of course, the beech—unlike the oak—is not characteristically associated, in human terms, with strength and stamina. Yet, I consulted the Lincoln Parish Library section on Southern trees and read that beech wood is hard, tight-grained and tough—the stuff of tool handles.

And this matching Jackson Parish pair, which I left guarding a dead spring at the foot of a gentle incline, would hold their bronze and gold leaves as long—or longer—than the most persistent oak in a forest of colored flags.

But there is more to beech wood than toughness and endurance and leaves that defy the winds of November. If the oak is a noble creature, somehow elevated above us mortals, the beech is friendly and sympathetic. A confidant, even.

MAYBE SOME THINGS ARE FOREVER

And though the Jackson beech twins were located well off the beaten path ("don't say exactly where they are," said our guide, "because some idiot may come and cut them down"), they displayed the marks of such contact with humankind.

"Jack Plus Mary" and "Tim Loves Susan" and a dozen other such tributes to romance were engraved on the white-gray trunks of the beech twosome. How many times, I wondered then, had a beech tree acted as a go-between in shy encounters of the heart?

Such beech trees have also preserved many a confidence of secret love, unbetrayed, for all time. Oftentimes a Mary or a Tim never knew that somebody cared, but that love was all the same written on the bark of a beech—there to withstand time and wind and river.

If the two old North Louisiana beeches I saw carried the literal knife-scars of love, they had also heard—and recorded—other human cries. A simple "1950" was carved deep into the great stem of one of the Old Vernon twins—consecrating, in that tranquil and turning wood, some event of gladness or sadness.

I don't know what confidence was poured out—or carved out, in this case—that day in 1950, but the beech tree knew. And if those beeches were engraved with unspoken pleas and prayers, they had also joined in the childhood play and laughter of a whole region.

No, I can't be sure that a gang of fourteen-year-olds dangled from the limbs of this particular Jackson Parish beech pair. But which of us has not, at one time or the other in the bright summer of our youth, hung from the kind arms of a beech that stood, inevitably, over the creek swimming hole?

And if the oak is a thing of beauty, who can deny the impossible balance, the perfect symmetry, of a beech tree's branch-spread? Those beech twins of Old Vernon, standing high in their gold halos, yielded nothing to beauty either—and yet were marked as down-to-earth confidants of humankind.

I think of them—in my mind's eye—as still mounting sentinels, this very hour, over a dry creek bed, and over the sentiments of a whole generation. And I think, picturing the beech pair, that maybe some things are forever. Maybe.

It was Kevin, exploring the rim of a wild-grown pond, who found another beech tree on my in-laws' property off the Rough Edge Road in Lincoln Parish. He showed it to me, just the other day, and I remembered the girl of my dreams.

"Bootsie Loves Ellen," I had carved into that tree, and there it was, worn but still clear.

That message was written on beech bark more than twenty-five years ago, most probably. And now, as the leaves bury this golden autumn of 1984, I think—again—that maybe, just maybe, some things are forever.

INDEX

A. E. Phillips School, 169
A Tale of Two Cities (Dickens), 116
Adib, Karim, 41-44
Air Force One, 18
Alexander, James, 5
Alexandria, La., 157
Alumni News. See Louisiana Tech University
Amal, 43
"America the Beautiful," 246
American Heritage Dictionary, 111, 153
American Lung Association, 195
American Name Society, 167
American South, The (Seay),
Andretti, Mario, 175
"Andy Griffith Show," 139-141
Antioch, La., 207, 209, 210, 237, 265
Antioch Methodist Church, 36-38, 209
Apocalypse Now, 40
Arkansas, University of, 187
Ashley, Leonard, R. N., 167, 169-170
Assad, al-, Hafez, 43
Associated Press, 167
Atchafalaya Basin, 95
Atlanta TV (Channel 17), 234
Atlanta, Ga., 215, 217, 218

Babe, (Creamer), 36
Baker, Wade, 38-40
Baker, La., 175
Barbados Islands, 262-265
Barham, C. E., 123, 189, 242, 275, 276
Barham, Carice, 241-242, 243
Barham, Charles, C., 86, 169, 275
Barham, Robert, 177, 188, 241-243, 275
Barnard, Sonny, 3-5, 18, 190-193, 201-203
Batman. *See* Hilburn, Kevin
Baton Rouge, La., 12, 90, 106, 108, 110, 114, 156, 288
Bayne, William, 4
Beard, Jack, 9

Beirut, Leb., 47, 157
Bergeron, Nancy, 34
Berri, Habih, 43
Best and the Brightest, The (Halberstam), 106
Bible, 51
Bienville Parish, 88, 198, 296, 308
Big Eight League, 8
Biloxi, Miss.: Chamber of Commerce, 250; mentioned, 251
Black Lake, 295
Blackwell, Lloyd P., 59-62
Boeuf Prairie, La., 284-285
Boeuf Prairie Methodist Church, 286
Boeuf River, 286
Book of Church Order, 51
Bourbons, 100
Bowa, Larry, 271
Bozeman, Eck, 12
Brezhnev, Leonid, 49
Bridgetown, Barbados, 264
Briggs, Joe Bob, 213
British League of Empire Loyalists, 160
Bronson, William, 129-130
Brooklyn College, 167
Brown, Buck, 4
Brown, Jim: defeated by Huckaby, 114, 115, 116; authors Open Meetings Law, 115; authors Architect Selection Act, 115; pushes Archives Building and oral history program, 115; and gubernatorial aspirations, 116-117; mentioned, 18, 86, 113
Brown, Jimmy, 159
Brown, Johnny Mack, 144
Butler, Kathleen, 21, 32, 33
Byrd High School, 133, 205
Byrnside, George, 157, 197

Caine Mutiny, The (Wouk), 30
Cajun Cavaliers, 101

315

INDEX

Cajun Restoration, 96, 110, 113
Calhoun, John, 59, 62
Calion, Ark., 307
Cambodia, 39
Cambridge University, 115, 116
Camelot. *See* Weaver, Loy
Cannon, Billy, 168, 215
Caray, Harry, 270, 271
Carter, Jimmy, 49, 84
Carter, Rosalynn, 16-19
Cassibry, Reginald, 9
Cassidy, Shaun, 258, 259
Cawthon, John Ardis, 54-55
Centenary College, 161
Center for Louisiana Studies, 308
Cey, Ron, 271
Chandler, Jeff, 144
Chapman, H. H., 60
Chicago Cubs, 269-272
Chicago, Ill., 269
"Chicago Sixteen," 259
Choudrant Creek, 294
Christian Observer, The, 222
Churchill, Winston, 130
Claiborne Parish, 107, 109, 116, 306, 308
Clay, La., 202
Clear Lake, 188, 190, 261
Clinton, Larry, 205-206
Cloud's Crossing, 305-306
Cobb, Gerald, 246
Coca-Cola, 215-218
Cochise, 144
Coke. *See* Coca-Cola
College Inn, 187
Columbia, La., 89, 102, 103, 287
Columbia Space Shuttle, 175
Colvin, Joe, 19
Colvin-Jones General Store, 14, 16
Communist Party, 39, 124
Congress, United States. *See* House of Representatives, United States; Senate, United States
Cook, Philip C., 55
Corbett, Lance. *See* Hilburn, Wiley W. Jr.
Cosby, Bill, 218
Cotton, Edith, 31
Creamer, Robert W., 36
Crockett, Davy, 305
Cubbies. *See* Chicago Cubs
Cuchi, Vietnam, 39
Cushing, Cardinal, 305

Dallas Cowboys, 270
Dalton Gang, 306
D'Arbonne, Lake, 295
Damascus, Syria, 43
Davis, Edwin Adams, 74, 90-91, 100
Davis, Jimmy, 76, 89, 92-94, 99, 101, 103
Davis, O. K., 47
Davis, Thomas McIlwaine, 283
Davison, Billy, 4
Day, Doris, 173-174
Dean's Wife, The, 214
DeBakey, Michael, 228
Delta Airlines, 58
"Diamond Dope," 44, 46
Dickens, Charles, 115
"Dirt Extractor," 3-5
Dixie Drugstore, 12-13
Dixie Inn, La., 206, 207
Dixie Theatre, 93, 143-145
Dorcheat Road, 48, 49
Dornbusch, Sanford, 272-273, 275-276
Downsville, La., 308
Doyline, La., 54
Dozier, Gil, 107
Dr. Pepper, 216
Dring, Maggie. *See* Price, Mrs. Bruce
Drocco, Pierre, 264
Drocco, Mrs. Pierre, 264
Druse, 43, 44
Dry Prong, La., 15
Dubach, La., 14, 177, 300
Duchesne, R. C., 242
Dugas, C. J., 124
Dulles, John Foster, 9
Durango Kid. *See* Starrett, Charles
Durrett, Craig, 307
Duty Ferry, 287-289
Duty, La., 287

E. M. Graham: North Louisianian (Thompson), 308-311
"Ebb Tide," 5, 6
Edwards, Edwin: and farmer-worker combine, 97; takes supporters to Paris, 110; popularity of, 111; proposes tax increase, 112; has mandate, 112-113; meets Wiley Hilburn, 150-152; mentioned, 86, 89, 95-96, 98, 100, 103, 114, 115, 116, 213, 274
Edwards, "Pee Wee," 18
1812, Overture, 280

316

INDEX

Eisenhower, Dwight David, 92
El Dorado, Ark., 307
Ellington, Lindy, 270
Emerson, Ralph Waldo, 44
Enterprise, La., 286
Erwin, Tom, 15
Evangeline Oak, 100
Evans, Dale, 144
Exxon Co., 179
Ewing, Donald M., 29, 161

Farley, Jewette, 304
Farmerville, La., 192
Farrar, Harry, 5
Faulk, Clarence, 146-148
Faulk, Mrs. Clarence, 146, 148
FDR. *See* Roosevelt, Franklin Delano
Ferriday, La., 86
Field & Stream, 203
Fife, Barney. *See* Knotts, Don
Finance Committee. *See* Senate, United States
Fitzmorris, Jimmy, 152
Fitzgerald, Roy, 152
Flournoy, Kendall, 19-21
Floyd's Bait Stand, 102
Fondren-Brown Building, 228
Ford, Gerald, 81
Forest Farmer, 60, 61
Fort Necessity, La., 285, 286
Foster, Elijah S., 168
Fox, Larry J., 44-47, 241
Fox, Shep, 46
"Fragments," 12, 14, 141, 155, 172
Frankenstein (Doctor), 4
Franklin, Battle of, 309
Franklin Parish, 88, 285
Fraser Field, 8, 10, 216
Freeman, Bobby, 114, 116
French Quarter, 157
French, Reggie, 134

Garrett, L. J., 134
Gates, Jack, 132
Gathering Storm, The (Churchill), 30
Gemayel, Amin, 44
"Georgia on My Mind," 17
Gerald, Mary B., 31-32
Gibsland, La., 19, 280, 296, 297
Gifford, Frank, 270
Glasgow's Men's Store, 173

Gleason, Jackie, 60
"Goals for Louisiana." *See* McKeithen, John
Goertz, John, 225, 226, 290
Good Earth, The, 273
Gore, Alvin, 205-206
Graham, Evander McNair, 308-310
Graham's Hill, 242, 308
Grambling College. *See* Grambling State University
Grambling State University: Tigers, 45; Band of, 240-241; mentioned, 97
Grant Parish, 297
Grapes of Wrath, The (Steinbeck), 226
"Grapevine," 146
Grayson, La., 287
Greece, 34
Green Clinic, 25
Greene, Allen, 308, 309
Grevemberg, Francis, 91
Grier, Rosey, 40
Griffith, Andy, 139-141
Grigsby, Billy, 47-50
Grigsby, Randy, 48-49
Gulf National Oil Building, 74
Gulf Oil Co., 164
Gutenberg Bible, 158
Guynes, Barron G., 13-16

Halberstam, David, 106
Hall, Emmett, 9
Hama, Syria, 43
Hamilton, Roy, 6
Hampton, Ark., 307
Hanna, Sam, 95
"Happy Days," 5
Harris Hotel, 240
Harrison, William, 9
Harrisonburg, La., 288
Hart, William, Larry, 32
Hatten, Jimmy, 132
Hays, John, 5, 15, 66-67, 269
Hays, Leslie, 67
Hayes, George Gabby, 144
Heatter, Gabriel, 221, 267
"Heaven's National Anthem," 93
Henry, E. L., 85, 152, 167
Herbert, Dr. Allen, 17, 18-19
Herbert, Wallace, 172-173
Herrin, Tommy, 9
Herrmann, Alice, 152

INDEX

Hester, James, 4
Hewings, Kenneth F., 22-24
Hilburn, Anne Marie, 21, 139, 225, 226-228, 244, 245, 250, 251, 258-260, 284, 287, 288, 289, 297
Hilburn, Chet, 295
Hilburn, E. W. (grandfather), finds monkey in bed, 221-223; integrates Grambling parade, 239-241; gin burns, 253-254; last days of, 266-269
Hilburn, Ellen: at Shreveport state fair, 137-139, not impressed by Ginsu knives, 235-236; and children take Wiley's clothes, 244-245, 247, and vacation frustrations, 249-251, vacations in Barbados, 261-265; mentioned, 21, 30, 51, 131, 154, 156, 165, 169, 172, 173, 176, 216, 225, 227, 232, 247, 255
Hilburn Gin Co., 254
Hilburn, Gregory: liked Beverley Steinfeldt, 224-225, wants senior ring, 232-233, and Ginsu knives, 234-236; takes father's razor and clothes, 243-245; graduates from high school, 245-246; celebrates Cubs divisional pennant, 269-272; mentioned, 21, 164, 166, 247, 255, 284
Hilburn, Kevin: takes father's razor, clothes and credit card, 244-245; as Batman, 260-261; mentioned, 11, 135, 225, 234, 236, 247, 249, 255, 284, 287, 289, 297, 313
Hilburn, Marie Trussell (mother), 154, 179, 207, 209
Hilburn, Roberta (grandmother), 221-223, 267
Hilburn, Wiley W., Jr.: envies teen-age rival, 5-8; admires Berry Hinton, 8-11; and Rosalynn Carter, 16-19; and Kendall Flournoy, 19-21; and Kenneth Hewings, 22-24; a patient of Henry Roane, 25-27; encounters Robert Snyder, 28-29; and Mrs. Upchurch, 29-30; describes his teachers, 31-33; and Bruce Price, 37-38; and Karim Adib, 41-43, 44; and Larry Fox, 44-47; meets Grigsbys, 48-49; and Curry Patton, 50-54; and Jay Taylor, 56-58, 183-184; lectured by Lloyd Blackwell, 59, 61-62; and Harold Smolinski, 64-65; and Joe Waggonner, 71; reverses *Times* slogan, 129-130; at *World*, 130-132; inglorious football career of, 132-135; wins teddy bears, 135-139; as Barney Fife, 139-141; assaulted by railroaders, 141-143; fired from *Ruston Leader*, 145-147; scolded by nurse, 148-150; meets Gov. Edwards, 150-152; fails to identify Treen, 152-153; mechanical abilities of, 153-155; has poor sense of direction, 156-157; deplores VDTs, 158-160; loses fight, 161-164; loses eraser in ear, 164-166; alias Lance Corbett, 168; credit card rejected, 170-171; receives compliment, 172-173; chews hair, 174; fails drivers exam, 175-176; fights Bill Upchurch, 178-180; encounters ghost, 189-190; best friends smoke, 193-194; tricks friends, 196-198; finds job for friend, 200-202; in barbershop, 203; insults watermelon farmer, 204-205; sees X-rated movie, 213-215; denounces Coke change, 215-218; tricks grandfather, 221-223; and Steinfeldts, 224-226; and Anne Marie, 226-228, 244, 258-260; at Houston Medical Center, 228-231; and senior ring, 231-233; and father's garden, 233-234; orders Ginsu knives, 234-236; visits Trussell homeplace, 237-239, 299-301; loses razor, clothing to sons, 243-245; at Greg's graduation, 245-246; and car problems, 246-248; vacations with children, 249-251; advises Little League dads, 255-257; misses Kevin as Batman, 260-261; in Barbados, 261-265; and grandfather's death, 266-269; celebrates Cubs' divisional pennant, 269-272; improves grades, 272-276; and rainstorms, 280; and old barns, 281-282; and church, 283-284; at Boeuf Prairie, 284-287; visits Duty Ferry, 287-289; fishes Morgan's Pond, 291, *ill*. 292, 293-295; on Thanksgiving, 296-297; at Cloud's Crossing, 305-306; on Beech tree initials, 313; mentioned, 5, 173, 177, 188, 243, 307
His political interviews and assessments. Sam Jones, 72-78; Russell Long, 78-85; Jerry Huckaby, 85-88; Robert Kennon, 89-92; Jimmy Davis, 92-94; David C.

INDEX

Treen, 94-96; half-century assessment, 96-101; John McKeithen, 102-106; Loy Weaver, 106-110; Edwin Edwards, 110-113; Jim Brown, 113-117; Huey Long, 117-119; Earl K. Long, 120-125
Hilburn, Wiley W., Sr.: has heart attack, 26; scores six touchdowns, 133; fails as a repairman, 154-155; loses bet, 186-187; chased by bull, 207, *ill.* 208, 209-210; in Medical Center ICU, 230-231; buys Wiley Jr. class ring, 232; makes garden, 233-234; crashes garage door, 248; and gin fire, 251, *ill.* 252, 253-254; and car-mule accident, 265-268; instills study habits in Wiley Jr., 273-276
Hinojosa, Albino Ray, 282
Hinton, Berry, 8-11
Hinton, Billy, 11
Hobgood, Mrs. Charles, 173
Hodge, La., 87
Hodgson, Reed, 272
Hogg, Ima, 168
Hogg, James, 168
Hollis, Sally Rose, 176
Holly Ridge, La., 253
Holstead, "Racer," 9
Holtman, Robert, 176
Holum, La., 287
Holy Grail, 11
Homer, La., 106, 110
Homer National Bank, 107
Hood, Eddie, 5, 188, 300
Hoover, J. Edgar, 108, 110
Hope, Bob, 40
House of Representatives, United States, 86, 87
Houston Astrodome, 249, 251
Houston Methodist Hospital, 229
Houston, Texas, 20, 21, 228, 249
Howe, Rolanda, 152
Huckaby, Jerry: with Rosalynn Carter, 18; and E. L. Henry, 85; defeats Otto Passman, 86; defeats Jim Brown, 86; political strategy of, 87; and "constituent service," 88; promotes wildlife refuge, 88; emphasizes defense and energy, 88; mentioned 114, 116
Huckaby, Sue, 18
Huddle House, 172, 177
Humphrey, Hubert, 168

Hunt, Mrs. Stewart, 120

"In Past Times," 130
"In the Garden," 37, 38
Indianapolis "500," 242
Inevitable Guest, The, (Cawthon), 54
Interstate Highway-20, 146, 148
Invasion of the Body-Snatchers, 159
"It's Your Life," 45, 46

Jackson Parish, 156, 198, 308, 311
James Gang, 306
Jerome, Frank, 27
Johnson, Lyndon Baines, 38, 83, 141
Johnston, J. Bennett, 85
Jolly Roger, 263
Jones, Sam Houston: angered by Earl Long, 73, 75; symbolizes reform, 74; defeats Earl Long, 75; fails to build machine, 76; proud of Civil Service, 77; laments failure of Shreveporters to vote, 77; mentioned, 97, 98, 99, 100, 101
Jones, Mrs. Sam Houston, 77
Jonesboro, High School, 186
Jonesboro, La., 105, 156, 186, 243, 306
Jonesville, La., 156
Jumblatt, Walid, 43
Junction City, Ark., 307

Karloff, Boris, 4
Kay, Melvin, 16
Kelly, Mellie Jo, 246
Kelso, Iris, 117
Kennedy, Edward, 83
Kennedy, John F., 99
Kennon, Robert Floyd: defeats Carlos Spaht, 90; and Civil Service League, 90; fails to maintain organization, 91; supports Eisenhower, 92; opposes integration, 92; mentioned, 77, 82, 89, 97, 98, 99, 103
Kerr, Ed, 60
Kilgore, George, 173
"Kingfish," *See* Long, Huey
KMOX (Saint Louis Radio Station), 270
Kisatchie National Forest, 61
Knotts, Don, 139-141, 163
Knox, L. D., 87
KSLA Channel 12 (Shreveport Television Station), 15

INDEX

Kuralt, Charles, 14
Kurtz, Michael L., 89-92

LABI (Louisiana Association of Business and Industry), 96, 97, 274
Lafayette, La., 184, 308
Lake Charles, La., 73, 74
Lambright, Maxie, 135
Lann, Benjamin, 9
LaRue, John, 4
LaRue, Lash, 144
Lawson, Steve, 287
Lebanon, 41-44
Lee, Jimmy, 171
Legend of the First Lick, 161, 163-164
Legislature. *See* Louisiana, State of
Lewis and Clark Expedition, 157
Lewis, S. X., 9
Lewis, Sinclair, 45
Life, 104
Lincoln General Hospital, 60, 149, 261
Lincoln Parish, 5, 6, 34, 59, 66, 144, 177, 190, 198, 205, 207, 223, 239, 280, 281, 308, 309, 313
Lincoln Parish Library, 29, 66, 164, 171, 311
Linder Motor Lodge, 106
Little League, 255-257, 260-261
Lombardi, Vince, 241
Long-Allen Bridge, 102
Long, Caroline, 83
Long, Earl Kemp: visits Ruston, 120; *ill.* 122; will run for governor, 123; friend of Negro, 124; recognizes Hilburn, 125; wins Congressional seat, 125; mentioned, 73, 75, 76, 77, 79, 81, 82, 90, 91, 97, 98, 99, 100, 103, 119
Long, Huey P., 75, 79, 84, 97, 99, 100, 117-119
Long, Russell B.: unlike Huey and Earl, 79; influence of, 79-80; proud of welfare legislation, 81; disclaims political organization, 82; denies gubernatorial aspirations, 82-83; problems in 1960s, 83; supported Lyndon Johnson, 83; feels Supreme Court permissive, 84; mentioned, 78, 85, 118
Louisiana, A Narrative History (Davis), 90
Louisiana, State of: Department of Transportation, 15; Legislature, 76, 90, 96, 97, 105, 108, 120; Civil Service League, 90; Right-to-Work Law, 90; Eleventh Congressional District, 106; Fourth Congressional District, 109; Fifth Congressional District, 114, 186; Architect Selection Act, 115; Archives Building, 115; Open Meetings Law, 115; National Guard, 118; Department of Highways, 145, 148; Board of Regents, 151; Office of Motor Vehicles, 175; *Driver's Guide*, 176
Louisiana Hayride, 118
Louisiana Life, 96, 99
Louisiana Press Association, 157
Louisiana Press Women, 156
Louisiana Progressive, 48
Louisiana Purchase Store, 217
Louisiana Scandals, 74, 100
Louisiana State Fair, 135
Louisiana State University (Baton Rouge), 63, 77, 175, 295
Louisiana Tech University: Memorial Gym, 19; *Lagniappe,* 23; Keeny Hall, 23, 72, 141, 150-151, 179, 196, 198; *Tech Talk*, 24, 72, 158, 159, 259; Old Engineering Building, 27-29; Athletic Council, 29, 63-64; Lady Techsters, 33; Theatre Players, 41; Student Government Association, 41; Bulldogs, 45; College of Education, 54; School of Forestry, 59; Lady of the Mist, 64, 141; School of Professional Accountancy, 63; Quadrangle, 64; *Alumni News*, 65; Thomas Assembly Center, 213; ROTC, 275, 296; Tech Rome, 276; mentioned, 7, 196, 199
Lynchburg, Va., 60

Madison Parish, 88
Mafia, 103-104
Main Street (Lewis), 145
Mallett, Lucien, 264
Mallett, Mrs. Lucien, 264
Mangham, La., 286
Massie, George, 164
Matthews, Gary, 270-271
Meadows, Marion Tillery, 169
Mercer, Fern, 5
Mercer, Tommy, 5
Michigan State University, 63

INDEX

Minden, La., 48, 63, 89, 187
Minnesota Fats, 59, 61, 62
Mississippi River, 99, 156, 157, 288
Monroe Morning World, 14, 86, 130-132, 150, 160
Monroe, La., 88
Montgomery, Jim, 17, 160
Montgomery Steak House, 173
Moore, Henson, 96, 114
Moran, Jack, 4
Morgan, Elemore, 60
Morgan's Pond, 291-295
Morris, Tom, 15
Mount Lebanon, La., 156
Murray, Jim, 45

McCrory, Sidney, 124
McDaniel, Raymond, 161
McKeithen, John: fuses Longs and anti-Longs, 99; supports Kennedy, 99; popularity of, 102, 103; denounces charges of Mafia influence, 103-104; improved highways, 104; pushed Superdome, 104; authors "Goals for Louisiana" amendments, 104; on segregation and integration, 104-105; pushes tax increase, 105; mentioned, 86, 89, 99, 106
McWilliams, Scott, 60

NAACP (National Association for the Advancement of Colored People), 124
Natchitoches, La., 88, 188
Neal, Dr. Larry, 165-166
New England Journal of Medicine, 25
New Journalism, 162
New Orleans, La., 101, 157, 170
New Orleans Superdome, 102, 104
New York, N. Y., 34, 179, 241
New York Times, 43
New York Yankees, 35, 36, 37
Nicholls, Francis T., 78
Nicoletti, Francis Xavier, 62
Norris, David, 16
North Carolina, University of, 116
Northeast Louisiana University: Band, 17; mentioned, 217
Northwestern State University, 23
Notre Dame, University of, 63

Old Arkansas Bar, 206
Old Vernon, La., 312

"On the Road," 14
"One Man's Opinion," 95
O'Neal, Bernice, 31
Opelousas, La., 91, 156
Orr, Virgil, 23-24
Ouachita River, 102, 287, 288, 307
Overton, John H., 82
"Ozymandias" (Shelley), 89, 92

Painter, Jack, 42
Parrot's Beak, Battle of, 39
Passman, Otto, 86
Patterson, Pat, 203
Patton, Curry, 50-51, *ill.* 52, 53-54
Pecan Island, 188
Pennington, Paul J., 168
Peoples, Morgan D., 101
Pepper, Maxine, 31
Pepsi-Cola, 216
Perez, Leander, 92, 124
Perritt, Johnny, 33-34
Peter the Great (Massie), 164, 165, 166
Phillips, R. W., 134
Pittard, Robert, 186-187
Plain Dealing, La., 38
Plato, 28
Poltava, Battle of, 165
Poltergeist, 262
Populists, 81, 116
Porter, Howard, A., 12-13
Portland, Ore., 61
Price, Bob, 35
Price, Bruce, 35-38
Price, Mrs. Bruce, 37, 38
Price, Larry, 36
Princeton, La., 206, 207
Prudhomme, Homer M., 9
Public Affairs Research Council, 96, 99, 100, 102
Purple Monster, The, 144

Quigg, H. D., 146

Radical Republicans, 308
Rainach, Willie, 92
Recent Editorial Research Reports, 194
Reagan, Ronald, 42
Reed, C. A. Jr., 9
Reeves, Steve, 177
Regan, Carroll, 87

INDEX

"Relationships," (*New York Times*), 272
Republic Pictures, 144
Republic (Plato), 27
Republican Party, 96, 110
Republican Roundheads, 101
Richardson, John, 226
Richardson, Mr. and Mrs. Tom, 225-226
Ride Him, Cowboy, 187
Ringheim, Amy, 287, 289
Riser, Ben, 216
River Queen Cafe, 102
Roane, Henry, 25-27
Rockhold, Jack, 205-206
Rodakis, John, 34-35
Rogers, Leola, 31, 32
Rogers, Roy, 93, 143, 144
Roosevelt, Franklin Delano, 118
Ropp, Ralph L., 28
Royal Sonesta Hotel, 170
Ruston Daily Leader, 14, 24, 44, 45, 46, 47, 61, 120, 121, 135, 145-148, 149, 160, 187, 198, 225, 238, 295
Ruston Episcopal Church of the Redeemer, 47
Ruston First Presbyterian Church, 51, 244, 282-284, 308
Ruston Hardware Store, 213, 214
Ruston High School: Bearcats, 45, 47, 187; mentioned, 19-20, 133-134, 138, 168-169, 171, 173-174, 178, 244-245, 247, 297
Ruston, La.: Model School, 31-32; Chatauqua, 46; Railroad Park, 46; Peach Festival, 46; Greenwood Cemetery, 65-66, 198, 240; Civic Center, 92; Centennial, 120; Soapbox Derby, 241-243; mentioned, 3, 20-21, 30, 64, 120, 128, 138, 168, 188, 201, 205, 212, 215, 216, 231, 239, 254, 274, 296, 308
Ruston Morning Paper, 5, 14, 15, 66, 269
Ruston Rebels, 8, 9
Ruston State Bank, 93
Ruston Temple Baptist Church, 198, 213, 222, 223, 239
Ruston Volunteers, 8, 9, 10, 11
Ruth, George Hermann, 35, 36, 37, 38

Saigon, Vietnam, 39
Salem United Methodist Church, 300-301
Saline Bayou, 297-299
Sawyer, Tom. *See* Barnard, Sonny
"Screaming Demons," 225
Seay, James, 291
Senate, United States, 79, 80, 85
Shadow, Hale, 216, 217
Shelley, Percy Bysshe, 89
Schick, Joe, 242
Shiites, 43, 44
Shipley's Cafe, 3, 5, 31, 153, 201, 247, 248, 300
Shreveport "Gassers," 35, 37
Shreveport Journal, 24
Shreveport, La., 34, 35, 36, 77, 135, 217, 231, 241, 270, 296
Shreveport State Fair, 135-139
Shreveport Times, 14, 17, 22-23, 24, 29, 50, 54, 74, 77, 103, 116, 129-130, 142, 149, 151, 153, 155, 156, 161, 171, 176, 186, 226, 285, 307
Shreveport Times Sunday Magazine, 117, 120
Simsboro, La., 51
Sin, Jaime, 168
Sindler, Allen, 75, 91
Smith, A. T., 242
Smolinski, Carl, 65
Smolinski, Dale, 65
Smolinski, Harold, 63-65
Smolinski, Jeanie, 65
Snyder, Robert C., 27-29
Society of American Foresters, 61
Southern California, University of, 63
Southern University (Baton Rouge), 105
Southwestern Louisiana, University of, 89
Spaght, Carlos, 90
Spooner, Frank, 86
Stark, Willie. *See* Warren, Robert Penn
Starrett, Charles, 93, 144
Steimel, Edward, 97
Steinfeldt, Beverley, 224, 225, 226
Steinfeldt, Joey, 225, 226
Steinfeldt, Karl, 225
Steinfeldt, Lyle, 224, 225, 226
Steinfeldt, Todd, 225
Stokley, Gary, 18
Stokley, Sandra, 17
Sumlin, William, 18

INDEX

Syria, 41-44
Syrian. *See* Syria

Tait, A. V. Jr., 305, 306
Tallulah High School, 184
Tallulah Madison Journal, 87
Tannehill, Charles, 269
Taylor, Ark., 280
Taylor, Sheriff Andy. *See* Griffith, Andy
Taylor, F. Jay: offers assistance to Mr. Hewings, 23; visits children's graves, 56-58; attends forestry convention, 61; introduces Wiley Hilburn to Gov. Edwards, 150-152; regrets letting Wiley Hilburn drive, 157, 176; ticketed by Turkey Creek constable, 183-184; mentioned, 153, 179, 196, 197
Taylor, Terry, 58
Tech Talk. *See* Louisiana Tech University
Tensas Parish, 88
Tensas Wildlife Refuge, 88
Texas (A&M) Aggies, 66
Texas (Baseball) League, 35
Thigpen, Jack, 9
Thing, The, 144
Thomas, Joe, 178
Thompson, H. H., 283
Thompson, William Y., 308, 309, 310
Thorn, Dale, 151
Tiner, Stan, 152-153
Tobacco Road (Caldwell), 116, 121, 189
Tobacco Roody, 214
Toledo Bend Lake, 295
Treen, David C.: settles Justice Department suit, 94; saves Atchafalaya Basin, 95; is "Mr. Clean," 95; at electoral disadvantage, 96; handicapped by Edwards' popularity, 96; first Republican governor since Reconstruction, 97; rather be right, 101; mentioned, 96, 98, 99, 103, 108, 109, 110, 152-153
Trees, The, 59
Tripoli, Leb., 42
Trussell, Chester, 207, 209
Trussell Country Store, 207
Trussell, Kate, 237-239, 296, 297, 299, 300
Tugwell, A. P., 124
Tulane University, 116, 270
"Tumbling, Tumbleweeds," 144

Turkey Creek, La., 183
25th Infantry Division, 39
269th Combat Aviation Battalion, 39

Union Parish, 107, 198, 306, 308
Unionville, La., 13, 14
United States: Bicentennial, 77; Capitol, 82; Constitutional Convention, 84; Farmers' Home Administration, 87; Justice Department, 94, 104; Surgeon General of, 195; Supreme Court, 239
Upchurch, Robert, 178
Upchurch, Mrs. Robert, 29-30, 178, 179
Upchurch, William, 30, 178, 291, 293-295
UPI Reporter, 146

VDT. *See* Video Display Terminal
Venezuela, 262
Vernon, La., 308
Versailles, Palace of, 110
Vicksburg, Miss., 250
Video Display Terminal, 158-160
Vienna, La., 302, 304, 308
Vietnam, 38-40
Ville Platte, La., 91
Vollner, James, 156
"Vulcan," 39-40

W. Prescott Foster, 288
Wade Correctional Institute, 107
Waggonner, Joe, 71-72
Walker, Gary, 54
Wall Street Journal, 80, 83
Warm Springs, Ga., 186
Warren, Robert Penn, 119
Washburn, Ethel, 31-32
Washington, D. C., 88
Watergate, 196
Wayne, John, 187
"Weaver Believers," 109-110
Weaver, Loy: retires from politics, 106-107; and roads, 107; and Wade Correctional Institute, 107; investigates Gil Dozier, 107; pushes for Louisiana Bureau of Investigation, 107-108; supports Treen, 108-109; defeated for Congress, 109; mentioned, 110
Webster Parish, 88
Weill, Gus, 111

INDEX

Wells, Mike, 4
West Carroll Parish, 253
West Monroe Convention Center, 16
WGN (Chicago TV Station), 269, 272
White, Neil Ron, 160
Whitman, Elliott Rabb, 66-67
Wildwood Express, 93
Willett, Bobby, 247-248
Willett, "Round Man," 10
Williams, A. L., 63
Williams, Blanche, 285
Williams, Hank, Sr., 34
Williams, T. Harry, 119
Williams, Tennessee, 119
Williamson, Huey, 9

Wilson, Woodrow, 78
Winkler, Henry, 6
Winn Parish, 57
Winnfield, La., 12, 13, 59, 100
Winnsboro, La., 253, 286
Winters, Mrs. Harry, 17
Wisner, La., 254
Woodward, Elizabeth, 259
Woods, Joe, 93
Worsnop, Richard L., 194-195
Wrigley Field, 270

"You Are My Sunshine," 94
"You'll Never Walk Alone," 6
Young, Kenneth, 4